IMAGES
*of America*

# LYNDON INSTITUTE

Dedicated to all Lyndon Institute (LI) alumni
sharing the heritage of our alma mater.

IMAGES
*of America*

# LYNDON INSTITUTE

Harriet Fletcher Fisher

ARCADIA
PUBLISHING

ISBN 978-0-7385-0093-5

Published by Arcadia Publishing
Charleton, South Carolina

Printed in the United States of America

Library of Congress Catalog Card Number: 99-069487

For all general information contact Arcadia Publishing at:
Telephone 843-853-2070
Fax 843-853-0044
E-mail sales@arcadiapublishing.com
For customer service and orders:
Toll-Free 1-888-313-2665

Visit us on the Internet at www.arcadiapublishing.com

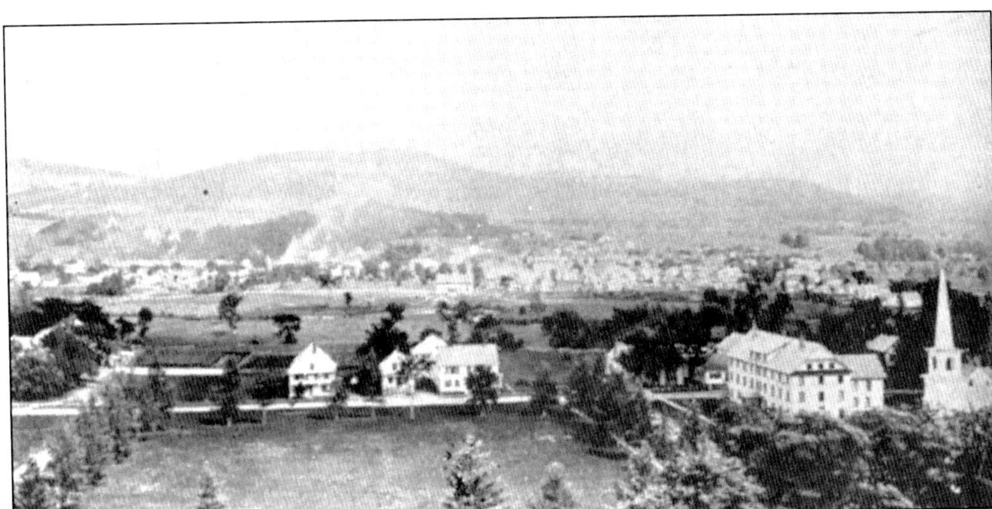

THE SETTING. An early scene of Lyndon Center taken from Lyndon Institute—perhaps from an upstairs window—overlooks the village common, which consists of the school athletic field, the post office and store, and other buildings on the street. Lyndonville is seen across the Passumpsic River; the Burke Mountain rises in the distance. Sanborn Hall, built in 1891, is at the left of the Baptist church. This ideal site for a secondary school was desired by those who incorporated the institution long before it became a reality

# Contents

THE LYNDON

Literary and Biblical Institution

WILL OPEN ITS FIRST TERM

AT

LYNDON CENTER, VERMONT,

On Tuesday, August 23, 1870.

FOR

THE ACADEMIC YEAR 1870-71.

---

CALENDAR:

*Fall Term begins August 23 ; ends November 4.*
*Winter Term begins Nov. 15 ; ends Jan. 20, 1871.*
*Spring Term begins Jan. 31 ; ends April 14, 1871.*
*Summer Term begins April 25 ; ends July 6, 1871.*

# ACKNOWLEDGMENTS

I wish to thank the many people who helped me with this book. First is the Lyndon Alumni Museum curator Gertrude (Angell) Grant '49, who opened the museum for me anytime so that I could browse through the yearbooks, catalogues, files, and photographs. I also thank those in the alumni offices: former headmaster Dwight Davis, alumni secretary Renee Simons, publicity director Lori Raymond, athletic director Merlyn Courser, and development director Paul Wheeler. I thank Jean Thompson who let me choose photographs from her Latin class trip to Rome, business teacher Cathy Tavares, and technology director Norman Legge. Others who were a great help were retired art teacher Bertha Koury, and alumni members Philip Mathewson '30, and Jean (Magill) Gilman '61. I also thank the *Caledonian-Record* for back issue photographs, the *Lyndon Independent*, and others who helped in any way. To all of you—your support was greatly appreciated.

# *One*

# THE EARLY YEARS

The idea of a secondary college preparatory school was conceived in 1855 when the Freewill Baptists held a yearly meeting and selected a committee for the purpose of locating a school in their eastern section. A seminary had already been established at Waterbury Center in the western section. It was not unusual at that time for religious denominations to act as the agency in the founding of many New England institutions. These religious organizations attempted to meet the educational needs of boys and girls and to provide further educational advantages for young men and women. Committee members chose a slope near the 1848 Baptist church in Lyndon Center as a site that they would like for the school.

At last, on November 20, 1867, 9 Baptist clergymen and 13 businessmen of Lyndon and the area, including Canada, became the charter members of the Lyndon Literary and Biblical Institution. Seventeen leading citizens of Lyndon and neighboring towns were selected to act as funds-soliciting agents. When the institute was actually erected, it was on the site they had hoped for: "A point of land in the rear of the house of S.S. Thompson, and that owned by the Parsonage Corporation." The school lot was ten acres, "more or less."

The Lyndon Literary and Biblical Institution opened its first term on August 23, 1870, with 50 pupils. In charge were George W. Worthen, principal (1870–71); Sarah E. Mason, preceptress; Hiram M. Pearl, commercial department and plain and ornamental penmanship; and Luella A. Meigs, music. Furthermore, English and classics were offered; these courses prepared the students for entrance to the best colleges and professional schools in the country. The next two principals were John C. Hopkins (1871–1872), a Civil War veteran and Freewill Baptist minister, and John S. Brown (1872–1881).

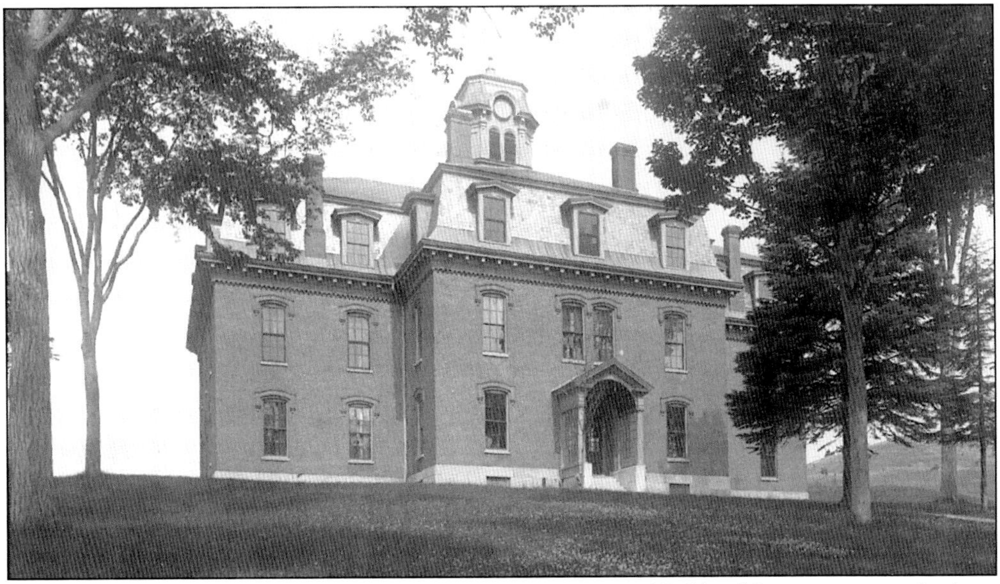

**A Reality.** After years of planning, the Lyndon Literary and Biblical Institution was built in 1869 on a knoll sloping gently toward the village common. The location was deemed ideal for secondary education and was described as "beautiful in all its surroundings, removed from the noise and excitement of a busy village like Lyndonville, yet near enough to make its advantages easily accessible to the students." (William H. Jaffrey, 1904.)

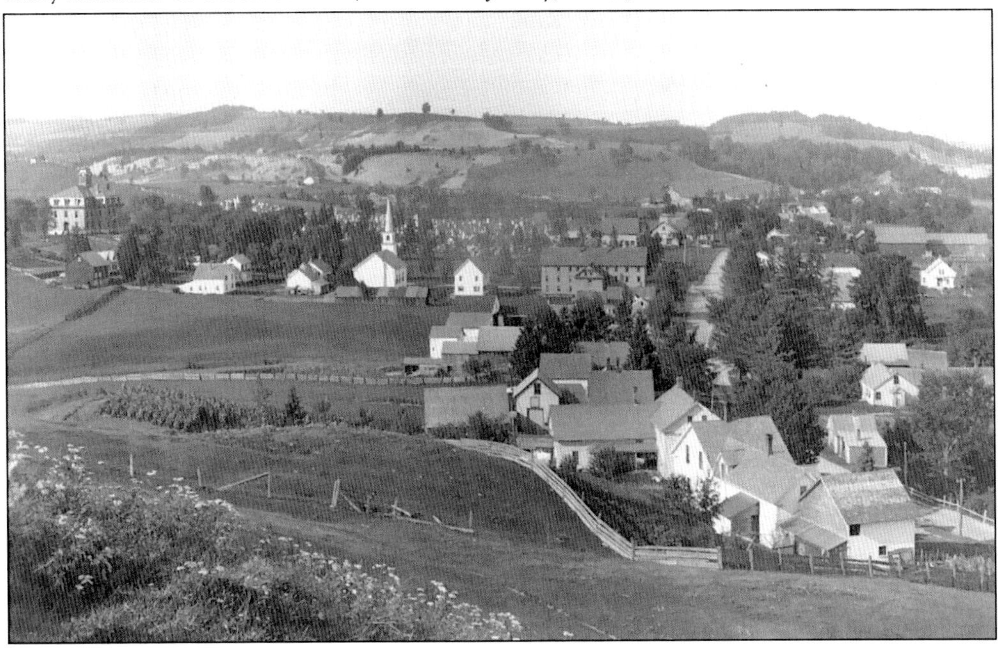

**Lyndon Center.** Seen to the far left is Thompson Hall, named in 1883 in memory of generous supporter Sumner Shaw Thompson, as it appeared in relation to the village of Lyndon Center. The Baptist church is the building with the steeple. To its right is the new Lyndon Center graded school, built in 1900. The large building next to the Lyndon Center school is Sanborn Hall. The cemetery is at the upper center and near it, seen above the roof of Sanborn Hall, is the town hall. The Universalist church is at the right of the town hall.

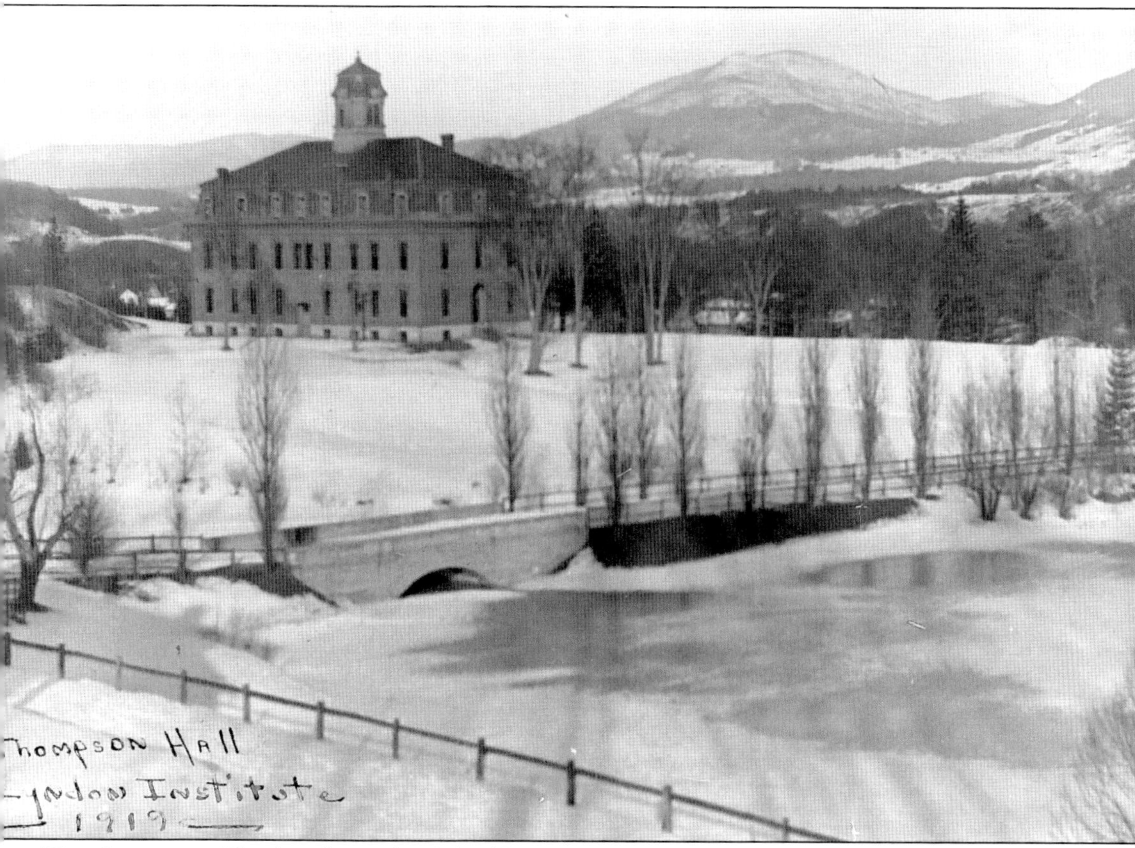


**The Seminary.** This handsome brick building was founded on August 27, 1869. Officers of the institution, clergymen, and citizens formed a procession at the Free Baptist Church and with music by the Lyndonville Band, marched to the site where a speaker's platform had been erected. The cornerstone was placed in an elevated position so that everyone could see it clearly. The building when completed was brick with granite trimming and measured 75 feet by 100 feet. Before 1887, only the chapel and three classrooms had been completed. More rooms were finished as the school grew. Wood stoves furnished heat until 1883 when steam heat was installed. That year, the top floor was finished into three rooms, which accommodated young women. In 1883, Sumner S. Thompson bought the liens upon the institute. He offered to give the building and its furnishings to the school, provided that a permanent endowment of $25,000 could be raised and that the school become nonsectarian. Burke Mountain, an area natural landmark, rises in the distance.

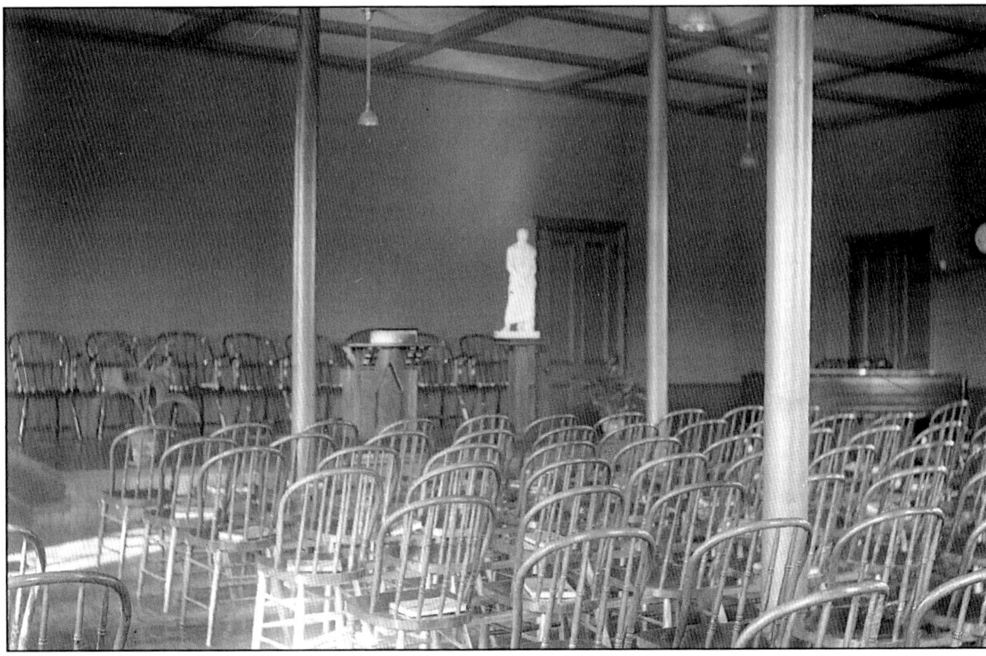

**The Chapel.** Students gathered here every morning for chapel exercises and school announcements. Sometimes noted speakers, such as college presidents and state commissioners, were on the program. Two or three times a week, selections from some composers were given on the pianola, together with a sketch of the featured composer's life.

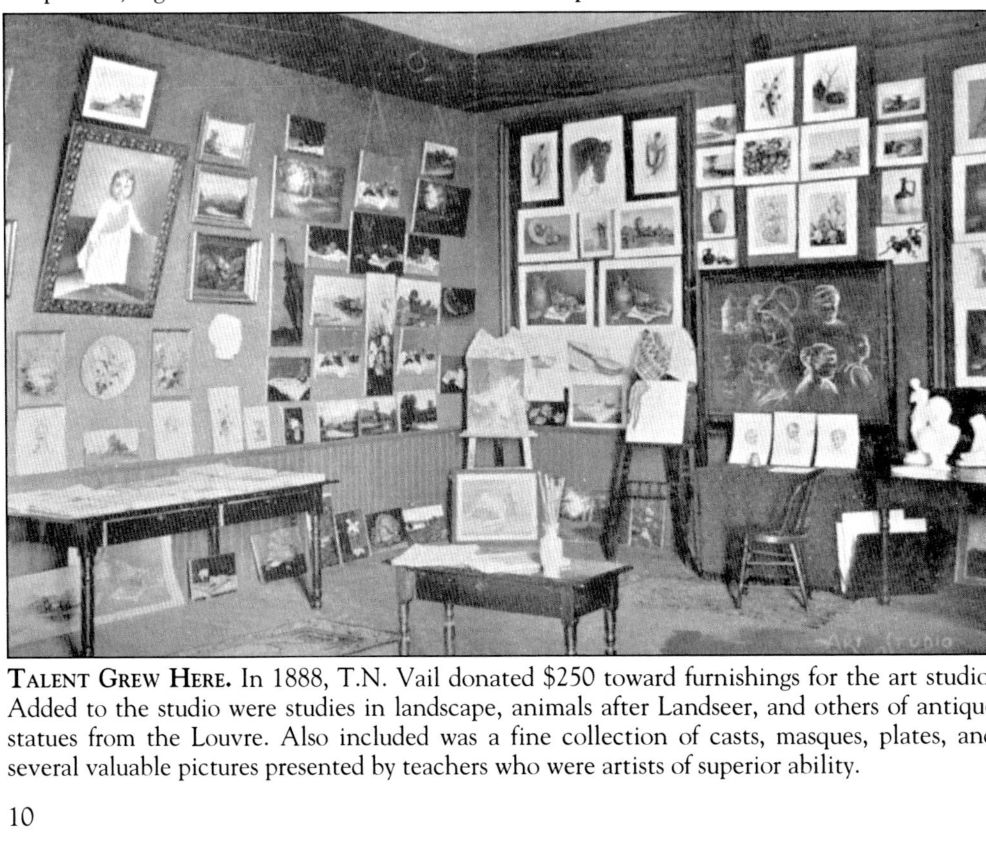

**Talent Grew Here.** In 1888, T.N. Vail donated $250 toward furnishings for the art studio. Added to the studio were studies in landscape, animals after Landseer, and others of antique statues from the Louvre. Also included was a fine collection of casts, masques, plates, and several valuable pictures presented by teachers who were artists of superior ability.

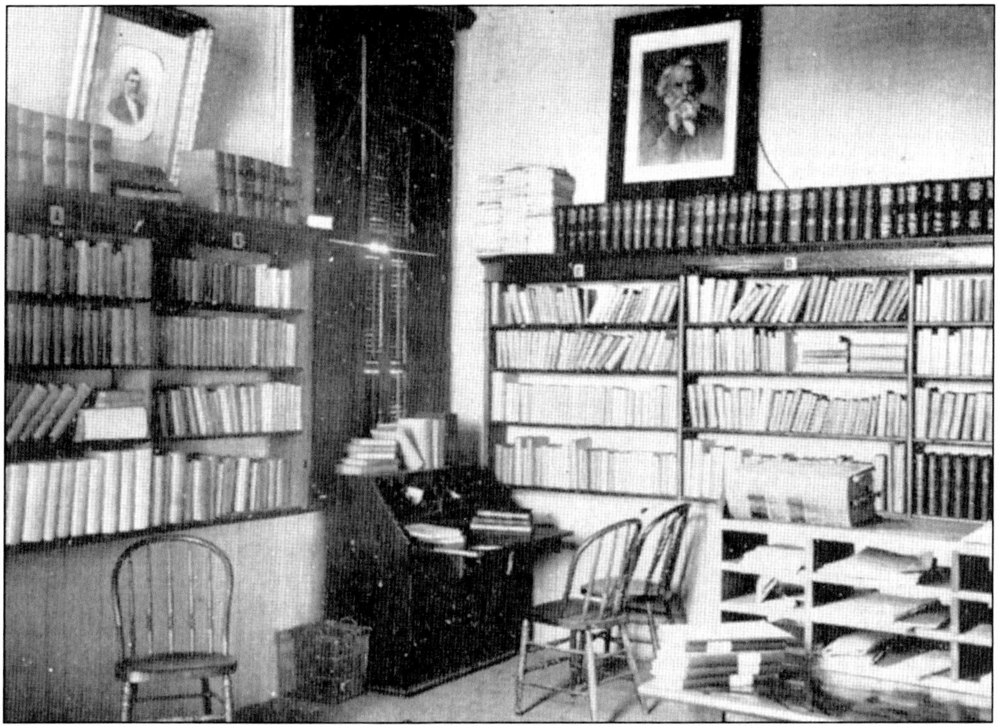

A CORNER OF THE LIBRARY. The 1894–1895 catalogue states that the library has more than 1,000 volumes in a well-lighted pleasant room, provides tables and chairs, and is open for reference work every day. During that year, nearly 100 books were added through the loyalty and generosity of Lyndon's alumni. A large number of leading newspapers and magazines were provided, including the *Lyndonville Journal*.

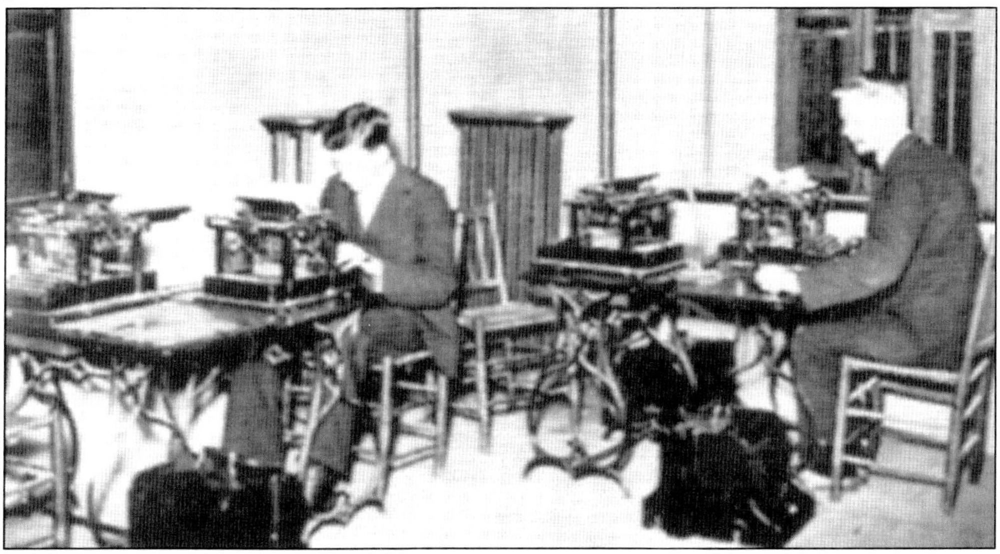

WHAT ARE THESE MACHINES? A commercial course was reestablished in 1884. Typewriting and phonography (phonetic shorthand) were added in 1888. These two students are using Remington No. 2 typewriters. The 1893 catalogue states, "Here is an opportunity for many to gain the means of an excellent livelihood."

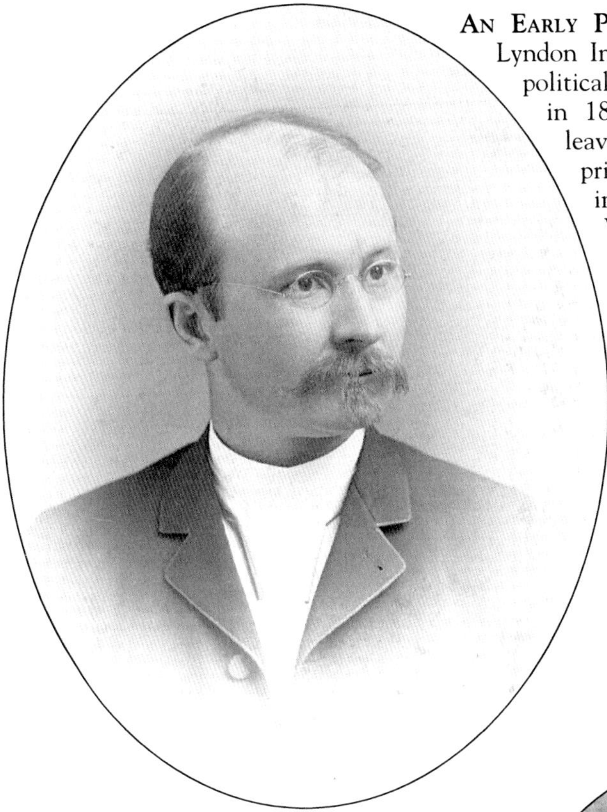

**AN EARLY PRINCIPAL.** Walter Ranger came to Lyndon Institute to teach Latin, Greek, and political science. He was named principal in 1883 and served until 1896. After leaving the institute, Ranger became principal of the Normal School in Johnson and was named the Vermont State Superintendent of Education in 1900.

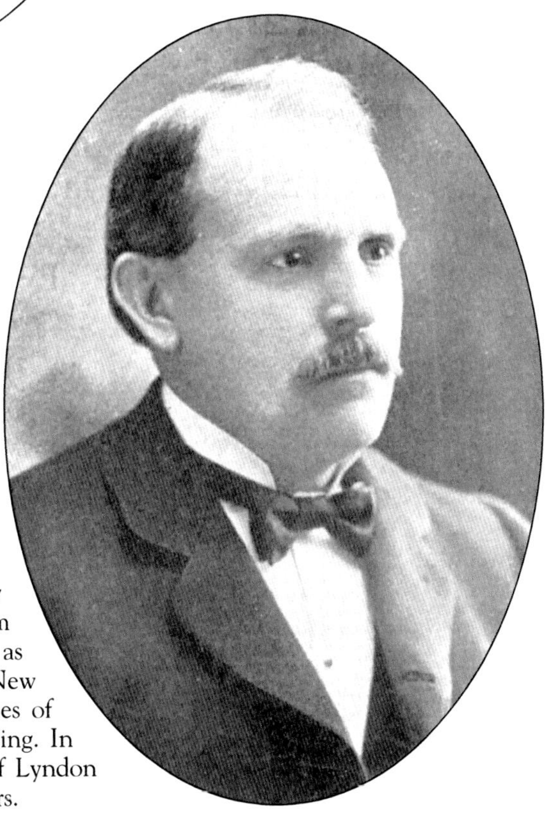

**PRINCIPAL PUGSLEY.** Freemont LaForest Pugsley was born in Rochester, New Hampshire, in 1839. He graduated from Bates College and served for five years as principal of the high school in Henniker, New Hampshire, where he laid out new courses of study and helped secure a fine new building. In 1896, he resigned to become principal of Lyndon Institute, where he remained for seven years.

**PRINCIPAL HARRIS.** Merritt Melvin Harris was born in West Chazy, New York, in 1866. He married Gertrude M. Loomis of Lyndonville, Vermont, and taught at the Troy Conference Academy at Poultney. He was sent to Ecuador to found normal schools. After his return, he was asked to take the position of teacher of science and modern language at Lyndon Institute. Harris filled this position so satisfactorily that upon the resignation of Fremont LaForest Pugsley, he was appointed principal in the fall term of 1903, staying until 1907.

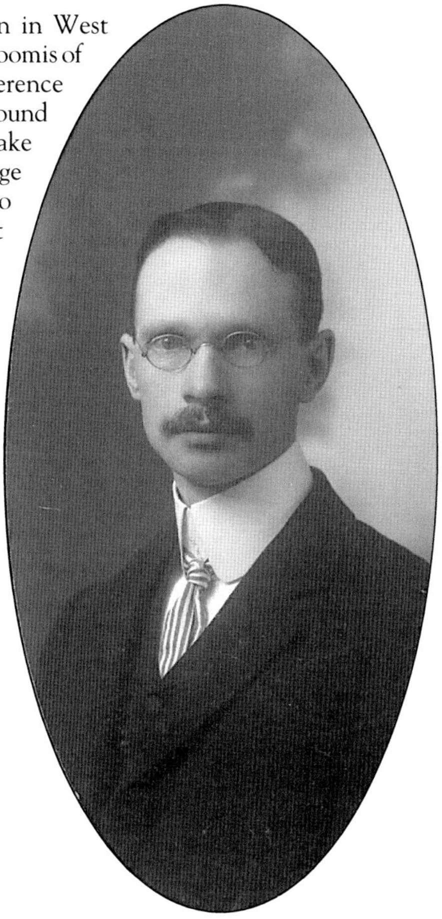

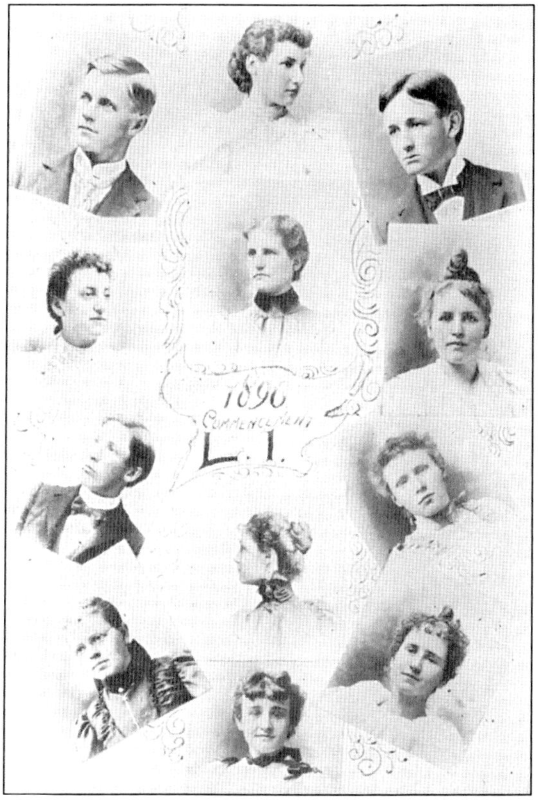


**CLASS PRESENTATION.** In a graduating class of 20 students in 1896, these 12 graduates from the classical and English departments were pictured on the front of the commencement program. The graduates are Lilla Carpenter, Homer Ford, Agnes Frost, Ora Gray, Elizabeth Howatt, Inez Howe, Emma Quimby, Gertrude Ruggles, Bertha Stern, Anna Thompson, Mary Wiggin, and Carlyle Willey.

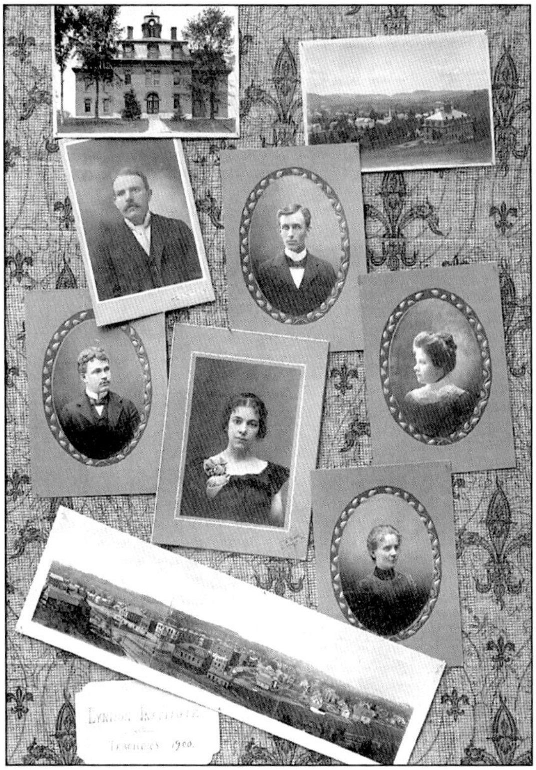

**Souvenir, 1900.** This image shows Lyndon Institute and its teachers. At the top right, Thompson Hall overlooks Lyndon Center. Pictured are, clockwise from top left, Freemont Pugsley, principal; Martin Daniels, commercial teacher; Grace Pugsley, Greek teacher; Cora Brock Daniels, teacher and the wife of Martin Daniels; unidentified; and J. Harold Fuller, science and history teacher. The lower photographs shows the village of Lyndonville.

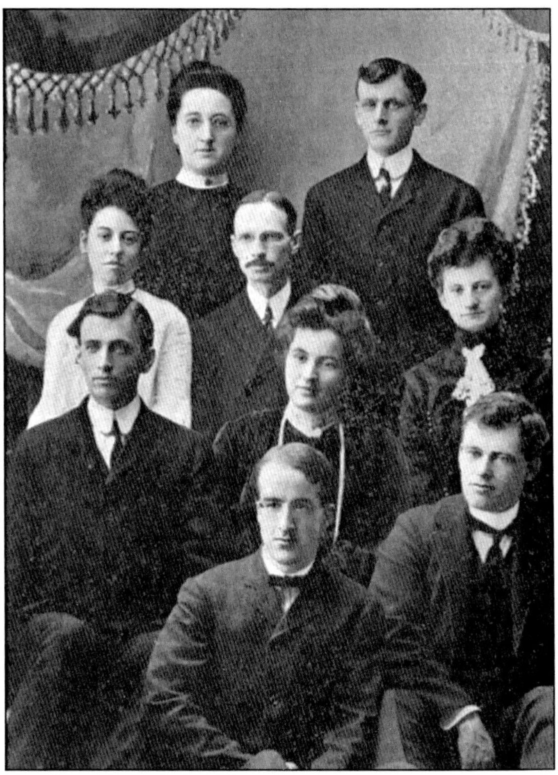

**Faculty, 1903–1904.** Faculty members identified in this photograph are Martin Daniels, principal of the Commercial College, second row, on the left; Merritt Harris, principal, third row, second from the left; and Edwin Daniels, shorthand and typing, fourth row, on the right. The others are John Fuller, Greek and Latin; Bessie Lull, preceptress and Latin, English, and history; Andrew Jackson, mathematics and sciences; Grace Joselyn, piano, organ, and harmony; Alice Hutchinson, voice; and Mabel Stewart, elocution.

**BASKETBALL, 1904.** With the letters L and I showing prominently on their collars, there is no mistaking where these young women are from. One cannot help but notice the sports uniform of 1904: middy blouses, knickers, stockings, and soft-soled shoes to protect the floor. These team members are Grace Deos, Nina Sheldon, Faye Newell, Hortense Murch, and Marguerite Newell.

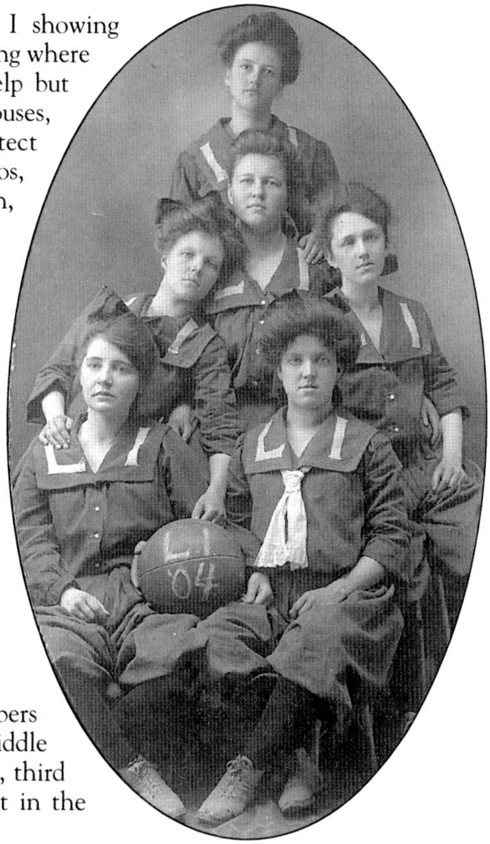


**FOOTBALL, 1904.** The two identified members of the 1904 football team are seated in the middle row: Albert Riley, left, and W. Arthur Simpson, third from left. Any team records were probably lost in the 1922 Thompson Hall fire.

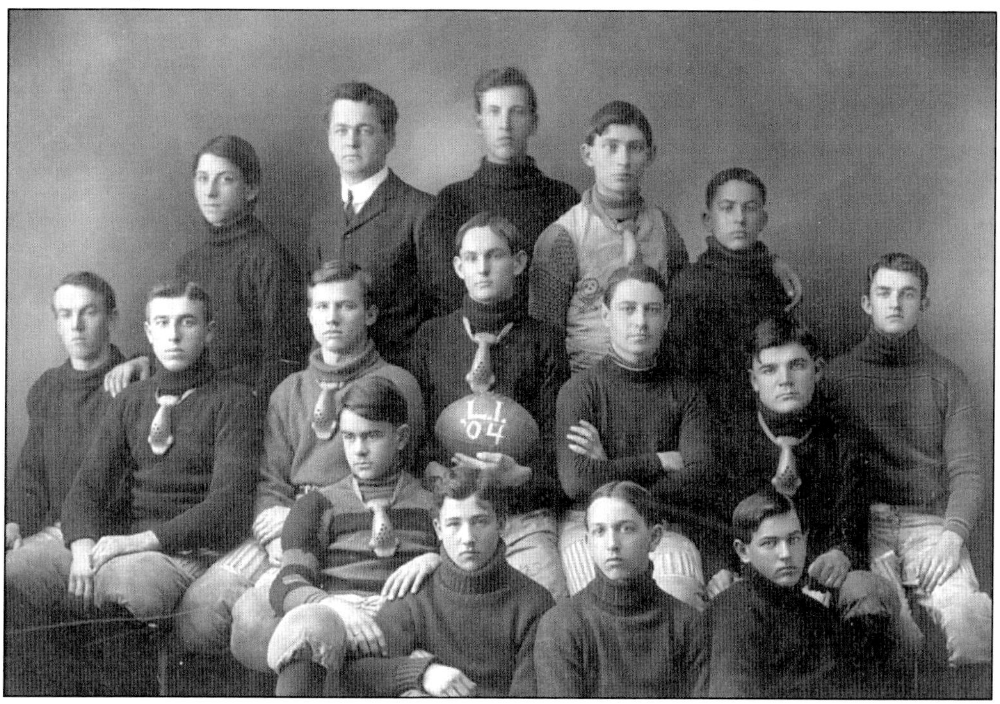

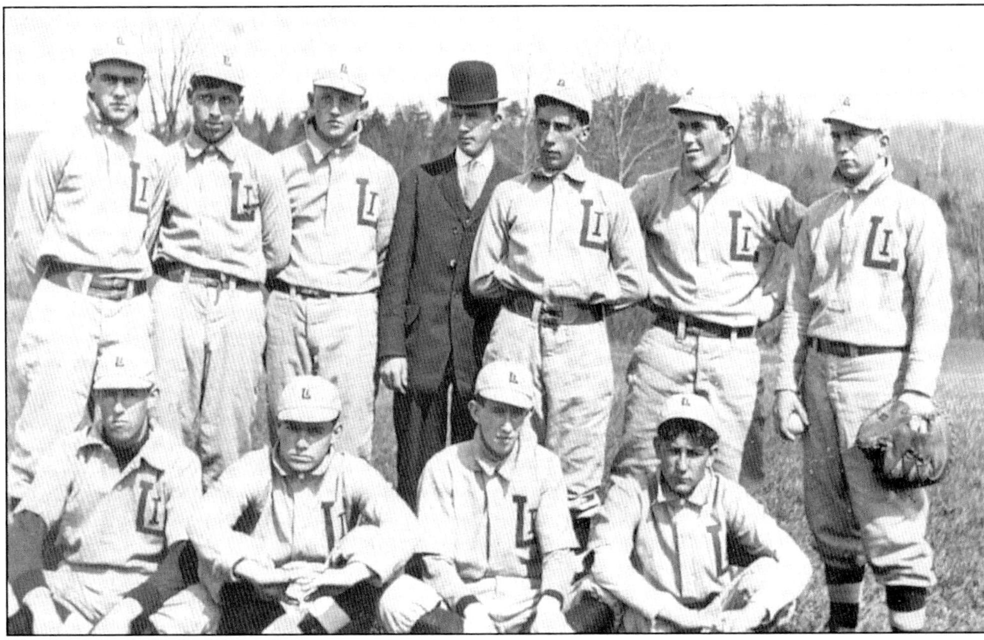

**MEN'S BASEBALL, 1909.** The members of this early baseball team are, from left to right, as follows: (front row) Phil Ferguson, Howard Hunter, ? Kelley, and ? LaFrance; (back row) Lincoln Wilson, Bill Campbell, Rusty Downer, ? Kibbe the trainer and coach, ? Wood, ? Jones, and Robert Wilson.

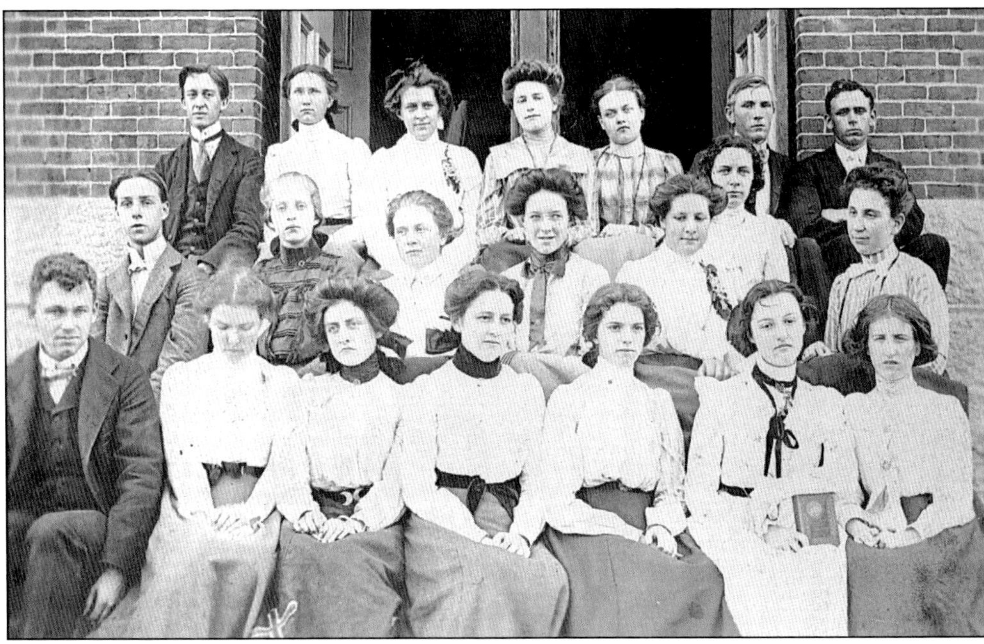

**THE GLEE CLUB, C. 1900.** Music was taught at that time by Gertrude Harris, the wife of Merritt Harris. Completion of the music course usually took three years, depending on previous attainment, talent, and diligence. Frequent performances were expected in both instrumental and vocal departments. Each candidate for graduation was required to give a public recital at the close of the course.

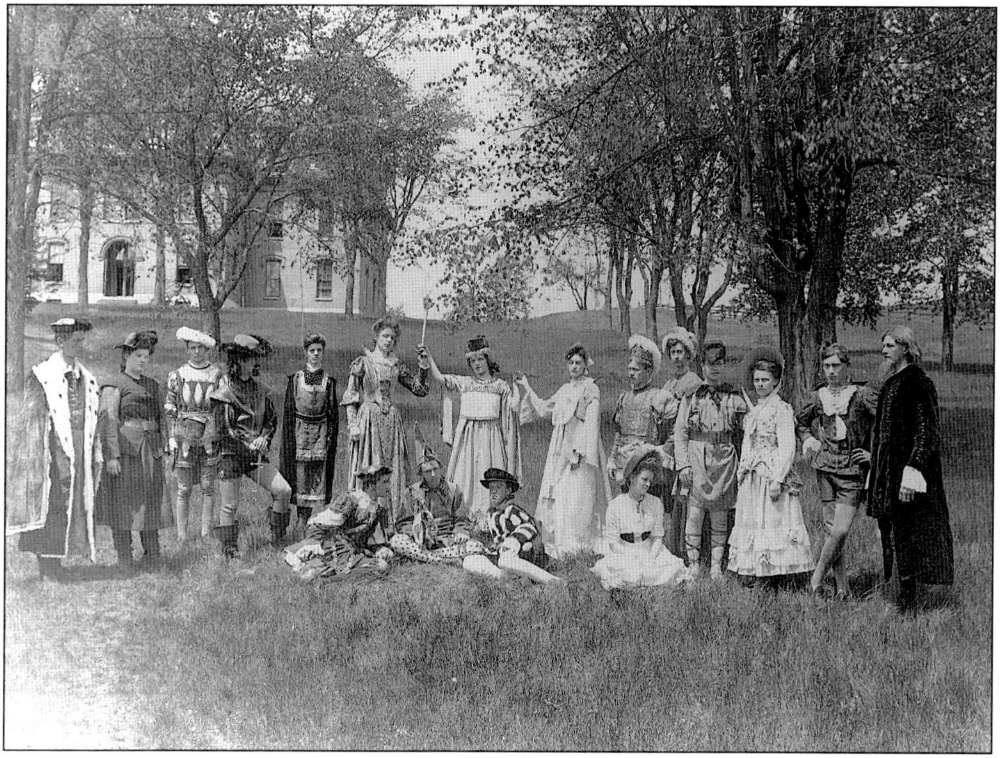

**AS YOU LIKE IT.** Undoubtedly the audience did like it. It appears that the class of 1905 went to their best efforts to make authentic period style costumes. The players are, from left to right, as follows: (front row) Earl Davis, Herbert Burnham, Albert Riley, and Grace Deos; (back row) Glenn Buck, Edith Gray, Ed Carpenter, Fred Rainey, Ida Flower, May Campbell, Faye Newell, Grace Finney, Arthur Simpson, Dana Smith, Walter Cleary, Flossie Chesley, Frank McGinnis, and Carl Smith.

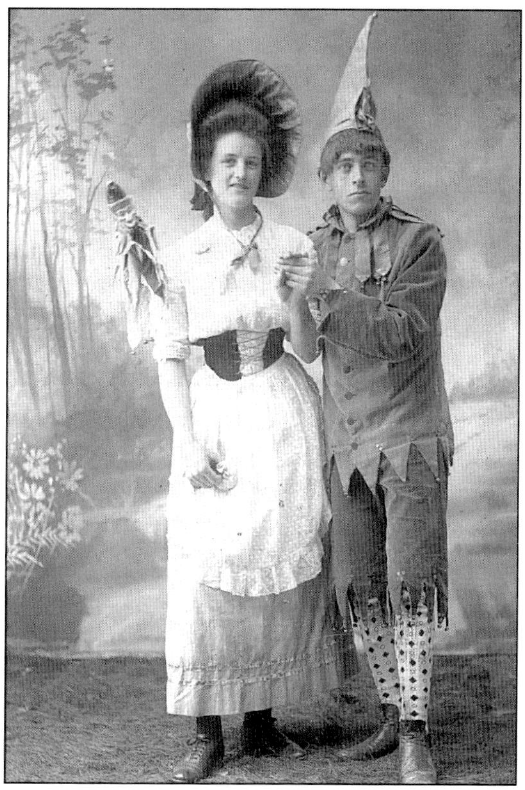

**THE SENIOR PLAY.** Grace Deos plays Audrey, a country wench, and Herbert Burnham is Touchstone, a clown, in *As You Like It*.

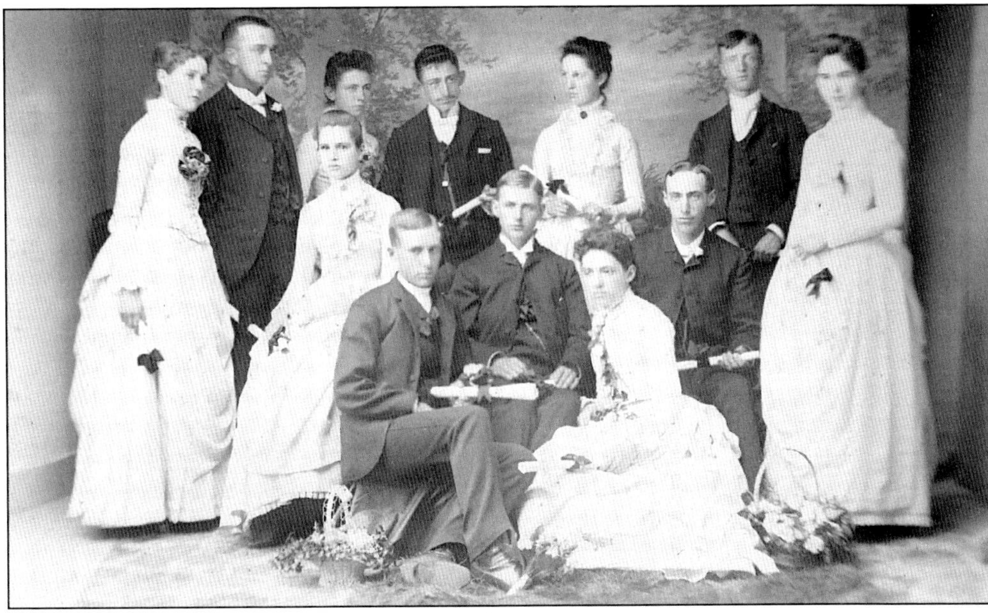

THE GRADUATES OF 1888. Six young men and six young women graduates are dressed in their suits and white dresses with diplomas in hand. They are, from left to right, as follows: (front row) Elvah Smith, Nathan Thompson, Trenholme Hidden, Mabel Dexter, and Nelson Wood;(back row) Clara Thompson, Fred Hoyt, Carrie Donaldson, Herbert Walter, Charlotte Cahoon, Forrest Brown, and Edith Smith.

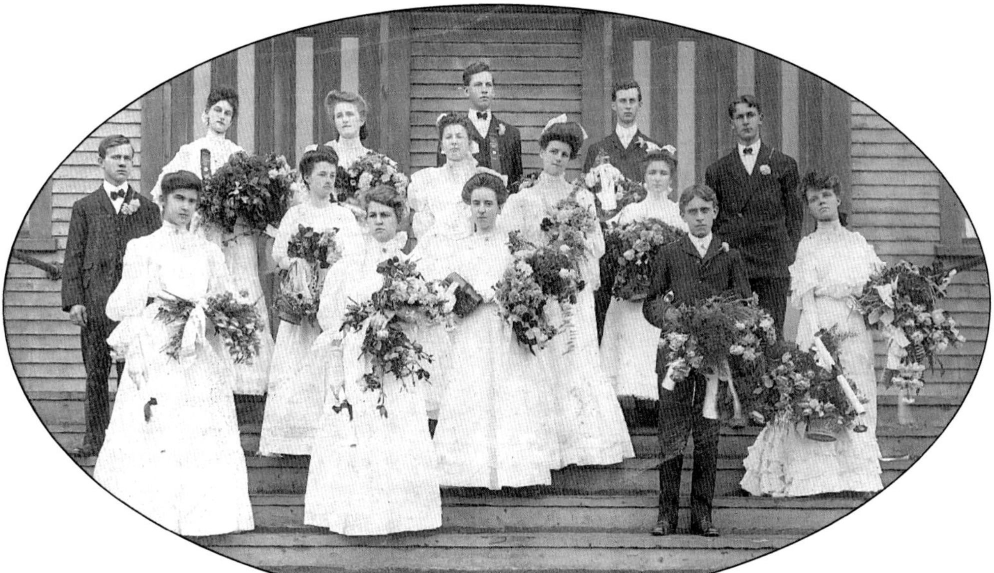

GRADUATION FINERY. Members of the Class of 1905 make a splendid picture in formal graduation attire—white dresses and bouquets, bow ties and boutonnieres—as they pose on the steps of the Music Hall in Lyndonville, where graduation ceremonies were held. At the far left are Arthur Simpson and Hazel Cunningham. For many years now, the graduation attire has been caps and gowns in the school colors: white for the young women and maroon for the young men.

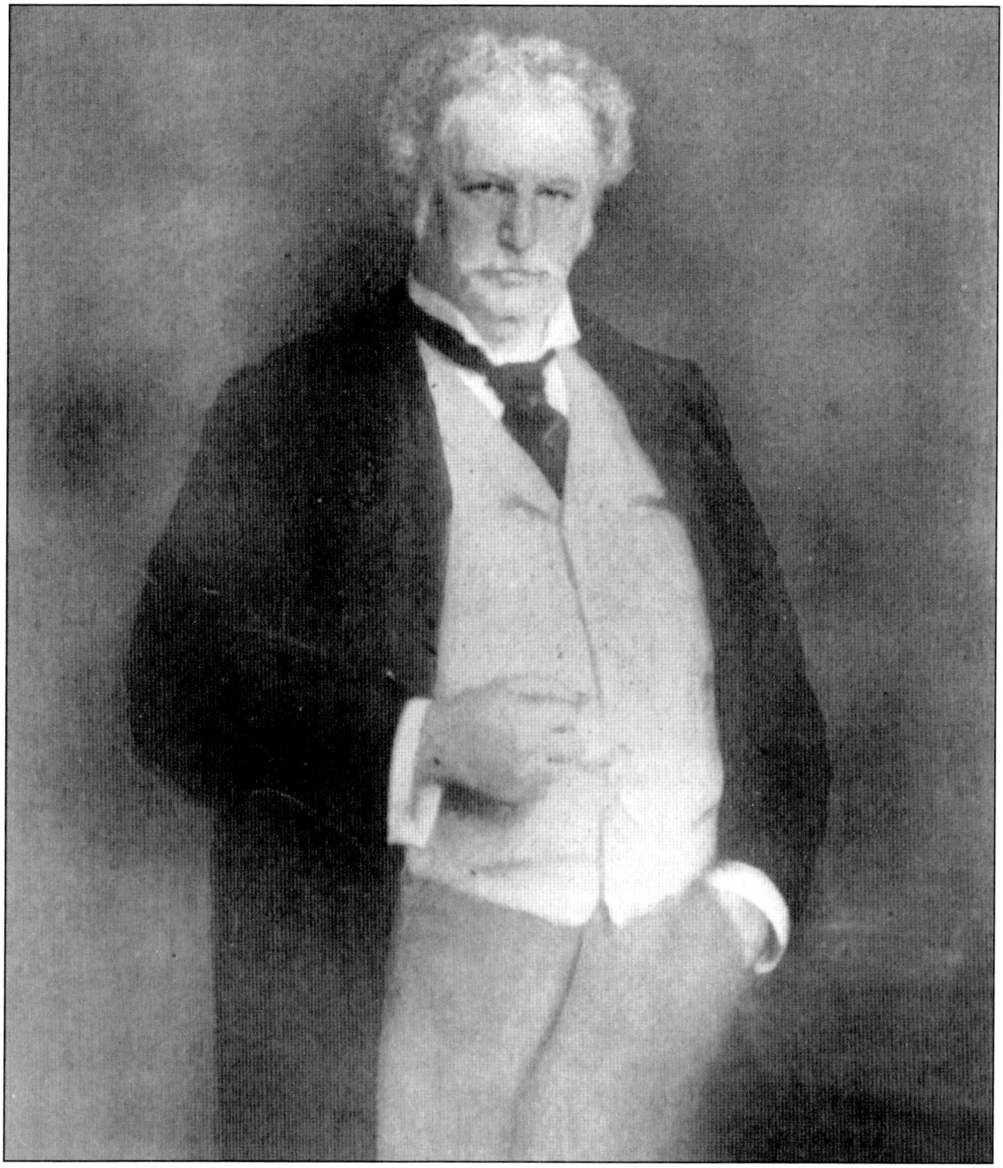

**THEODORE NEWTON VAIL (1845–1920).** Theodore Vail was from a family who were connected with his uncle's Speedwell Iron Works in Morristown, New Jersey. As the head mail clerk for the Union Pacific Railroad, Vail became friends with Luther B. Harris, a civil engineer from Lyndon Center who was building bridges for the same railroad. While visiting Harris at his home in Lyndon Center, Vail was so taken with the area that in 1883, he bought the Calvin Bigelow farm on the hill above Lyndon Center and changed it into a twin-towered mansion. Earlier, in 1878, he had been made general manager of the newly formed American Bell Telephone Company. He later founded the American Telephone and Telegraph Company and was its first president. He bought other property on the hill, which became "Vail Hill," and stocked the resulting Speedwell Farms with French coach horses, Jersey cattle, Shropshire Dorsett sheep, and Welsh ponies. He conducted much of his business from his home with the elaborate telephone system he had installed. He served as president of the Lyndon Institute Board of Trustees for many years.

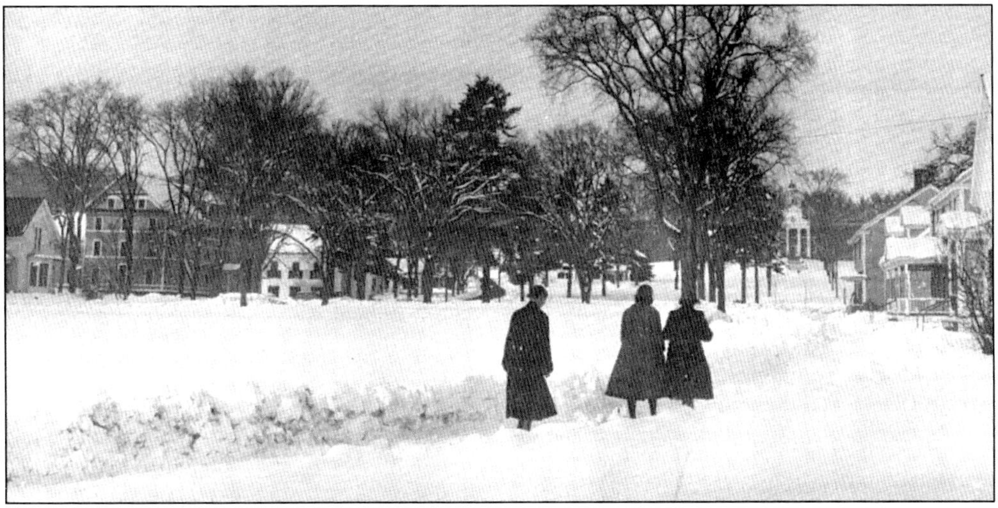

**The Quadrangle.** In 1912, Theodore Vail assumed full management of Lyndon Institute. He bought up all the property in the middle of Lyndon Center and moved buildings to form the present quadrangle, now known as the Vail Campus. Seen on the left are the Willey House and the Sanborn House. On the right are the back of the store and post office, the Tavern, and Smith Cottage. In 1915, Vail made a gift of these properties to the institute. Also seen to the right of the Sanborn House are windows of the Baptist church, which was not the property of the institute.

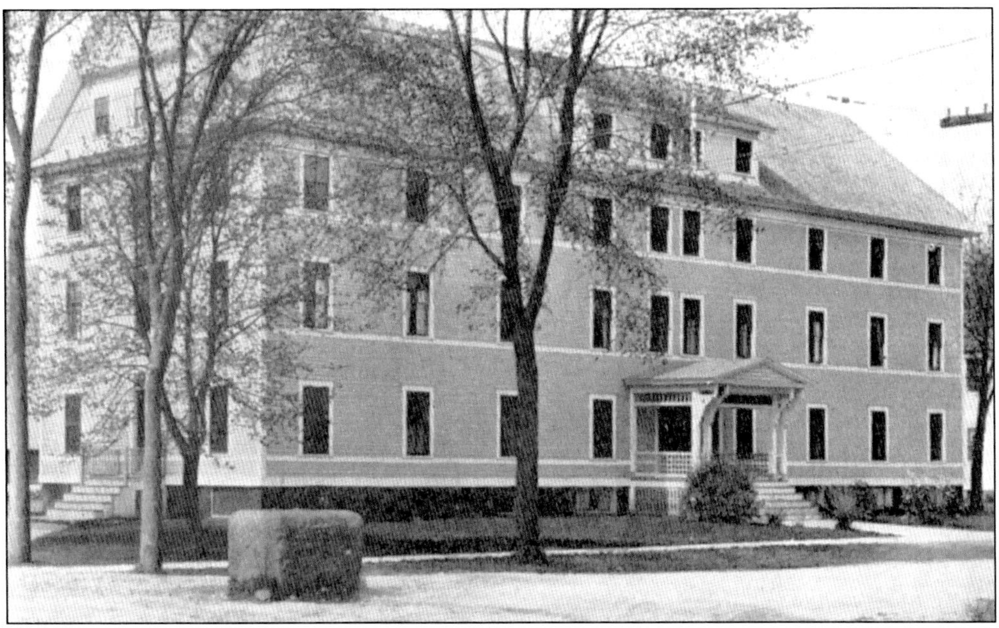

**Sanborn Hall.** Built in 1891, this hall was named for Isaac W. Sanborn, the Lyndon town clerk and treasurer from 1888 to 1902, secretary and treasurer of the institute, and constant benefactor. The hall was divided into two parts: West Hall for young ladies with the resident preceptress, Aby Lyle Eveleth; and East Hall for young men, managed by teacher William Bunker. In 1916, it became a dormitory for the Vail Agricultural School and in 1922, a dormitory for Lyndon Normal School. The water tub in front was chiseled out of a granite block by Luther B. Harris, an institute benefactor. The tub still stands today.

# *Two*

# A New Era

On a bitter cold night in January 1922, Ernest Grant was tending the fire in his tenement when he went to the door to look at the thermometer, according to the *Vermont Union Journal*. He happened to look up at the institute and saw a small blaze flashing from the belfry. The alarm was spread quickly and the Lyndonville and Lyndon Center fire companies responded, but the fire was caught in an upward draft and it was impossible to save the building.

In the morning, most of the 300 students began arriving for the first day of the winter term. Chapel exercises were held in the Baptist church and a recess was called so that arrangements could be made to resume school on January 9, using temporary quarters. Eighteen of the Institute trustees met that same morning and formed a committee to reconstruct the building. The trustees who were present pledged $30,000. Insurance adjusters came quickly and determined that the full amount would be paid: $4,000 on the building and $2,000 on the contents. Townspeople and organizations rallied around to help raise the additional funds needed to rebuild.

The new $200,000 building was dedicated on December 21, 1922, with impressive ceremonies in the beautiful chapel and Elmer A. Darling, president of the Board of Trustees, presiding. Among the dignitaries present was former Gov. Samuel W. McCall of Massachusetts, whose wife, a Lyndon Institute graduate of 1873, was the daughter of the first institute president, Sumner S. Thompson. The day's program included two receptions and tours of the building.

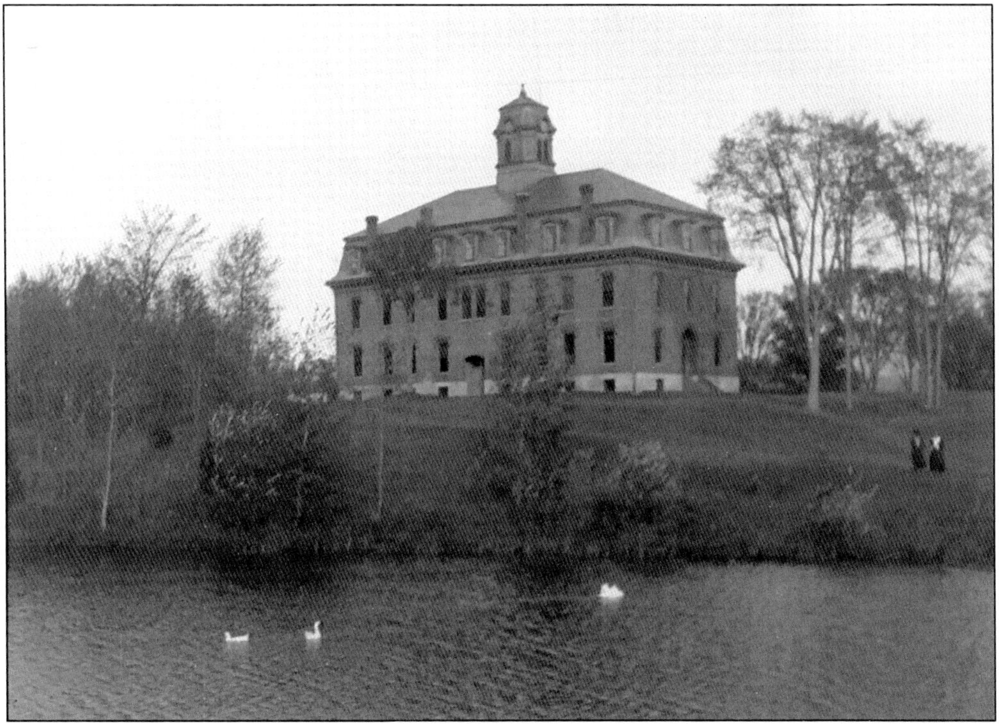

**The Demise of Thompson Hall.** This beautiful school building, the pride of the area, fell to the flames that cold January night. The fire had apparently been smoldering under the roof, and the attic part was a mass of flames before it was discovered. When the bell and belfry crashed to the floor, flames shot up so high in the air that the wind carried burning scraps of paper a mile or more away. At the time of the fire, the swans that are shown here were in their winter quarters behind Principal Mathewson's home.

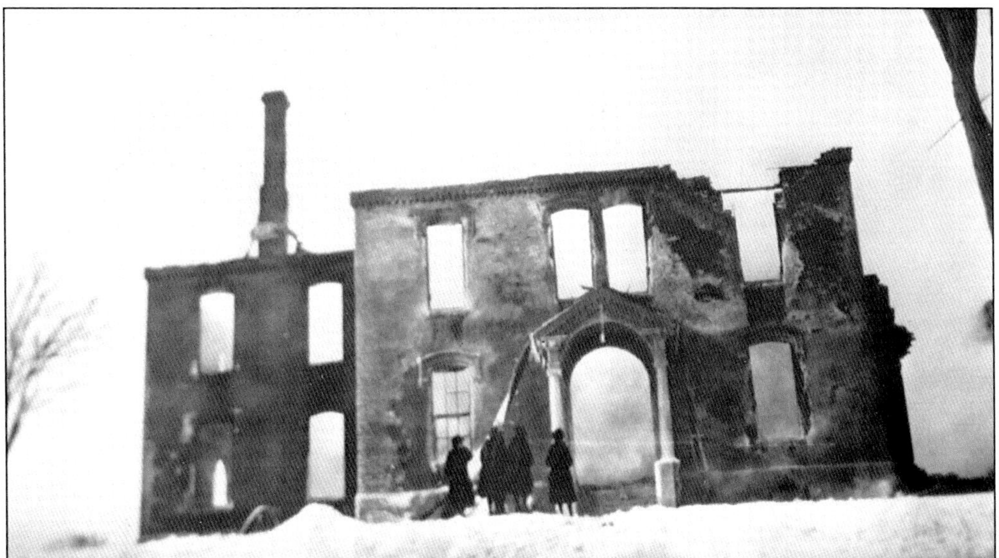

**Viewing the Ruins.** Observers stare in disbelief at what is left of Thompson Hall. This photograph was taken before the chimney was removed for safety's sake.

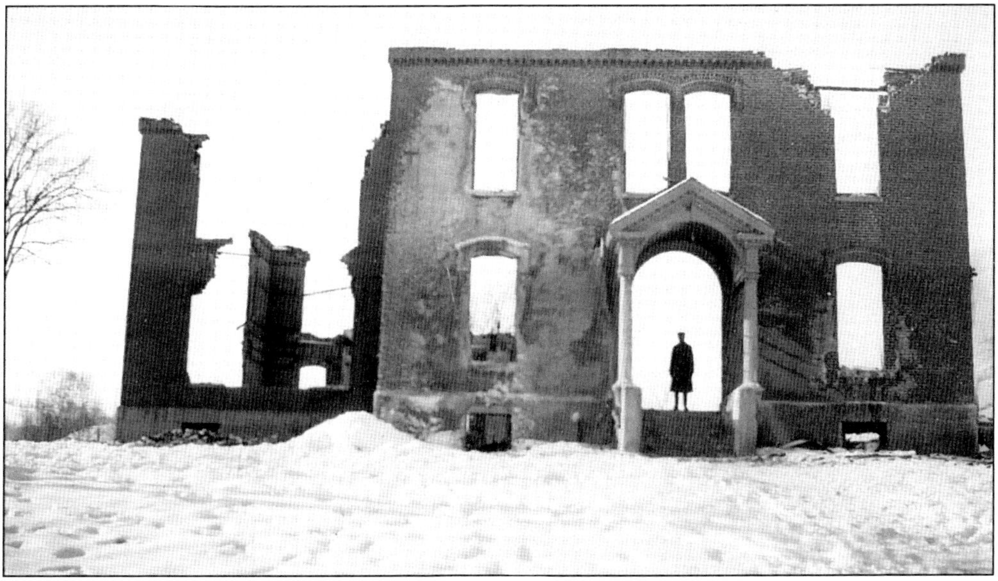

**Our School Will Rise Again.** William Bemis stands framed in the doorway of the Thompson Hall ruins. Townspeople and organizations rallied together to help raise the funds for rebuilding.

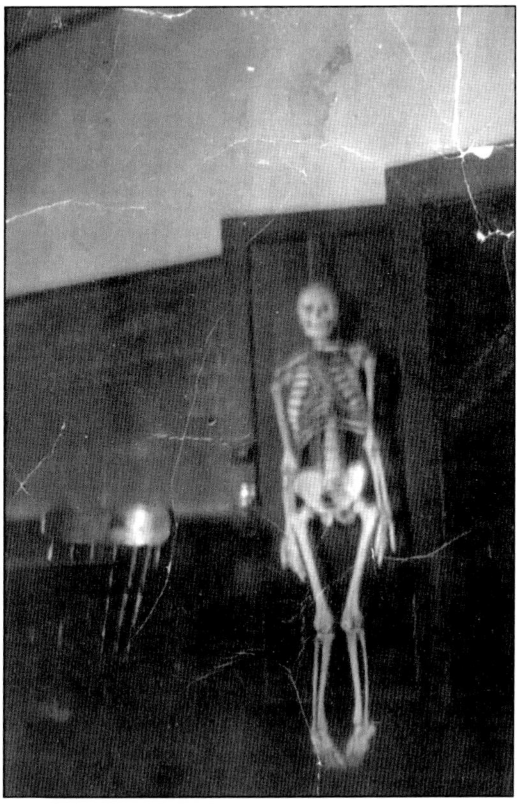

**Just Hanging Around.** As one might guess, this bony classmate was the butt of jokes among the students who, nevertheless, learned more than "the hip bone connected to the thigh bone" in biology class with her help. Sadly, Bessie the skeleton lost her "life" in the Thompson Hall fire. One student was heard to remark, "What will we do without our dear departed skeleton?"

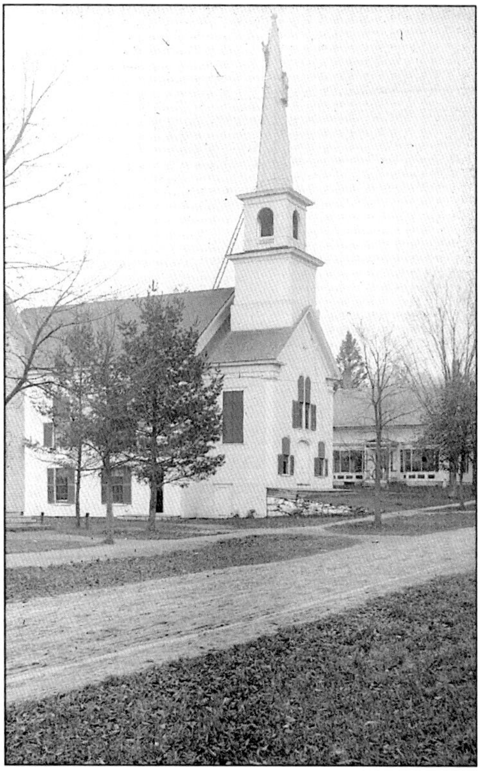

**THE TEMPORARY CLASSROOMS.** School resumed within a week after the fire, and schoolwork continued in the best and most thorough manner possible. Classes were held not only in the dormitories Sanborn Hall and the Mathewson House but also in the nearby Baptist church and the town hall, seen below.

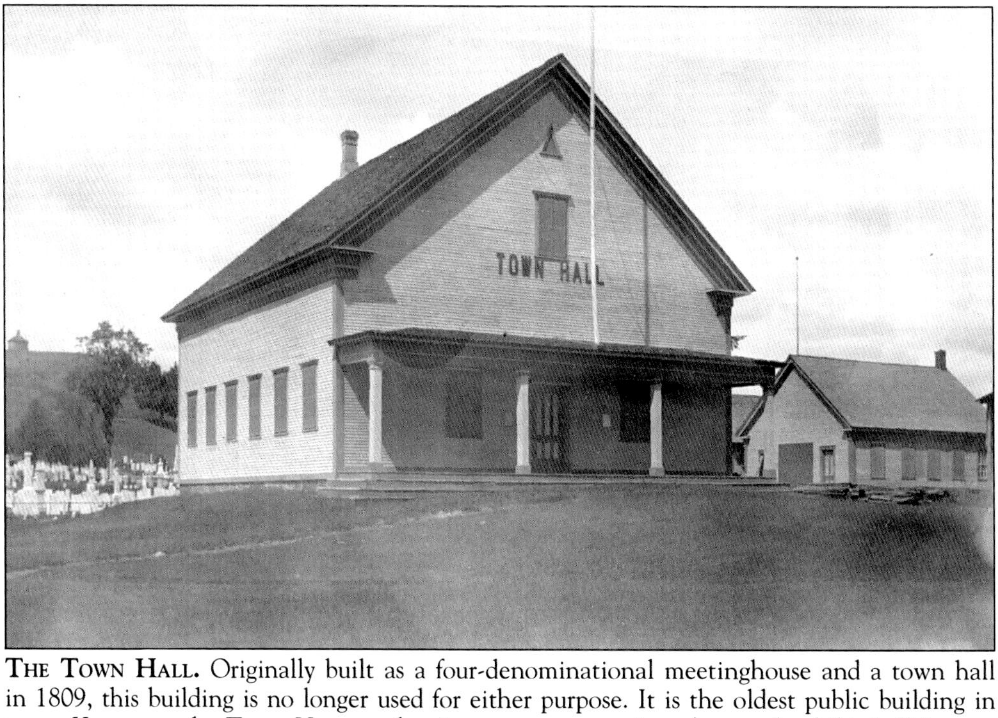


**THE TOWN HALL.** Originally built as a four-denominational meetinghouse and a town hall in 1809, this building is no longer used for either purpose. It is the oldest public building in town. Known as the Town House today, it serves as a meeting place and exhibit hall for any organizations wishing to use it.

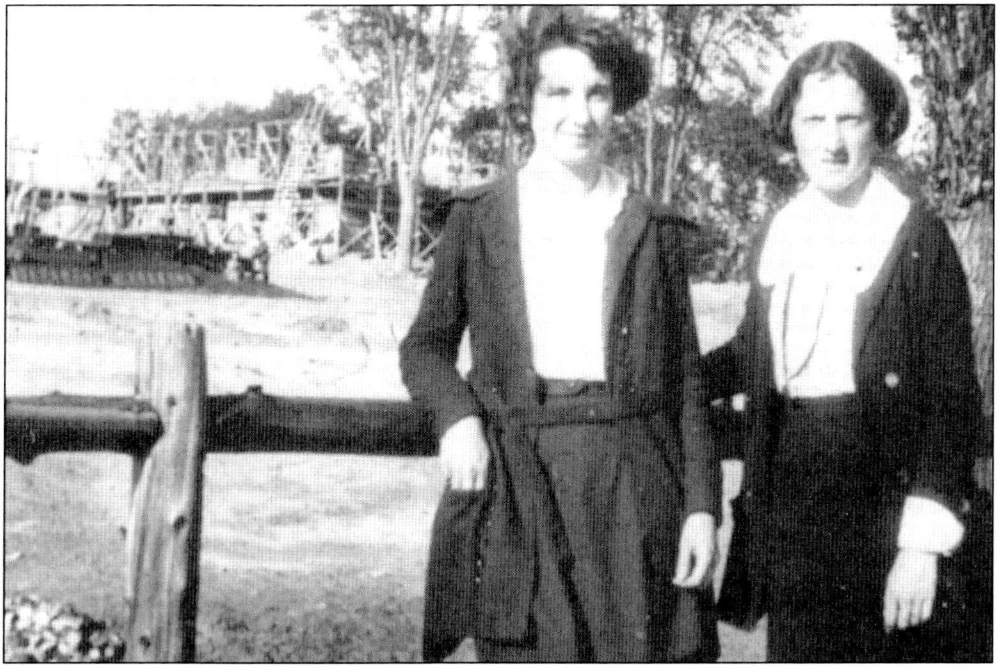

**Classmates of 1922.** Elizabeth (Harris) Brown and Helen Dexter pause near the site of the new Lyndon Institute construction. Elizabeth Brown was a major contributor to the renovation project that made the former Lyndon Center graded school (also known as the Campus School) the E.H. Brown Commercial Business Center. That campus was named the L.B. Harris Campus for her grandfather, an early benefactor. Helen Dexter was the physical education instructor for the young women at Lyndon Institute from 1929 to 1937.

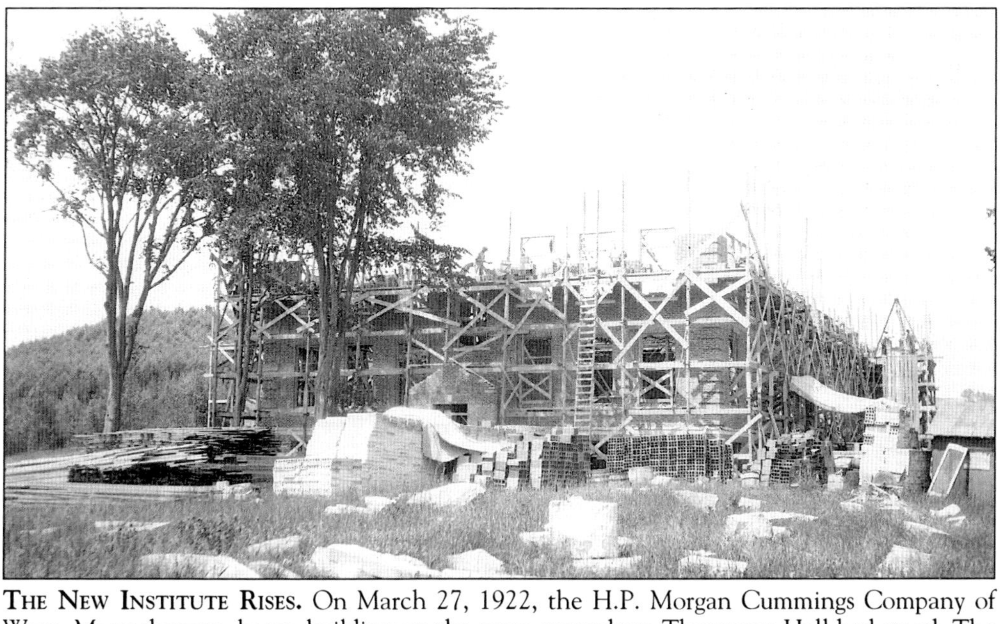

**The New Institute Rises.** On March 27, 1922, the H.P. Morgan Cummings Company of Ware, Massachusetts, began building on the same spot where Thompson Hall had stood. The new building measured 160 feet long by 68 feet wide, with a rear wing of 50 feet by 43 feet to contain the chapel and the gymnasium beneath it.

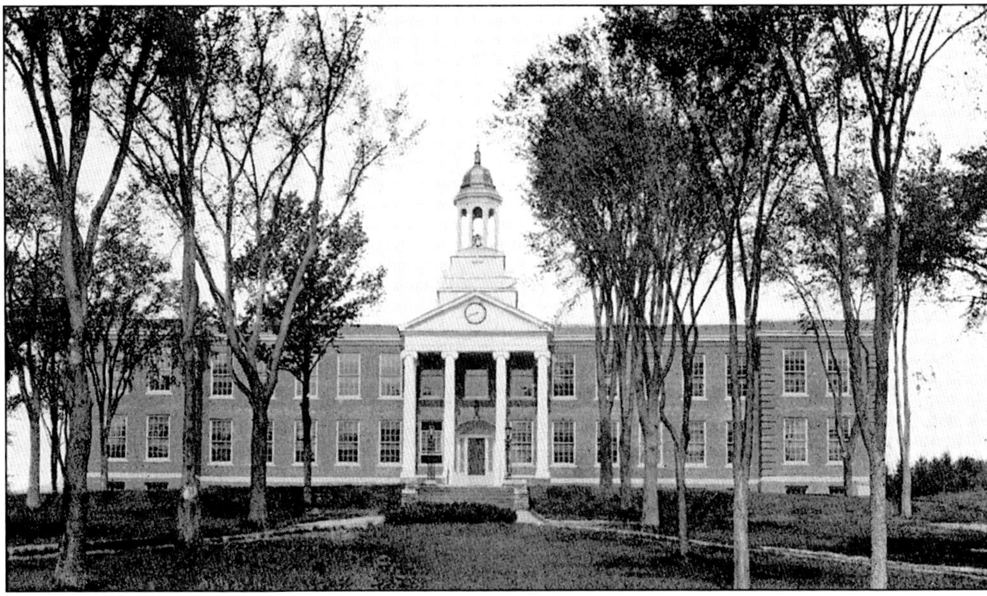

**The New Institute.** The weekly newspaper, the *Vermont Union*, said that the building "is fireproof with modern heating, lighting, ventilation, and sanitation, with furnishings and equipment entirely new and thoroughly modern. It is one of the best secondary school buildings in New England." The building has simple lines enhanced by fluted columns and a graceful belfry. It was dedicated on December 21, 1922, less than a year after fire destroyed Thompson Hall. The winter term opened in the new institute on January 9, 1923, with approximately 300 students.

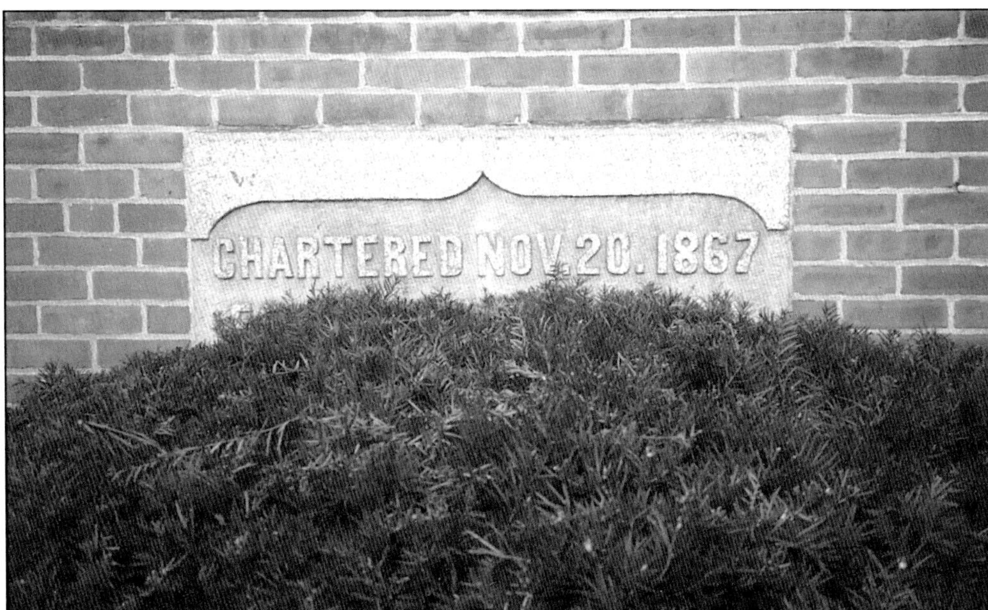


**The Cornerstone.** Resurfaced and relettered, the old cornerstone now reads, "Chartered Nov. 30, 1867. Founded Aug. 27, 1869. Rebuilt 1922." Though partly hidden behind hedges today, what is showing of the granite cornerstone stands out against the red brick. It is set into the front left corner of the building.

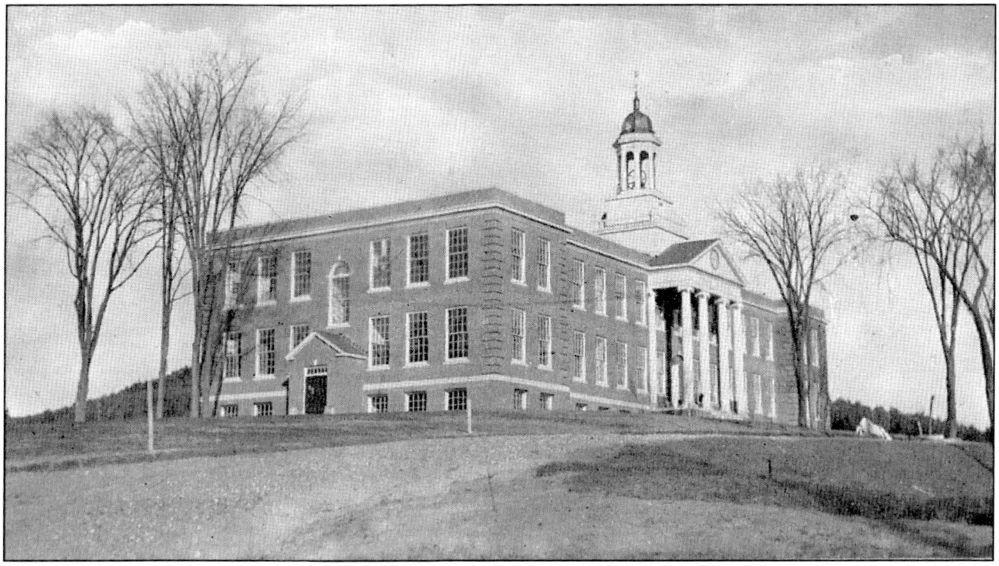

**THE SOUTH END OF LYNDON INSTITUTE.** The reverse side of this postcard reads, "Ideal location. Large campus and beautiful grounds. Modern buildings and equipment. Excellent gymnasium. Strong athletic teams. Lyndon Institute offers College Preparatory Course, English Scientific Course, Household Economics and Arts, Agriculture." The side door was the boys' entrance; a matching one on the north end was for the girls. The two-entrance custom continued for many years, as it had at Thompson Hall.

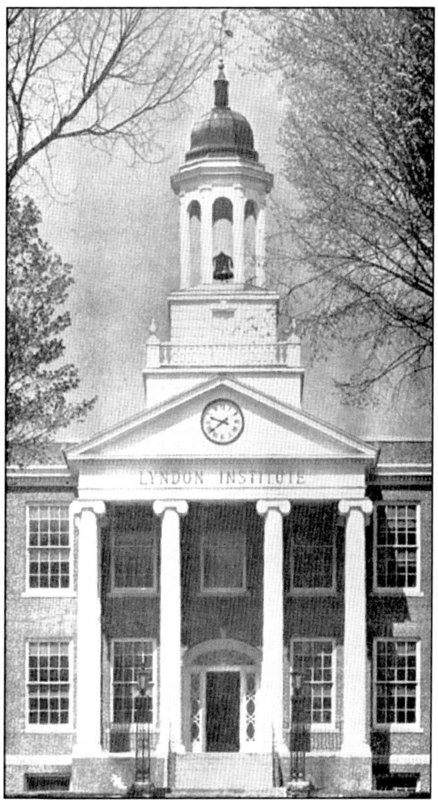


**STRONG AND BEAUTIFUL.** This view appeared in many catalogues of Lyndon Institute, with the following words: "Beautiful both in location and architecture."

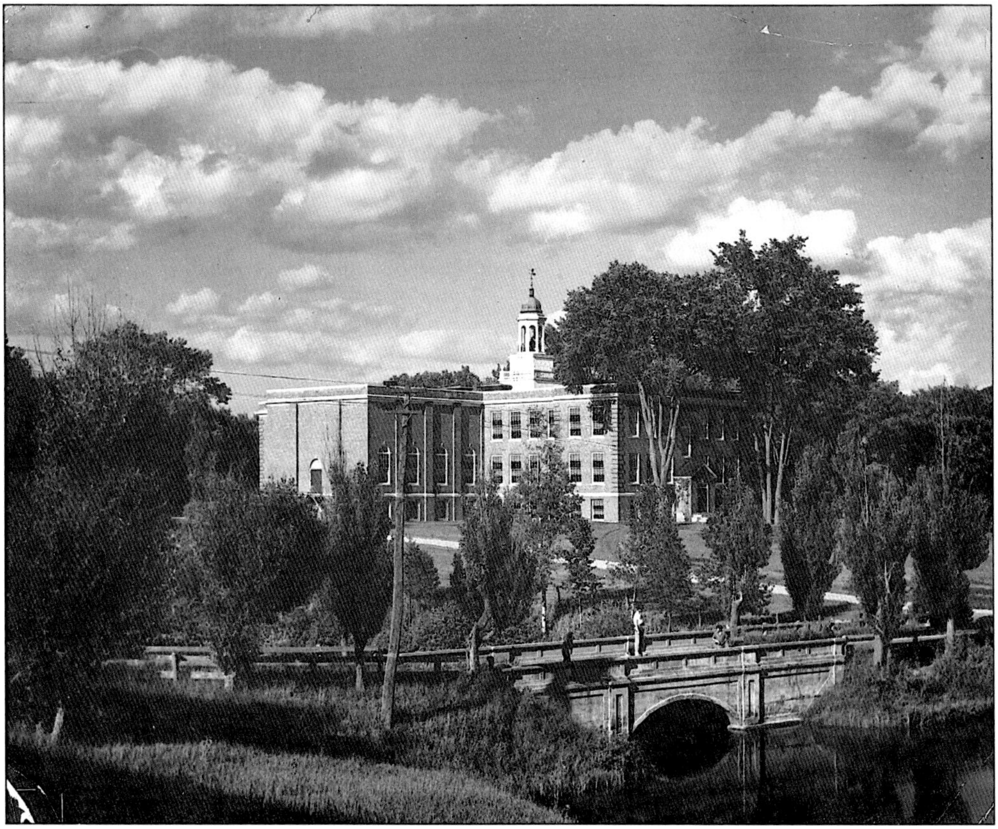

**THE CHERISHED VIEW.** The photographer caught this scenic rear view of Lyndon Institute, showing the chapel, the wing, the elm trees, and Matty's Pond flowing under the Vail Bridge. The elm trees are long gone and the bridge became a highway culvert when the road leading to Vail Hill and Lyndon State College was widened to accommodate more traffic. This image of the institute is a nice comparison to the one of the first building, Thompson Hall, on page 9.

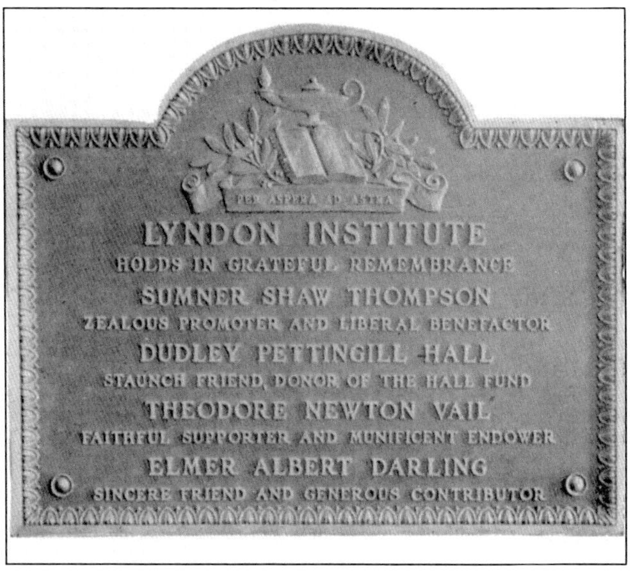


**IN MEMORY.** A bronze tablet on the wall near the main entrance bears the following inscription: "*Per Aspera Ad Astra* [Through hope to the stars]. Lyndon Institute holds in grateful remembrance Sumner Shaw Thompson, zealous promoter and liberal benefactor; Dudley Pettingill Hall, staunch friend, donor of the Hall Fund; Theodore Newton Vail, faithful supporter and munificent endower; Elmer Albert Darling, sincere friend and generous contributor." These loyal men were the first four presidents of Lyndon Institute.

**THE ZEALOUS PROMOTER AND LIBERAL BENEFACTOR.** Sumner Shaw Thompson (1823–1889) came to Lyndon from Massachusetts in 1856. He was a railroad contractor, a financial director, and a lumber businessman associated with the Lyndon Mill. He was a liberal supporter of church and school. His donations to Lyndon Institute amounted to more than $30,000. In 1883, he bought the institute for the liens upon it with the provision that a permanent endowment of $25,000 be raised and that the school become nonsectarian.

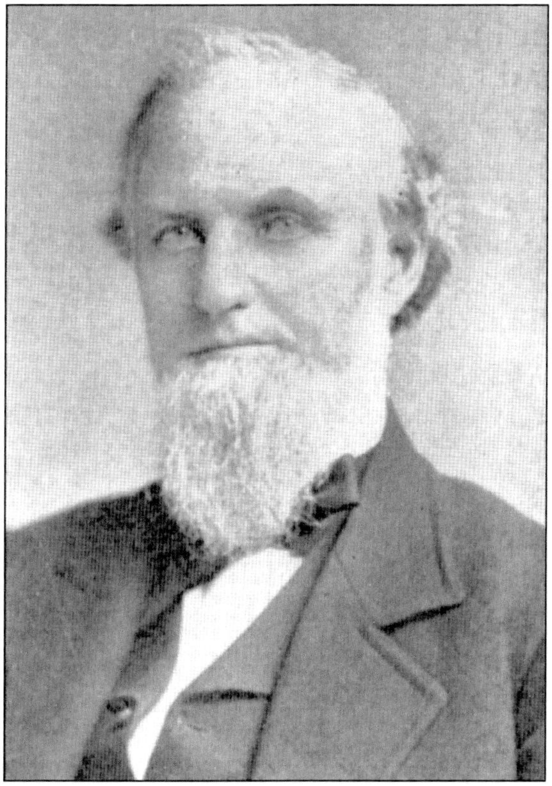

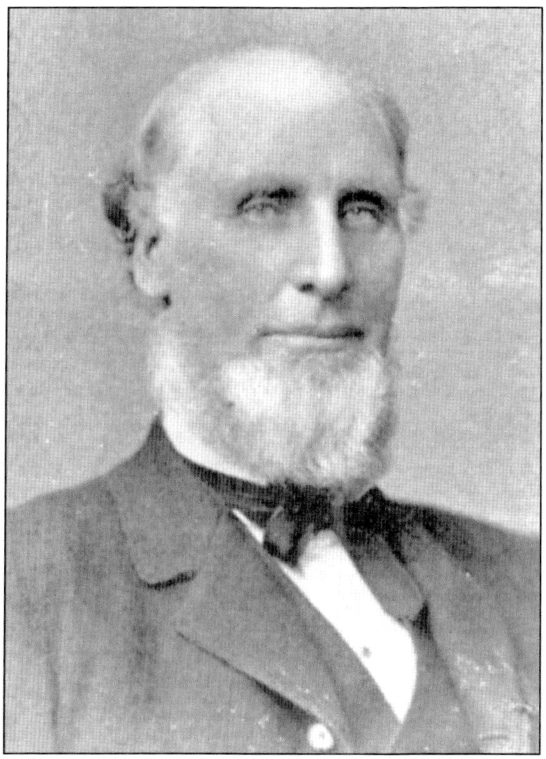

**THE STAUNCH FRIEND AND DONOR OF THE HALL FUND.** Dudley Pettingill Hall (1820–1885) was born in Hart's Location, New Hampshire. He built mills in Concord, Vermont, and moved to East Burke, where he bought a gristmill and a sawmill. He came to Lyndon in 1864, was in business in the Lyndon Mill Company, and built a home that was called Riverside. The home remained a private until 1981 when it became a private school for grades four through eight.

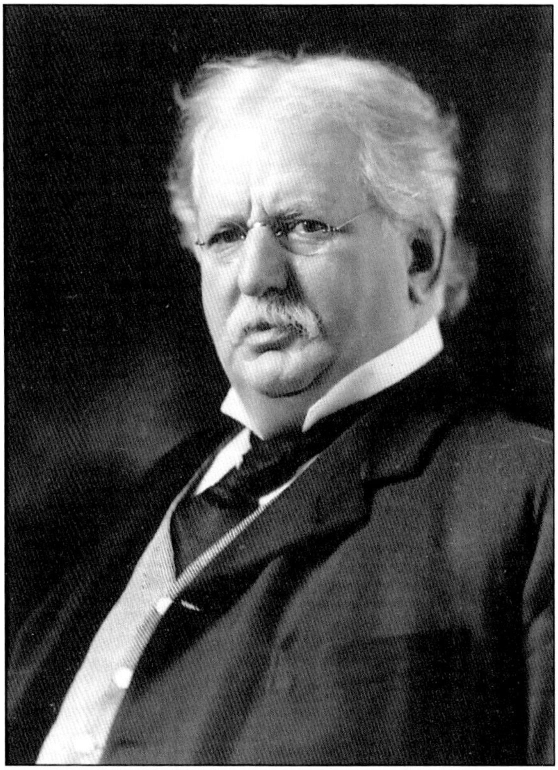

**THE FAITHFUL SUPPORTER AND MUNIFICENT ENDOWER.** Though Theodore N. Vail (1845–1920) traveled a great deal on business, Lyndon remained his beloved home after 1889, when he made it his official residence. Everyone in town knew when he was "in residence" because the American flag flew from the tallest flagpole in Vermont on the hill behind his mansion. His generosity to the institute is detailed in the previous chapter.

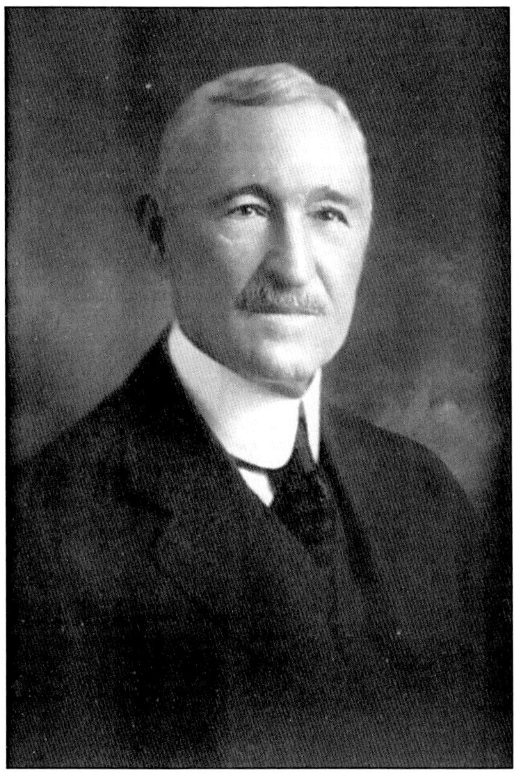

**THE SINCERE FRIEND AND GENEROUS CONTRIBUTOR.** The 1926 yearbook (*Cynosure*) was dedicated to Elmer Albert Darling (1851–1931), president of the Board of Trustees and largely responsible for the new building. A native of Burke, he became wealthy through his long association with the Fifth Avenue Hotel in New York City. He built a mansion on the Burke–Lyndon town line, and contributed generously to his native town and the area. He bequeathed funds to the Lyndon Institute in memory of his sister Louise and his brother Scott Darling.

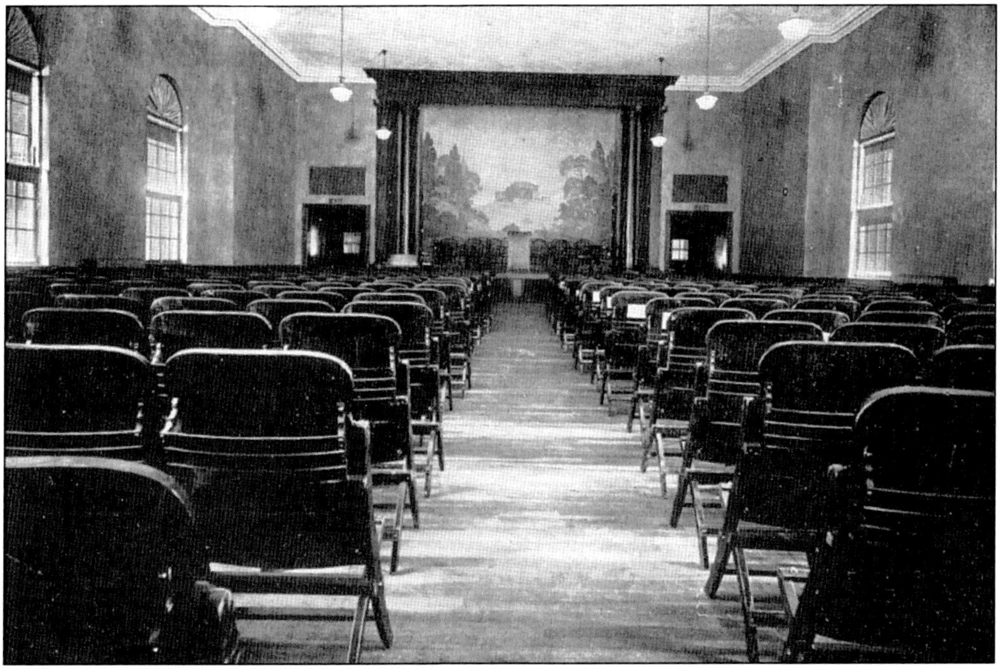

**The Chapel.** When the new classic-style building replaced the burned Thompson Hall, an unknown benefactor commissioned the 15-foot by 20-foot painting of the Parthenon for the new assembly hall (chapel). Symbolizing the classical roots of Lyndon Institute, the painting is framed within the walls of the stage. As in the former chapel, the custom of all students and faculty assembling here every morning continued for many years.

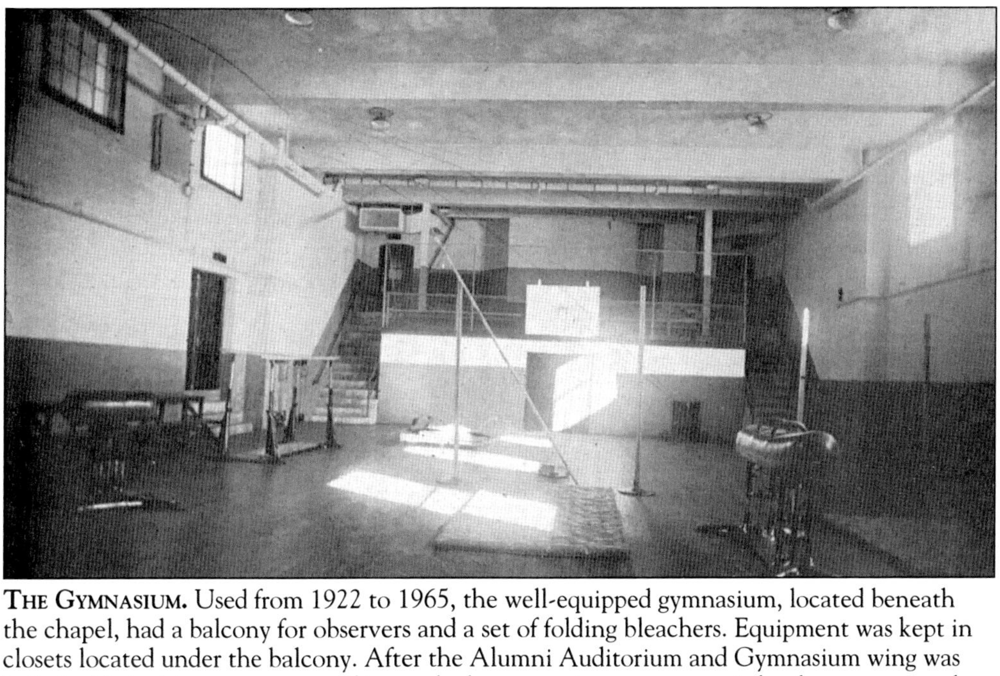

**The Gymnasium.** Used from 1922 to 1965, the well-equipped gymnasium, located beneath the chapel, had a balcony for observers and a set of folding bleachers. Equipment was kept in closets located under the balcony. After the Alumni Auditorium and Gymnasium wing was built in 1965, this gym was turned into a locker room. In recent years it has been converted to a state-of-the-art library with the latest in computer technology.

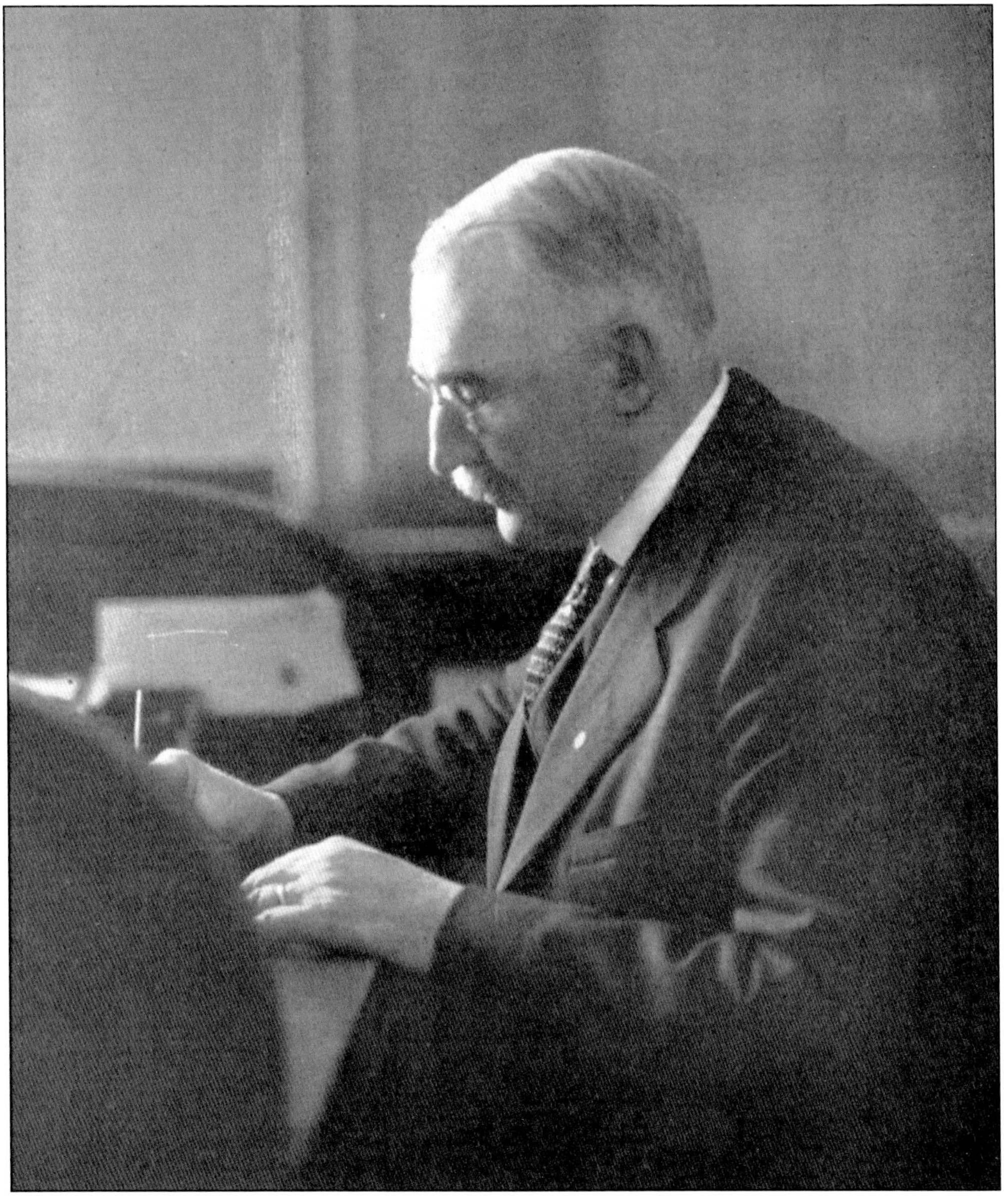

**A Familiar Portrait.** Born in Wheelock, Ozias D. Mathewson (1864–1944) graduated from Lyndon Institute in 1886 and from Dartmouth, Phi Beta Kappa, in 1890. He helped form the permanent organization of Lyndon Institute graduates in 1889 that became the Lyndon Institute Alumni Association, effective in 1900 to 1991. After 22 years as principal and superintendent in the Barre School System, he was hired by Theodore N. Vail to become principal of Lyndon Institute. During his 31 years as principal, he was strong on discipline but was always fair. He taught many classes and was public spirited, serving the community in many ways. His high educational standards and long service earned him the reputation of being one of Vermont's outstanding educators. He and his wife, Grace Hoyt Mathewson,'02, lived in the house by the pond across from the institute with their twin girls, Marion '28 and Miriam '28, and their son Philip '30, who now resides there with his wife.

*Three*

# The Vail Agricultural School

In 1910, Theodore N. Vail as trustee organized and supported from his private funds the School of Agriculture at Lyndon Institute. Classes were conducted in rooms in the basement and all of the third floor of Thompson Hall, and Vail's Speedwell Farms on the hill above the institute was used for practical farm practices. The school was the first agricultural school in the state of Vermont on a high school level. Although the school was separate from Lyndon Institute, the two schools cooperated in the use of buildings and the employment of some teachers. Agricultural students could elect to take courses from Lyndon Institute, and institute students could elect subjects from the School of Agriculture. All students were required to maintain a high standard of scholarship.

Haying, raising crops, logging, sugaring, and many other agricultural activities and practical lessons were learned at Vail's Speedwell properties. In 1915, Vail gave the Agricultural School to the state of Vermont. It was managed by the State Board of Agriculture and the State Board of Education.

When Vail died in 1920, the state gave up the agricultural school in order to concentrate its efforts at Randolph. The Vail Agricultural School and Speedwell Farms, including Vail's mansion, reverted to Lyndon Institute. The institute sold the Speedwell properties and mansion and in 1924, began its own vocational agricultural courses.

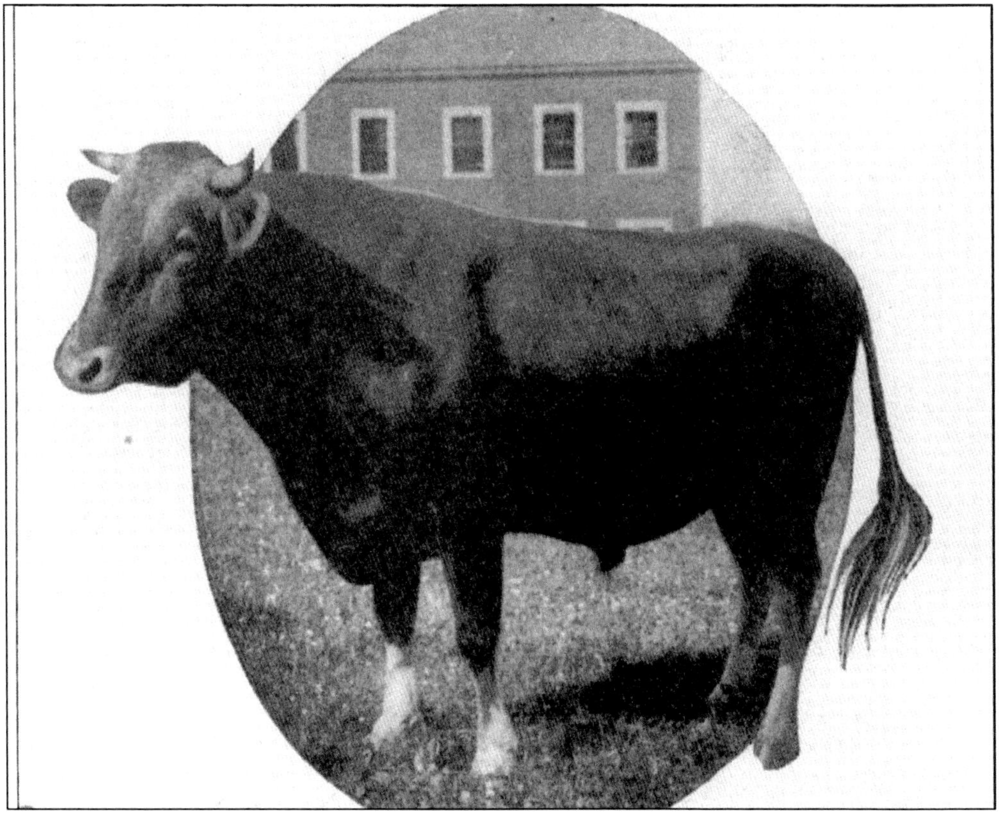

**A Registered Guernsey Sire.** This proud animal pictured in a Vail Agricultural School catalog, *c.* 1918, stands by the agricultural barn at Lyndon Institute.

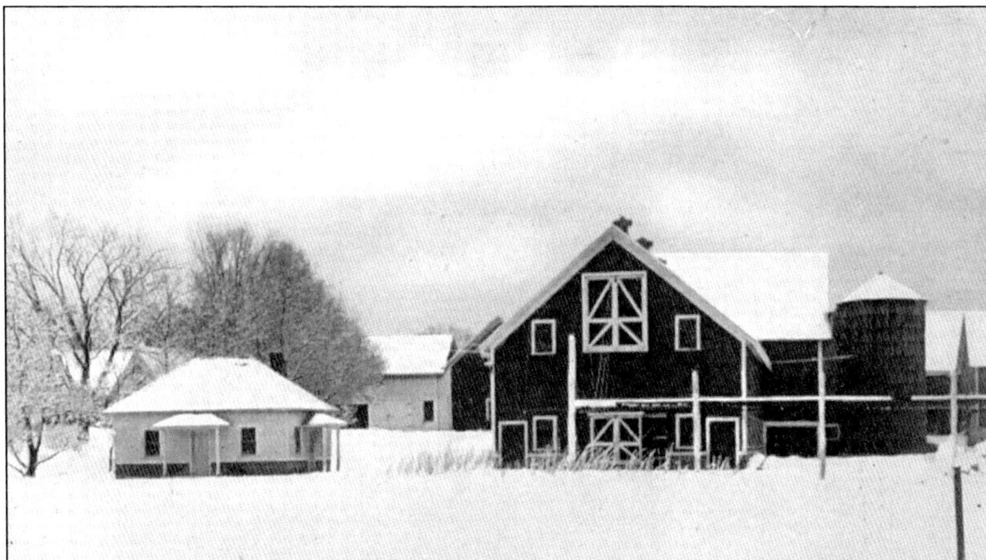

**The Lyndon Agricultural School.** The Aggies, as the agricultural students were called, built this dairy barn and the creamery near the lower campus in 1913. Cows were pastured on the meadow by the Passumpsic River.

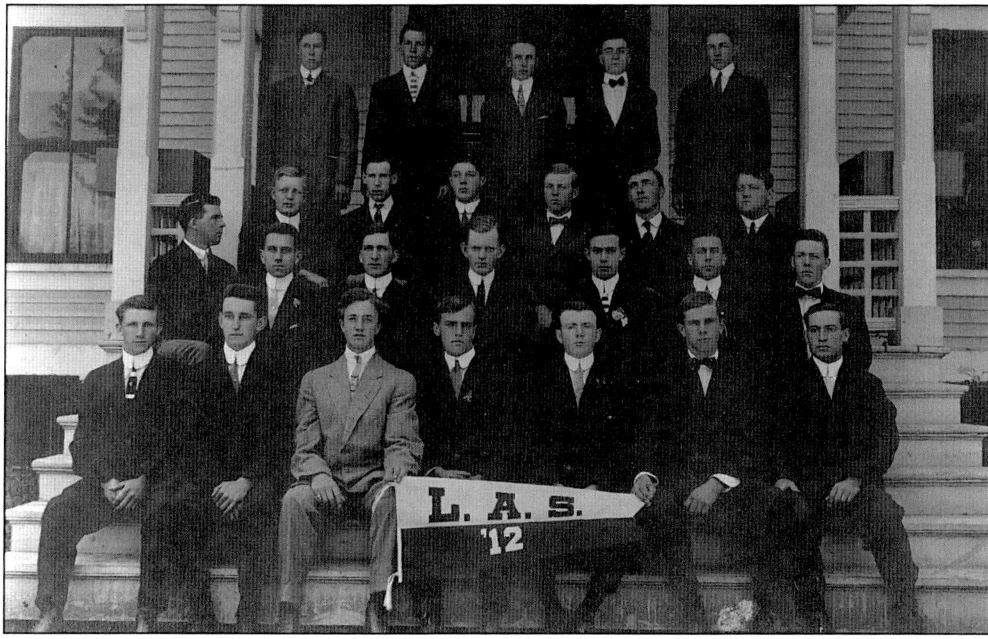


**GRADUATES OF 1912.** They came from many places in Vermont as well as locally, and Sanborn House was their dormitory. These agricultural students are pictured sitting on the front steps of Sanborn House on graduation day. Vermonters were granted free tuition to the Lyndon Agricultural School.

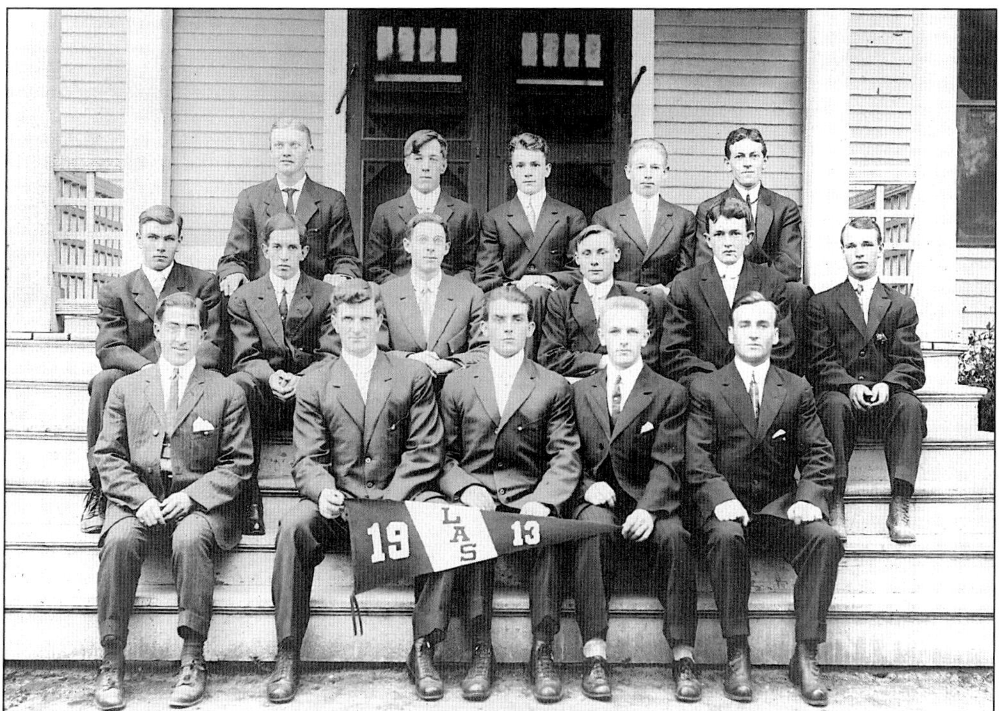


**THE CLASS OF 1913.** The Lyndon Agricultural School graduating class of the following year poses on the front steps of the Sanborn House dormitory.

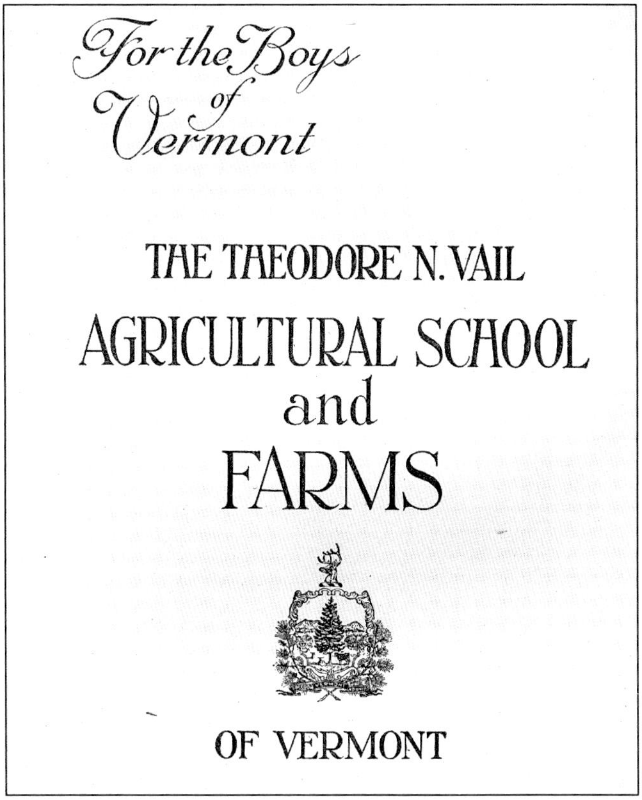

*For the Boys of Vermont*

THE THEODORE N. VAIL

AGRICULTURAL SCHOOL and FARMS

OF VERMONT

**VAIL'S GIFT TO VERMONT.** After Theodore N. Vail gave the Vail Agricultural School to the state of Vermont in 1915, the school was renamed the Theodore N. Vail Agricultural School and Farms of Vermont. It was not a school of agricultural specialties but a course of general farming, based on the belief that general farming is a trade, a business proposition, and a science. Students learned how to do things by doing them. One week out of every month, they were required to work on the main farm for wages, in part to train them to work under commercial competition.

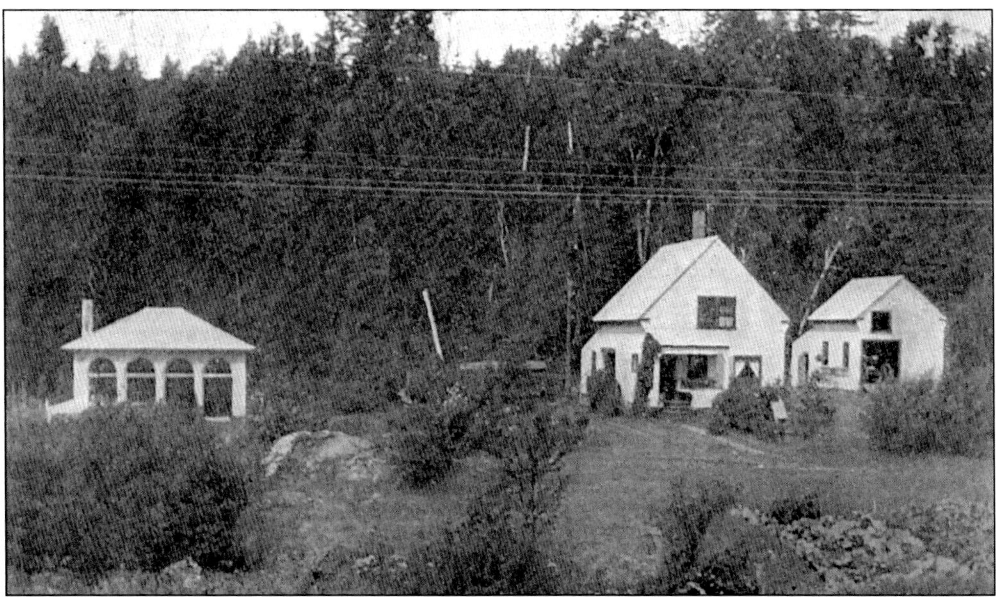

**VAIL'S HYDROELECTRIC PLANT.** T.N. Vail built the first electric plant in Lyndon on the Passumpsic River; he used it to generate power for his home and the Speedwell Farms. The superintendent lived in the house shown in this image. Vail also built the first "hard" road in town. It went from Lyndon Center to his property on the hill that became known as Vail Hill. These improvements were made before the town of Lyndon itself had electricity or paved roads.

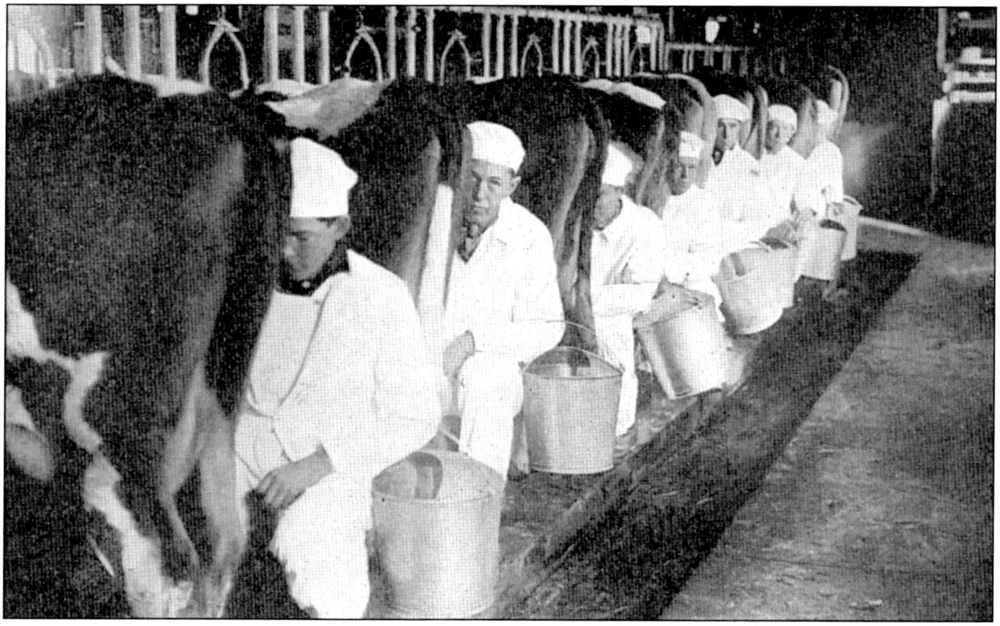

**THEIR OWN HERD.** Vail Agricultural students learn how to "draw Vermont's biggest dividends" (milk the cows).

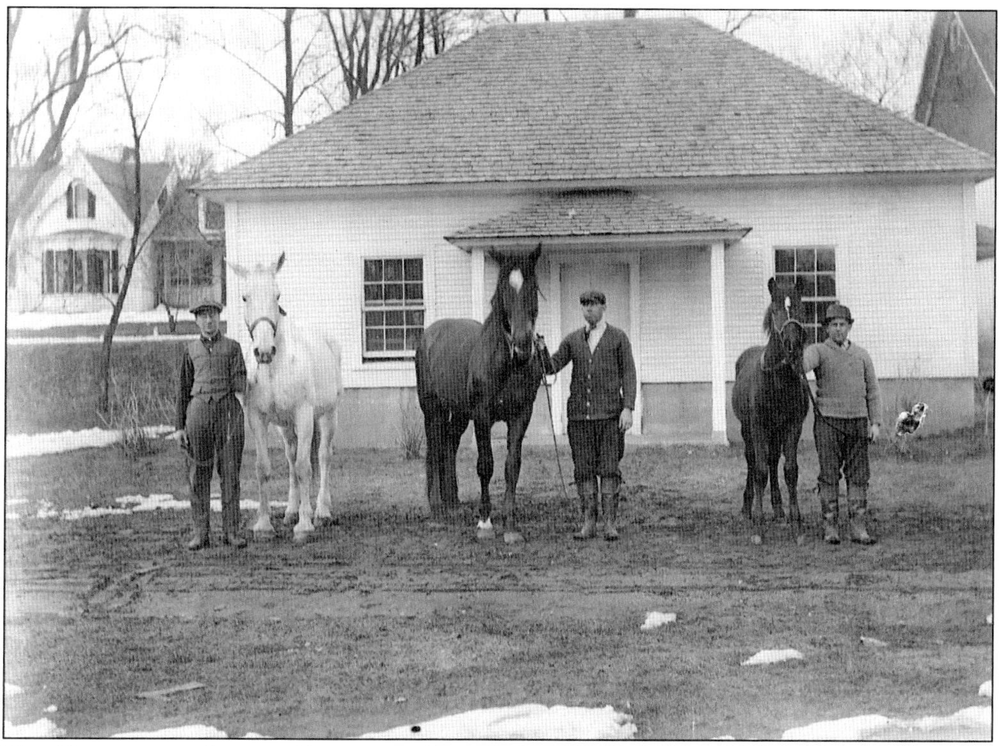

**THE CREAMERY AT LYNDON INSTITUTE.** Outside the creamery are agricultural instructors, from left to right, Stanley Judd, B.S.A., animal husbandry and dairying; Morton Downing, B.S., agronomy and farm mechanics; and ? Fink.

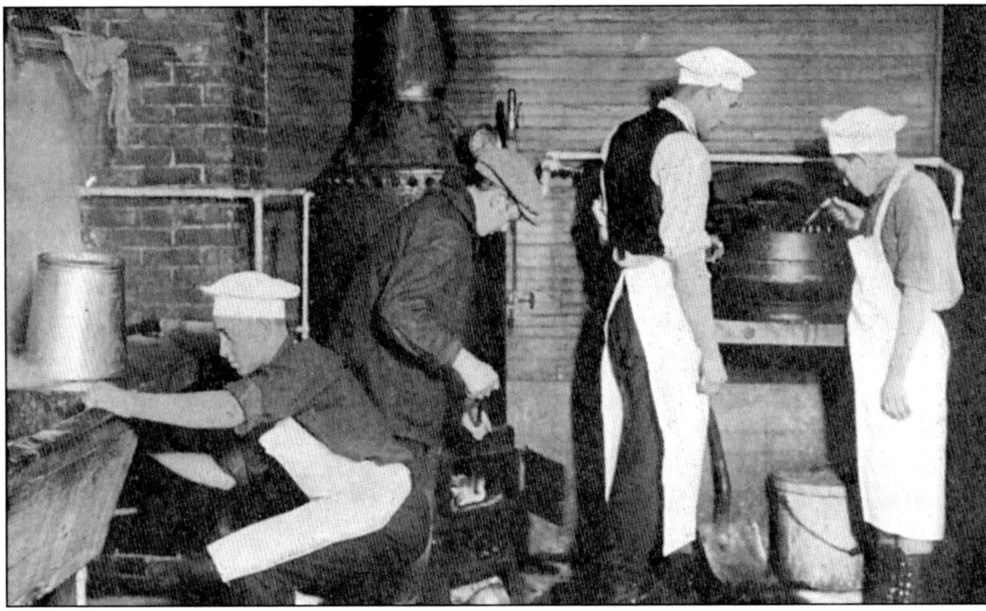

**SEPARATOR AND WASHROOM.** The creamery is where the agricultural students learned what to do with "Vermont's biggest dividends." With agricultural programs no longer in demand, the building is now offices of the Technology Center.

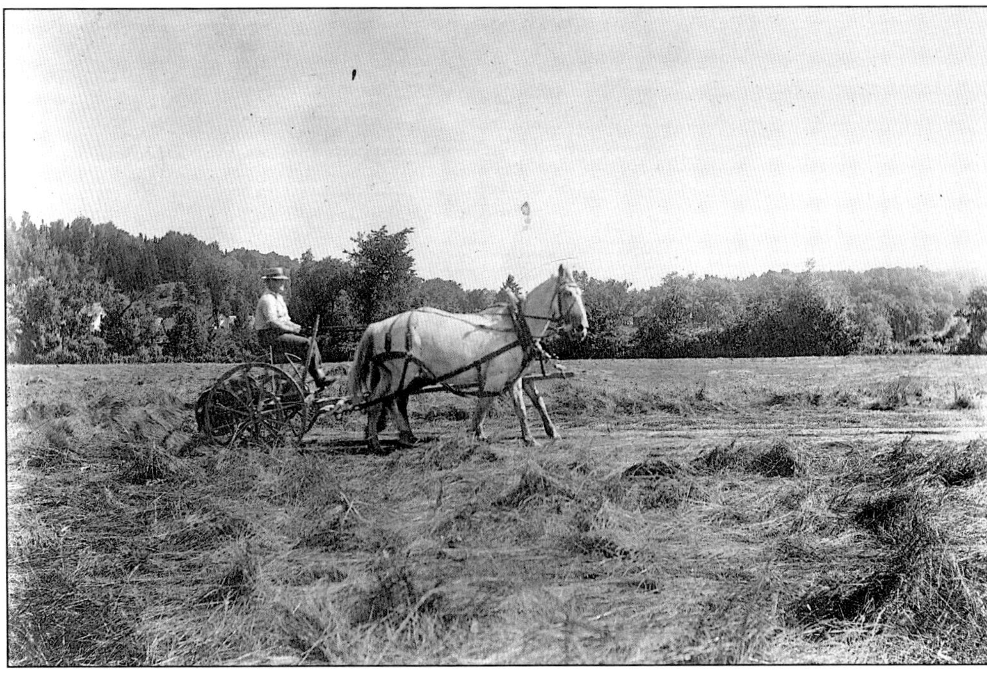

**CUTTING THE INSTITUTE MEADOW.** The agriculture program was a two-year school and included the following seasonal courses: agronomy, agricultural engineering, animal husbandry, dairy husbandry, horticulture, rural economics, and miscellaneous subjects, such as arithmetic, agricultural chemistry, civics, English, and farm drawing—the study of the methods of constructing farm buildings, making farm maps, drawing plans for drainage systems, and other farm conveniences.

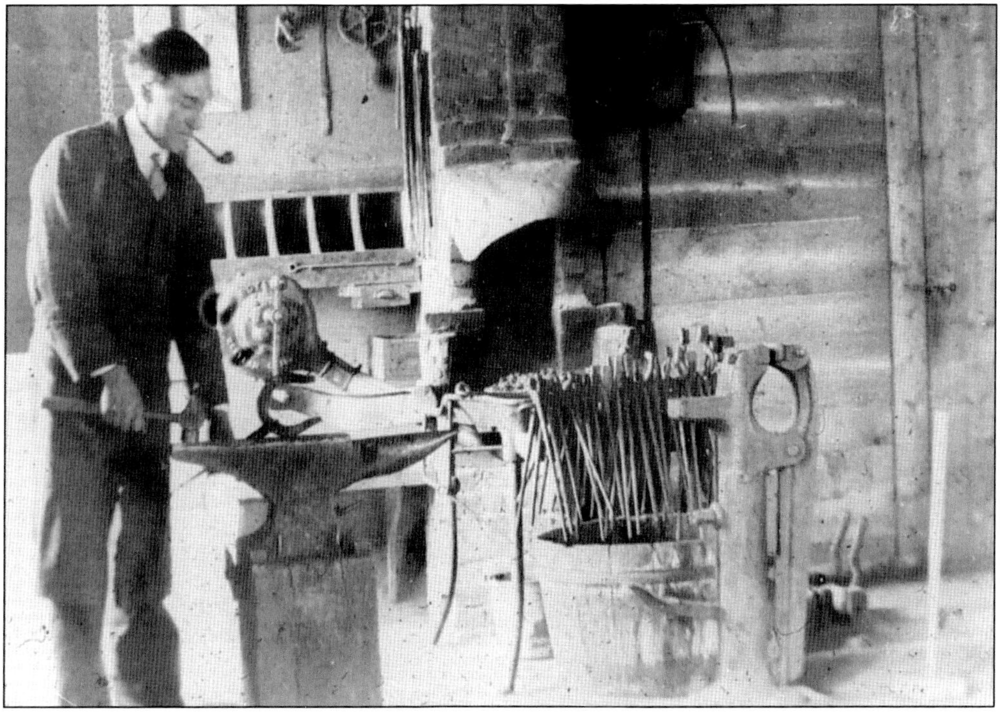

**The Blacksmith Shop.** An instructor demonstrates the use of the anvil, while smoke rolls up from the forge. Blacksmithing skills and the making of tools were part of the agricultural training.

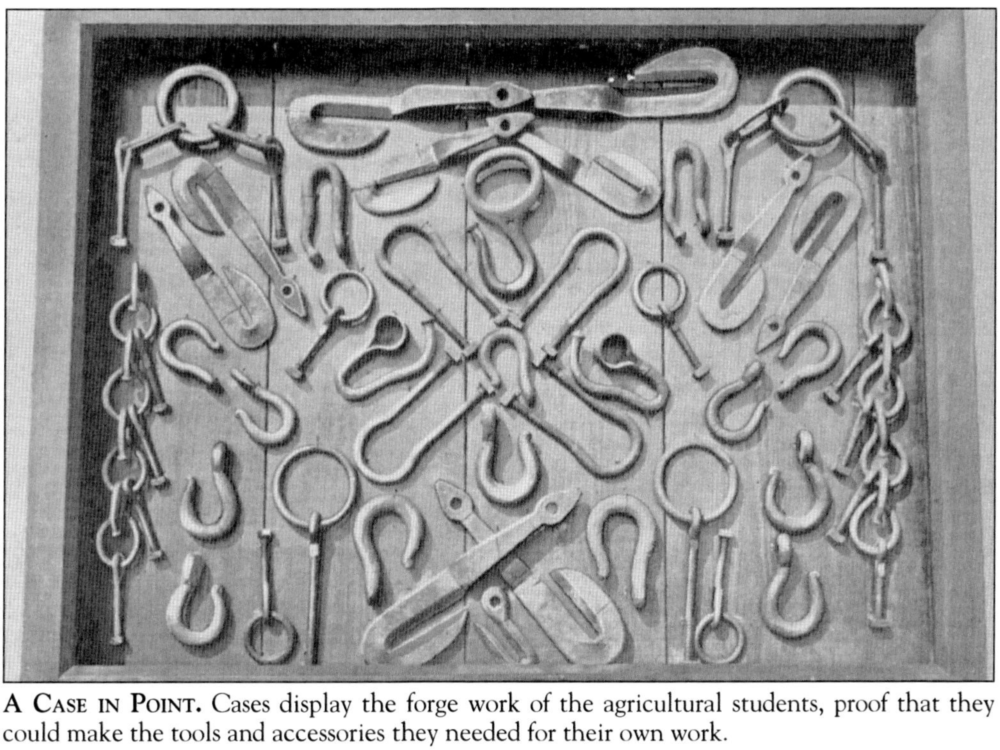

**A Case in Point.** Cases display the forge work of the agricultural students, proof that they could make the tools and accessories they needed for their own work.

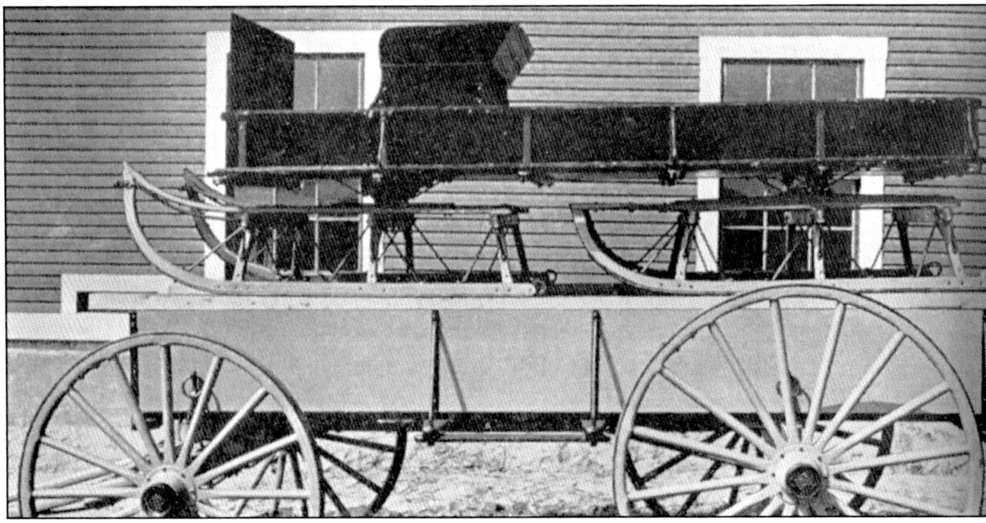

**WORK BEYOND JUST TOOLS.** This image shows a farm wagon and an express sleigh made by students in the agricultural school.

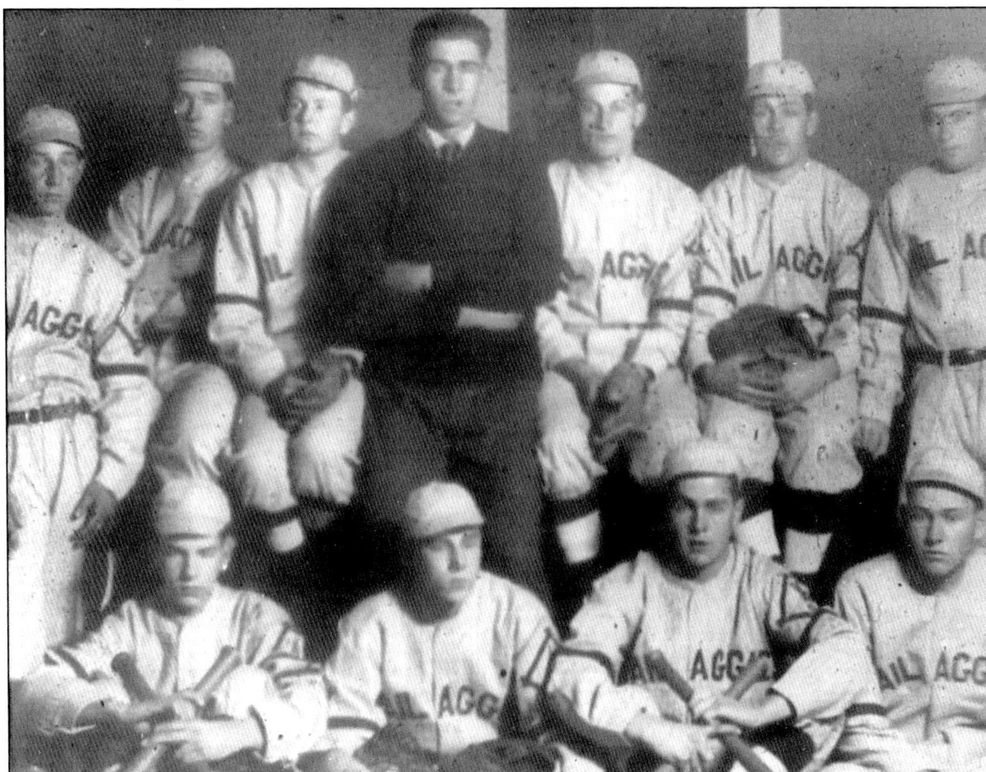

**THE VAIL AGGIES BASEBALL TEAM.** Along with their farm work, agricultural students had time for fun, too. Pictured here is the school's baseball team. There was a basketball team as well and opportunities for winter sports, such as snowshoeing, skating, and skiing. From time to time, social evenings and parties were held by both the Vail Agricultural School and the Lyndon Institute. "This permits of a social life between the girls and boys which is desirable," said the Vail School catalogues.

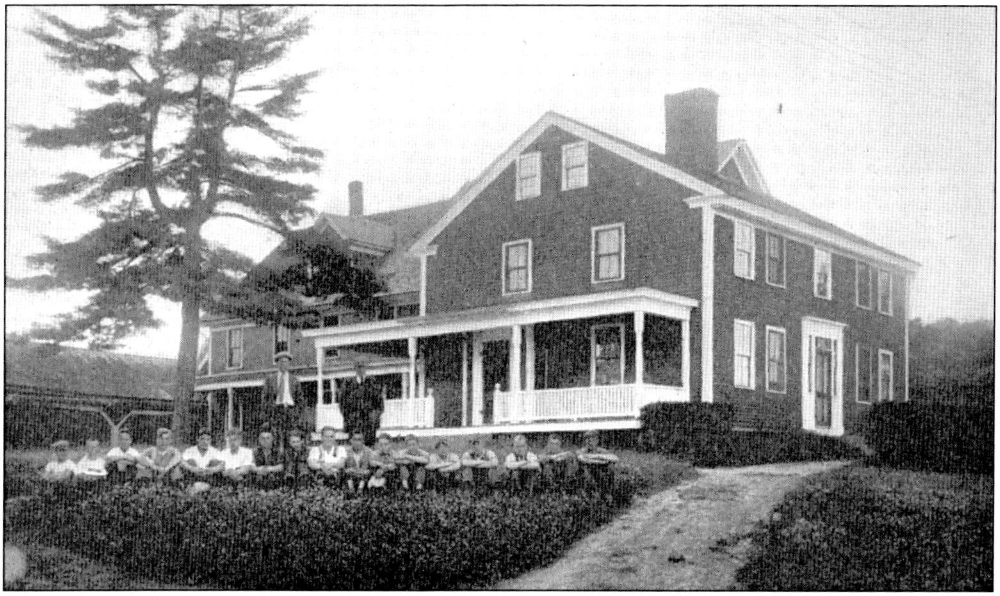

**The Speedwell Dormitory.** Vail Aggies lived in this modern home. A recreation room was fitted with a player piano, a victrola, a pool table, and various other games. There were magazines, state and national newspapers, and agricultural periodicals for the boys to read. Rooms were also available at the Sanborn House on the Lyndon Institute campus.

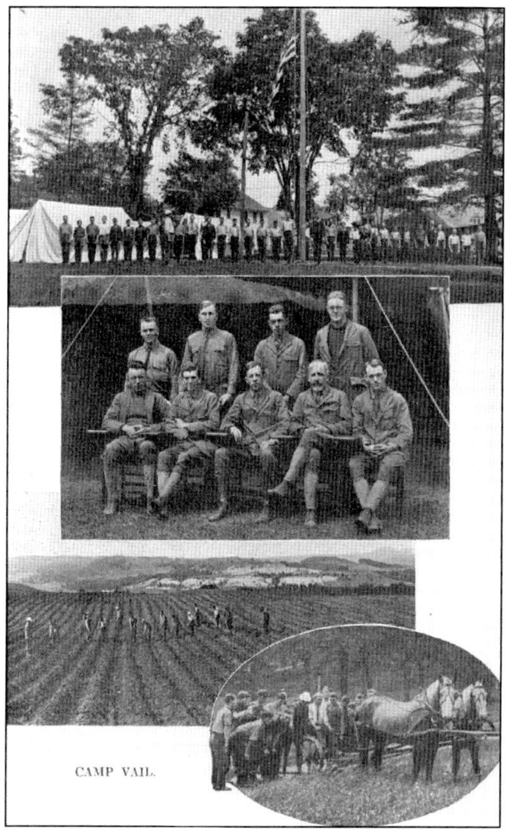


**Camp Vail.** In the spring of 1918, to help ease Vermont's farm labor shortage during World War I, Camp Vail was conducted by the Vail Agricultural School and financed by the Departments of Agriculture and Education. A total of 155 boys from Vermont cities and towns were given farm training for two weeks per session. They were placed on farms recommended by the Agricultural Department county agents. The tents in which they lived were pitched on the institute campus.

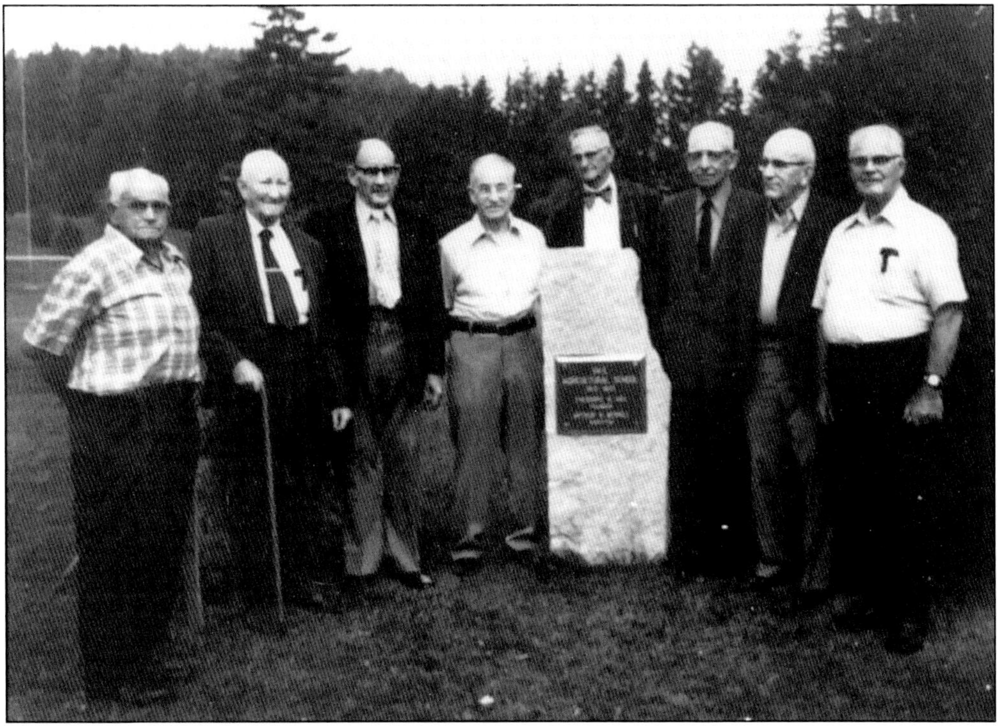

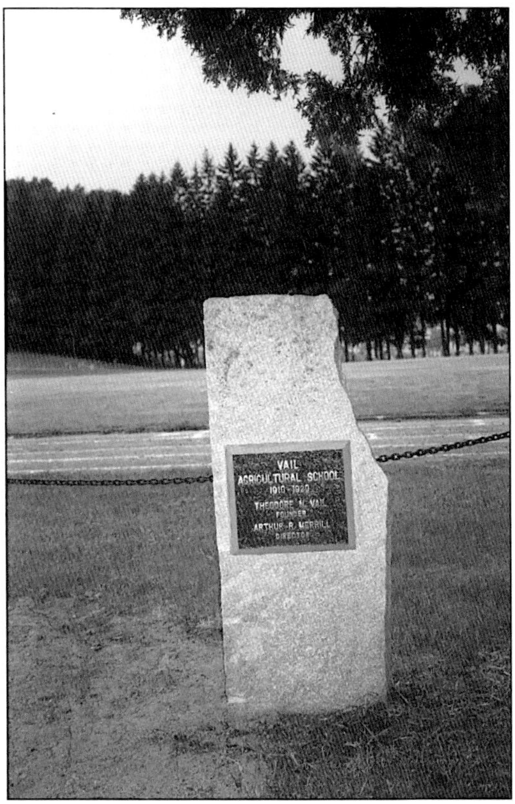


**THE VAIL SCHOOL REUNION.** The Vail Agricultural School marker, donated by Bunal Cheney, president of the Vail Agricultural School Alumni Association, was dedicated on August 18, 1974. From left to right, the alumni are Howard Varney '16, Wyman Hubbard '14, Ira Dodge '17, Bunal Cheney '16, George Cate '13, Ralph Gibson '12, and Carl Morrison '16.

**THE VAIL SCHOOL MARKER.** This marker is located on the southeast corner of the main campus, across the street from the original Sanborn Hall, which for a time was the dormitory for the agricultural students. The plaque, with its black background and brass frame and lettering, is set into a granite block. It reads, "Vail Agricultural School 1910–1920. Theodore N. Vail, founder, Arthur R. Merrill, director."

# *Four*

# The Lyndon Normal School

When the shortage of elementary teachers in this country caused the closing of many schools, the Vermont Legislature in 1910 sought to remedy this situation by an Enabling Act that provided teacher training courses for seniors in high schools. A one-year teacher training course started at Lyndon Institute under this act. The first facility was one room on the third floor of Thompson Hall.

In 1912, the legislature made provisions for teacher training courses in secondary schools for students who were graduates of approved high schools or with an equivalent education, or for students who had completed two years, without condition, in a four-year high school and had taught 50 weeks in public schools. Teacher training was under the direction of the Vermont State Board of Education.

By 1923, two years of teacher training was offered in the Normal Department. In 1933, three-year certificates were being granted. Certain professional colleges granted credit for satisfactory completion of important courses toward college degrees. In 1927, Rita L. Bole was named principal of Lyndon Normal School. "The name changed to Lyndon Teachers College in 1949, and Miss Bole's title to president. When the Normal School moved to the Vail property on Vail Hill, Miss Bole 'led the charge up the hill.' Students hauled the 12,000 volumes, and every available vehicle was recruited to move the equipment. The early morning hours, Monday July 1, 1951, witnessed the establishment of Lyndon Teachers College at Vail Manor," the *Lyn News* reported on October 5, 1989, after Miss Bole's death. It was a later owner after Theodore Vail's death that named his mansion Vail Manor. The Lyndon Teachers College became Lyndon State College in 1963.

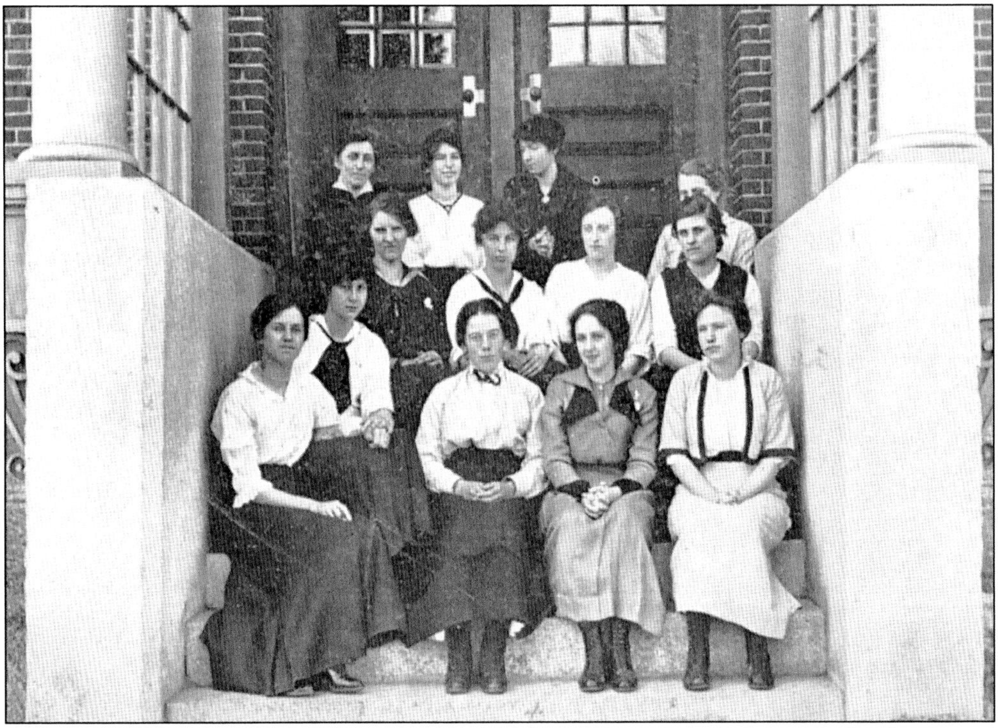

**Aspiring to Teach.** The teacher training class from 1916 to 1917 poses on the front steps of Thompson Hall. Student Rita L. Bole is in the front row, second from the right. Training teacher Eliza Allen reminisces in the July 23, 1955 Lyndon Teachers College *Lyn News* that "It is a source of pride to me that one of 'my girls,' Miss Rita Bole, is now principal of the State Normal School at Lyndon Center."

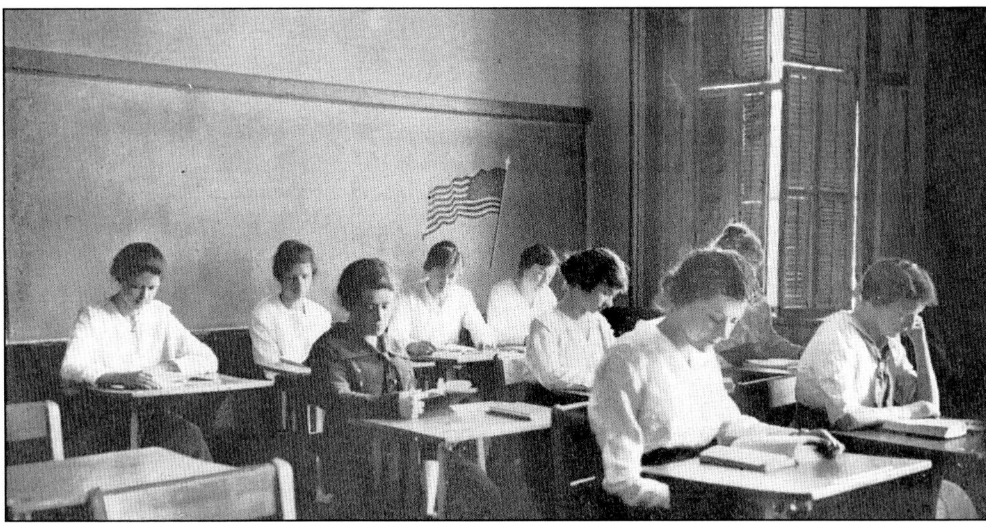

**Learning to Teach, c. 1918.** These teacher training students are intent on their classwork in a room on the third floor of Thompson Hall. Practice teaching was done in the spring term at nearby rural one-room schools and village schools. When these "older" teacher training students were seen passing by to their residence halls or to classes, they were dubbed "TTs" by the regular Lyndon Institute students

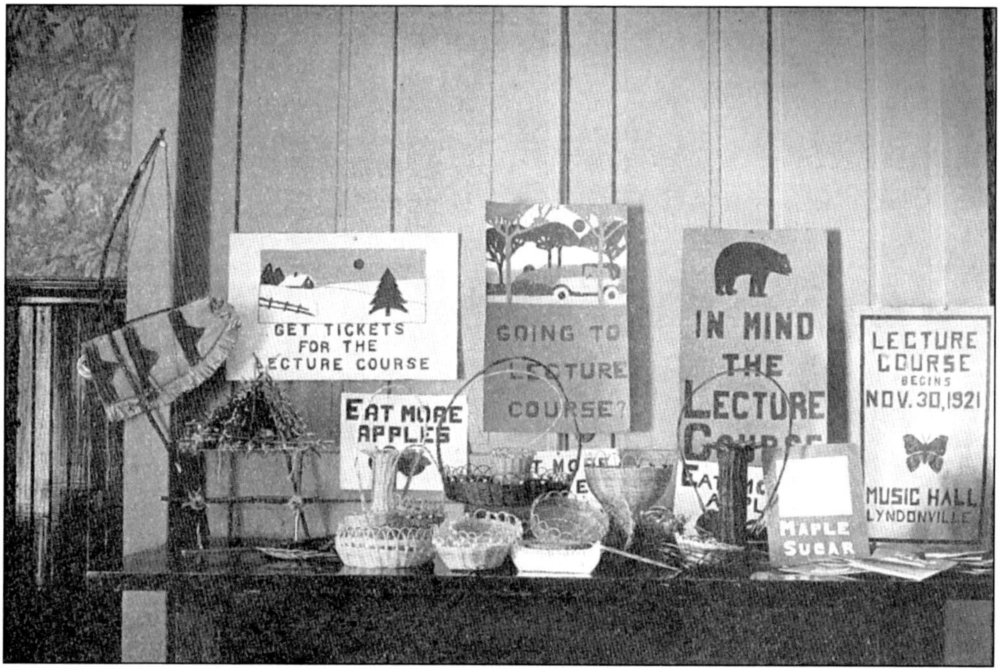


**The Teacher Training Work, c. 1923.** Drawing, art, and method was part of the curriculum. It was expected that the graduates would gain therefrom some degree of enrichment, initiative, progression, and understanding.

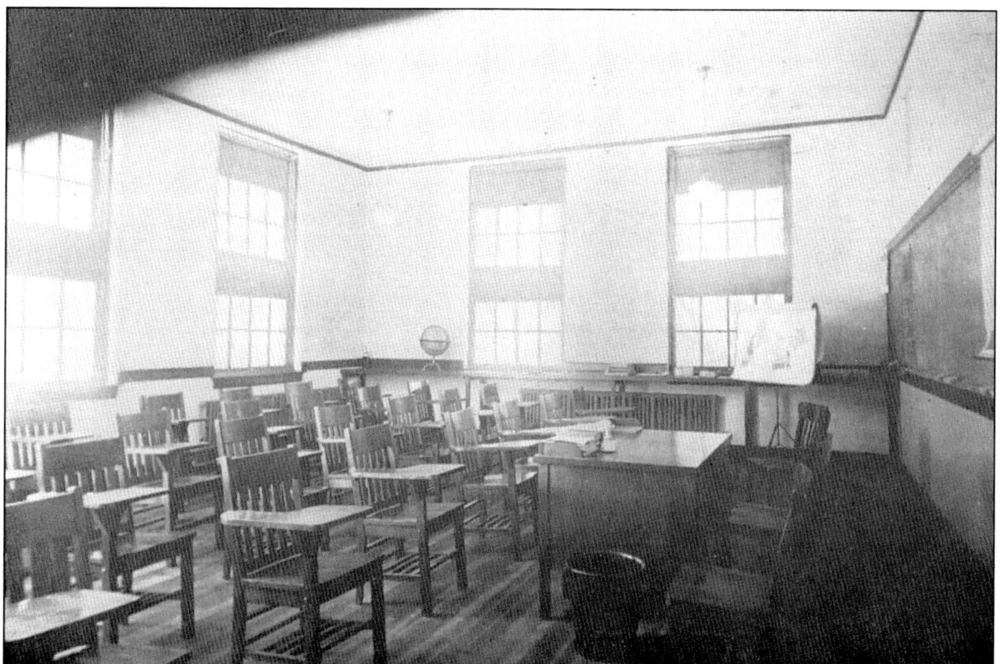

**The Teacher Training Room, 1926.** The teacher training classes were held in classrooms on the third floor of the new institute, built after the destruction of Thompson Hall by fire in 1922. The tall windows let in a lot of light.

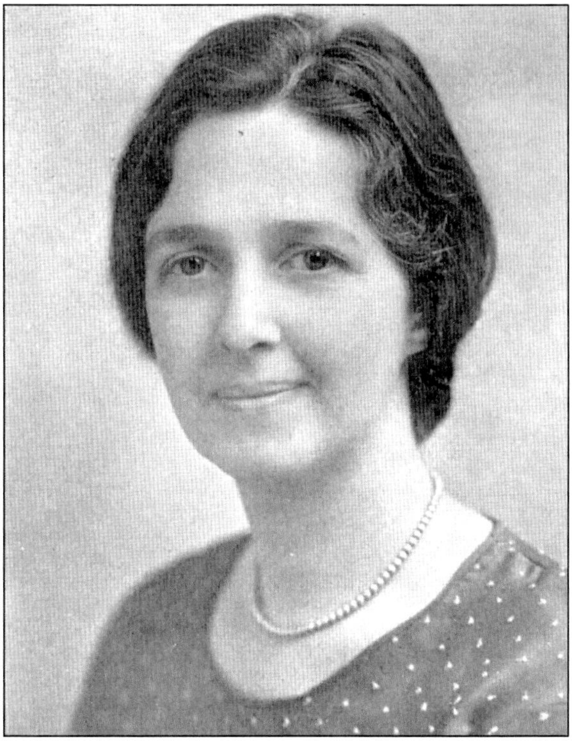

**A Lyndon Normal School Principal.** Rita L. Bole, A.B. (1895–1989), was born in Bangor, Maine. After her year at Lyndon in the teacher training course, she taught teacher training in several schools and then became principal of Lyndon Normal School in 1927. In 1935–36, she took a year for graduate study at Teachers College, Columbia University, where she received her master's degree.

**A Laughing Matter.** Rita Bole, former Lyndon Teachers College president, center, says something that amuses Clive Veri, Lyndon State College president, and Susan Gallagher, former acting president. They are attending the Brunch in the Park in Lyndonville, held on July 26, 1987, during the LSC Foundation's Stars and Stripes Festival. (Photographed by Harriet Fisher for the *Caledonian-Record*.)

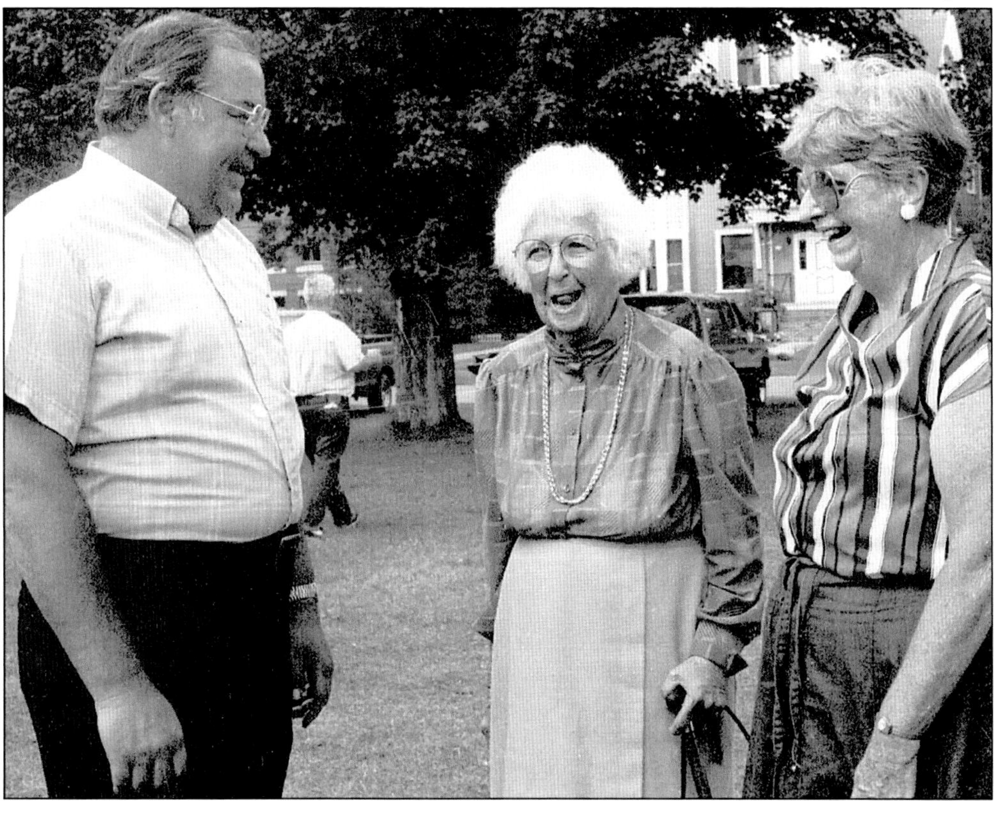

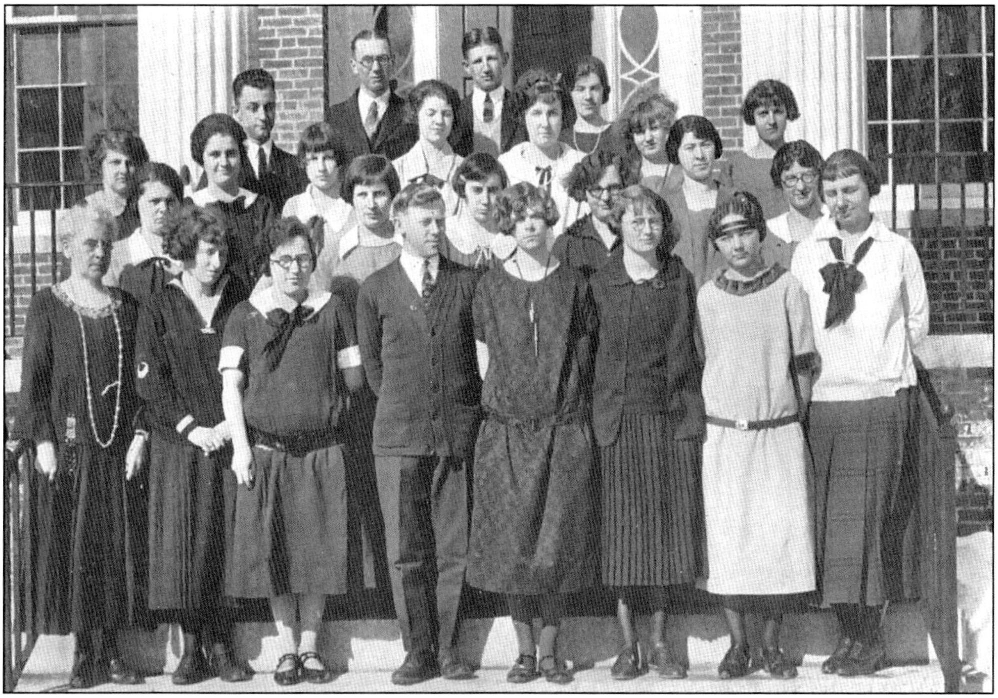

**A Teacher Training Class.** In the 1925–26 Lyndon Institute catalogue, 26 teacher training students, including three men, are listed. In 1926–27 catalogue, there are 42 students, including six men. This large increase was due to the premise that becoming a teacher could now be a promising career, not just a stopgap for a woman until she married.

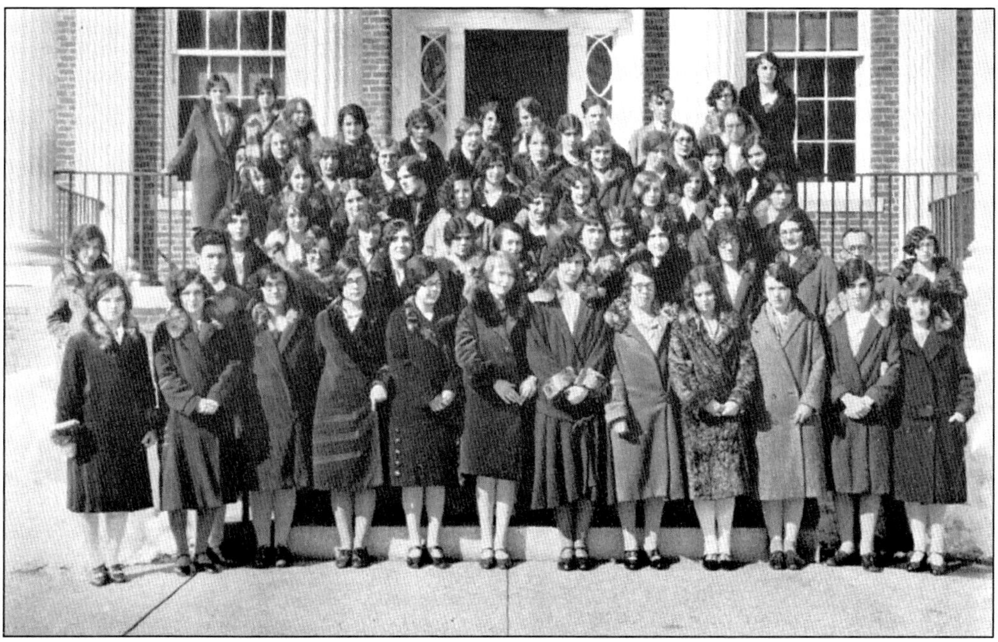

**A Teacher Training Class, c. 1929.** The classes grew as the years progressed and teachers were needed for the many schools in Vermont, which included rural one-room schools as well as village schools.

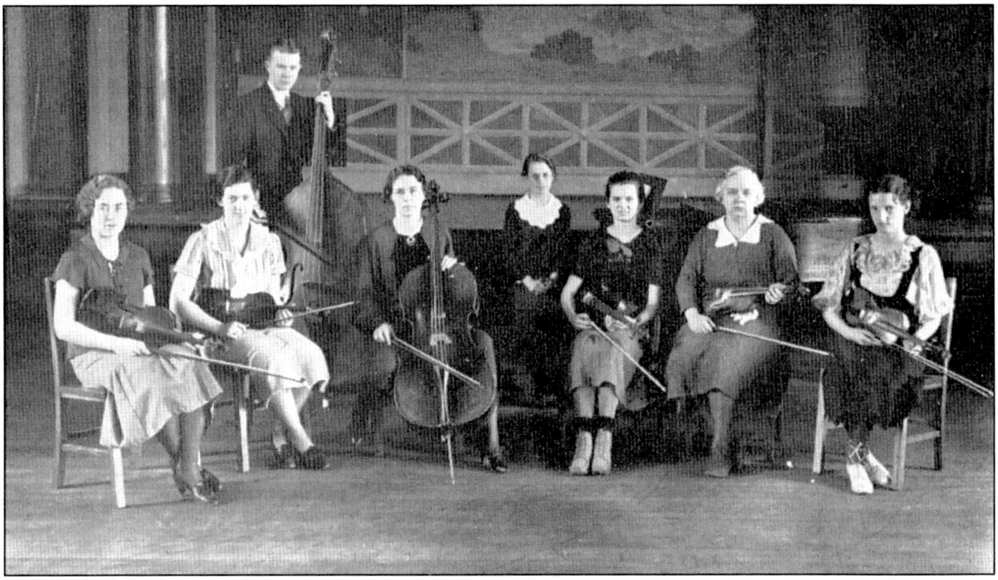

**MUSIC.** Ruby Blaine, music teacher at Lyndon Institute, was also the music teacher for the teacher training classes. In this photograph, she is playing the cello. There was a girls' glee club and a Normal School orchestra. The Normal School boys joined the Lyndon Institute boys' glee club. There were quartets and other musical groups as well. Care was taken to play music of varying degrees of difficulty so that all performers, from beginners to advanced, could participate.

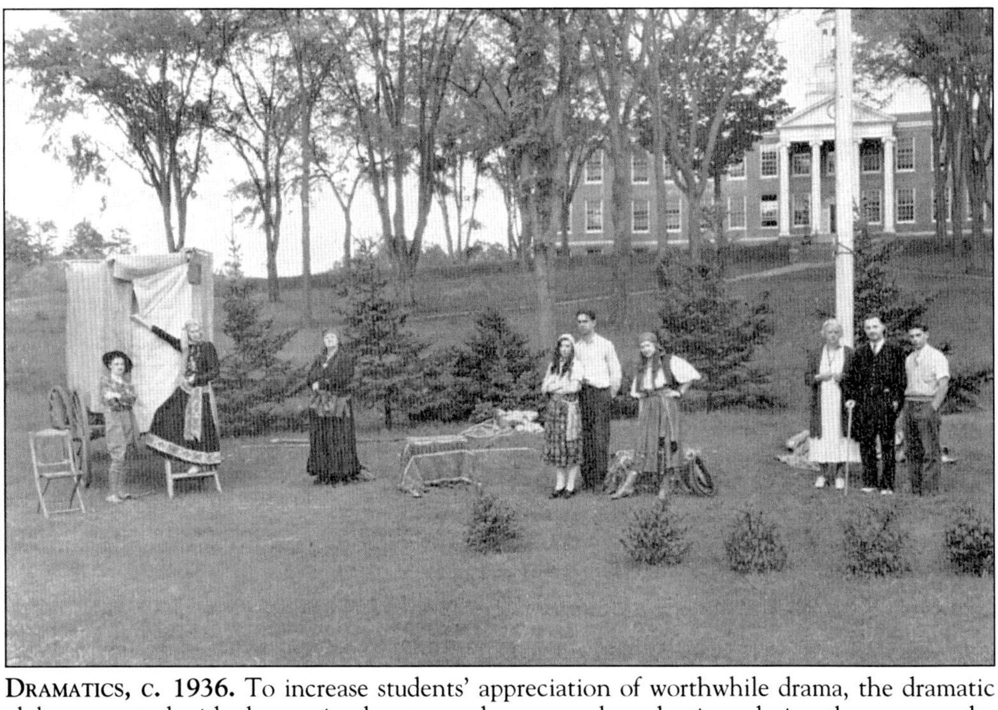

**DRAMATICS, C. 1936.** To increase students' appreciation of worthwhile drama, the dramatic club cooperated with the music class to produce several productions during the year on the Lyndon Institute campus. Productions included *The Mikado* and *Gypsy Fires*, which is shown here. Drama was also a means of practicing good oral and interpretative reading.

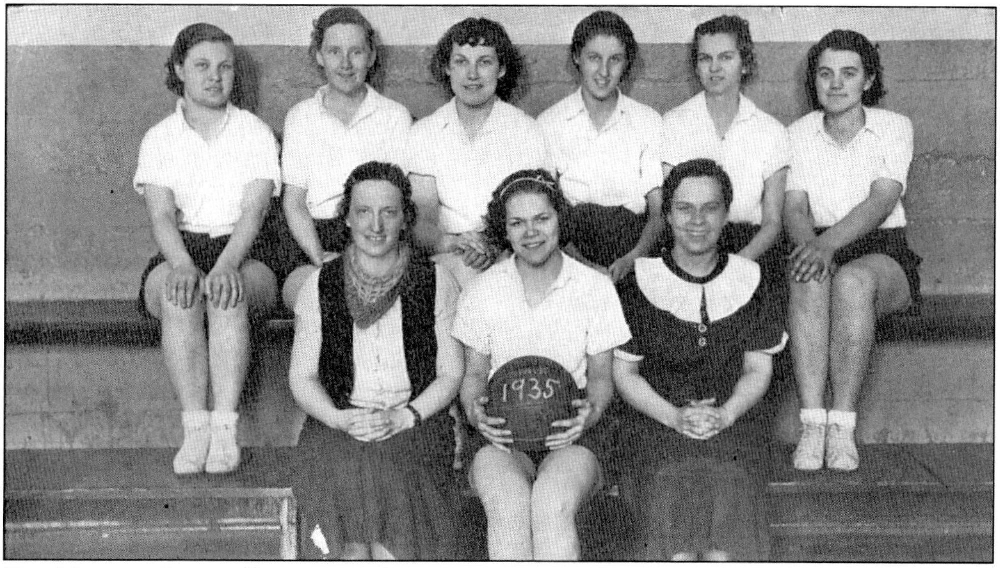


**THE NORMAL SCHOOL BASKETBALL TEAM OF 1935.** Helen Dexter, Lyndon Institute Class of 1922, front row on the left, was athletic instructor for both the Lyndon Institute and the Normal School girls. The Normal School girls' basketball team enjoyed playing against the Johnson Normal School. The Lyndon Normal School Athletic Association also enjoyed Mountain Day on Burke Mountain, annual barge rides, winter carnival, and the annual sugar party. Credits were given for participation in these events, some of which included hiking.

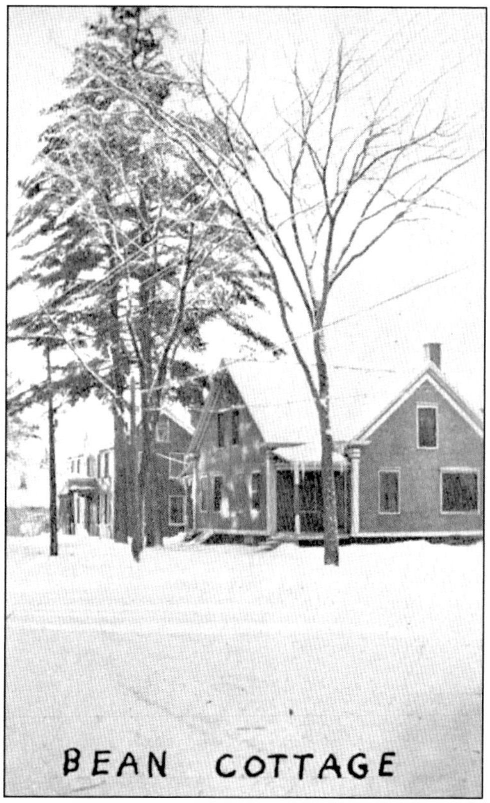


**HOME AWAY FROM HOME.** In 1938, the Lyndon Normal School consisted of four classrooms on the top floor of the institute building, the new library, the Sanborn House, the Willey House, and Bean Cottage, shown here.

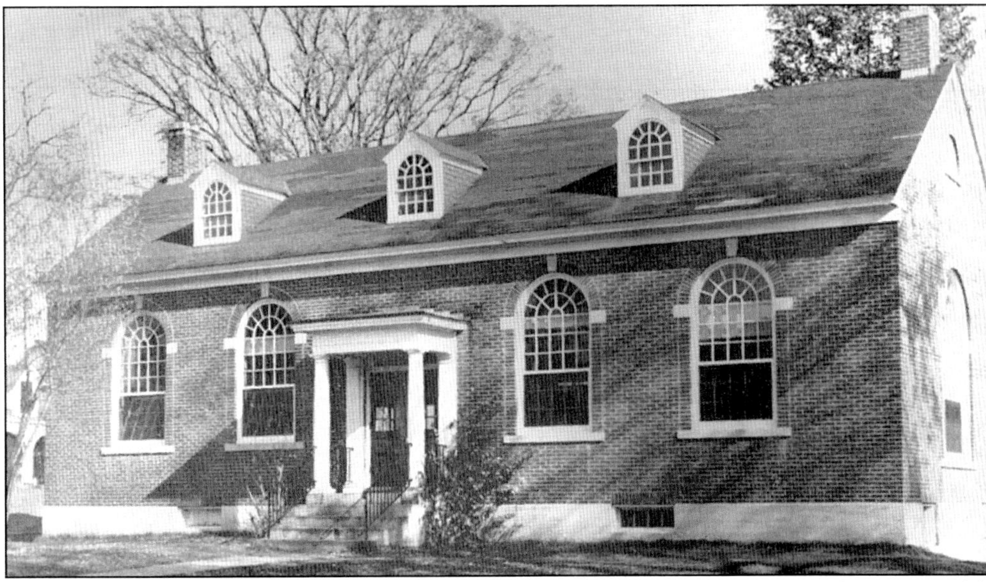

**The Normal School Library.** In order to give adequate accommodations and more suitable opportunity for social and recreational life at the Normal School, the Lyndon Institute built a colonial-style brick library in 1938. After the Lyndon Normal School moved to the Vail property, the institute moved its library here and named it the Theta Helen Baker Hall, after the teacher who taught English and Latin at Lyndon Institute for many years.

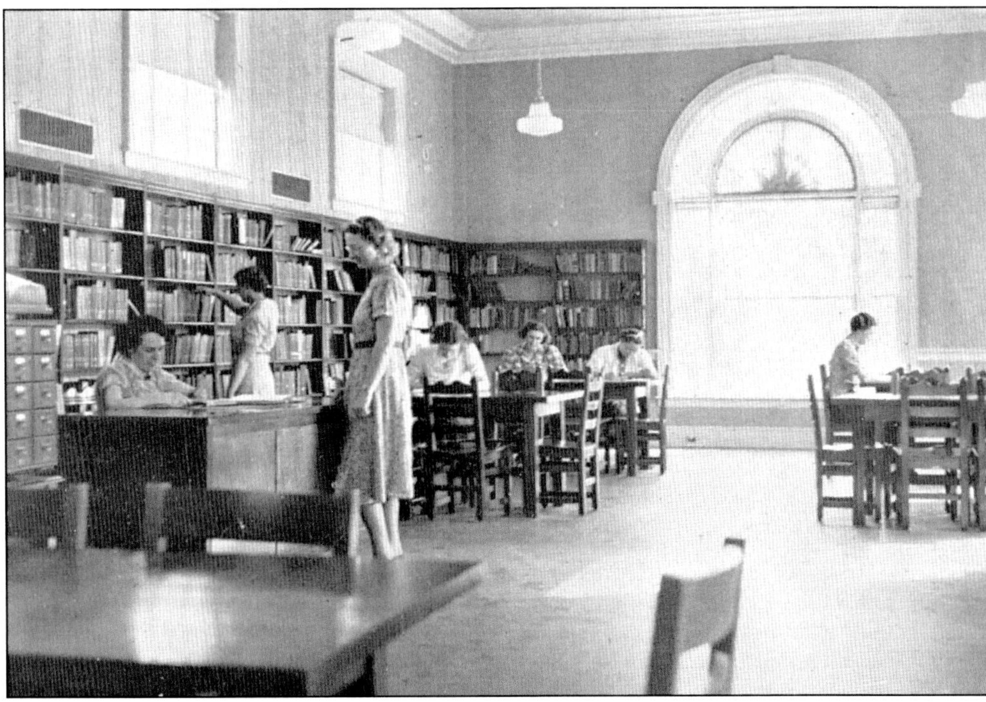

**The Interior of the Library.** The capacity of the library ranged from 12,000 to 15,000 volumes. The whole main floor was one large room, well lighted and furnished in beautiful maple—stacks, tables, chairs, and librarian's desk all included. Now, Baker Hall houses Lyndon Institute classrooms, and the LI Alumni Museum has the whole lower split-level area.

## *Five*

# Around the Campus

Lyndon Institute is made up of 34 buildings, several campuses, and the huge meadow, which is now an athletic field named for Albert Forrest, beloved teacher and coach for many years. Some of the buildings have been seen in other chapters. The main building on the Darling Campus remains the largest classroom facility, but most of the other buildings have been adapted to classrooms or to other uses as needs arose.

The main campus, including the football and track field and the site of outdoor graduations—the Robert K. Lewis Field—was once the town green. In 1801, Job Sheldon donated three properties to the town: 4 acres for a town cemetery (the town later bought 2 more); the Union Meetinghouse, which also served as the hall for town meetings; and the green, or common, which he specified would be used for the militia on June Training Day. The town of Lyndon still owns the green; however, Lyndon Institute holds a 50-year lease on the land and for $1 a year, uses it and maintains it.

This chapter includes a sampling of staff members who keep the Lyndon Institute buildings sparkling and the grounds in good order. Photographs are not available of all of the staff. However, memories of them remain. Many people remember the only secretary at the time, Helen Pride, who lived up to her name in keeping Lyndon Institute records. Also, the school janitor who served for many years was Fred Chapman. Students who took their lunch down to eat in the boiler room in winter used to race to see which one would get "Chappie"'s swivel chair and desk, under the basement stairway.

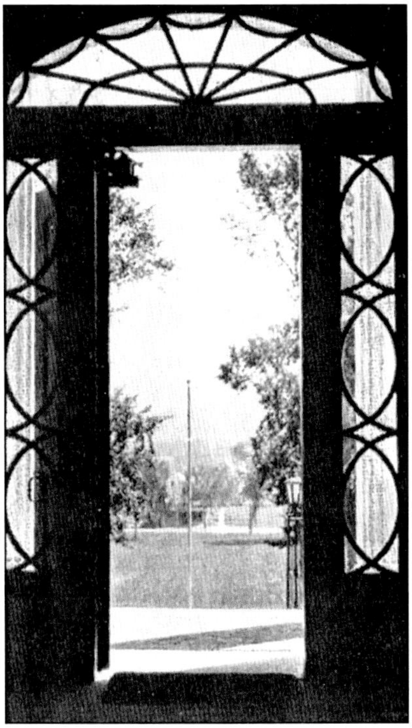

**THE DOORWAY TO THE FUTURE.** Using the front door is a senior privilege. When seniors walk through this beautiful doorway for the last time, they step into the next phase of their life. This image was used for many years in catalogues on the page that stated that Lyndon Institute was a place of opportunity.

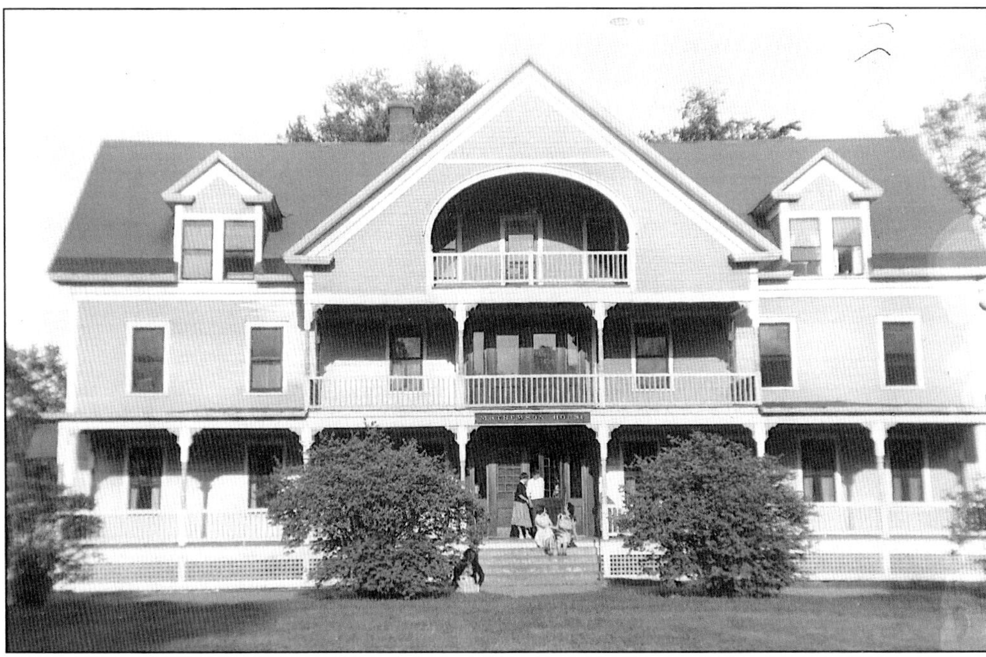

**THE MATHEWSON HOUSE.** This attractive dormitory for girls was built in 1913 and named for Principal Ozias D. Mathewson, graduate of 1886. There was a large living room on the first floor and exercise equipment for physical training in a basement room. After the the dormitory program ended in 1986, the Mathewson House was used as the Alumni Museum and office and as classroom space. The museum later moved to the Baker Building, and the Mathewson House is currently rented by Lyndon State College for extra dormitory space.

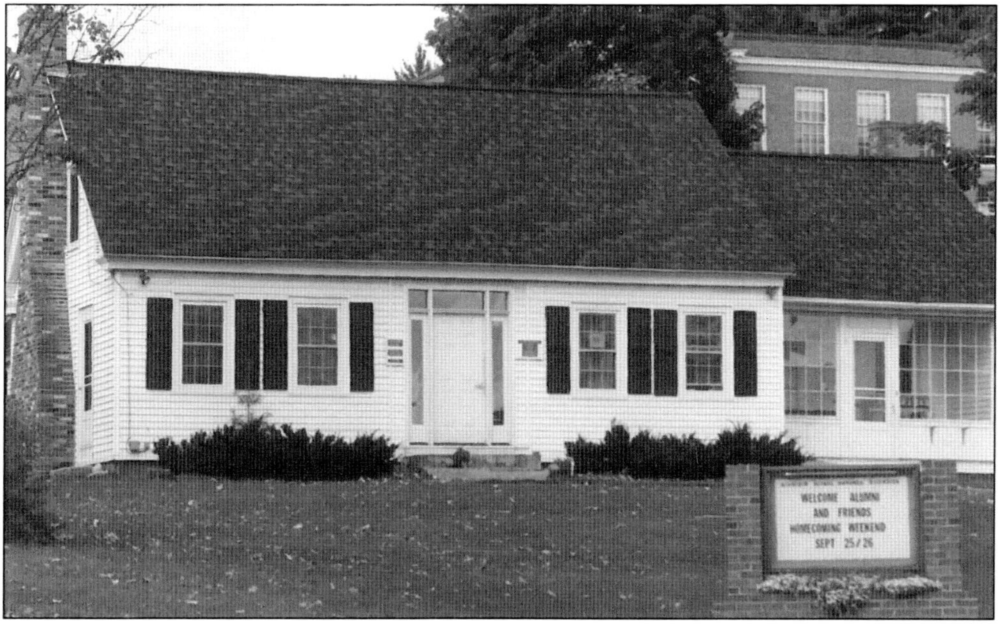


**THE THOMPSON COTTAGE.** Located on the campus, this house, once the home of Sumner Shaw Thompson, has served as a residence for teachers and occasionally as the headmaster's home. At the time of this publication, it houses offices of the alumni secretary, development director, athletic director, and publicity director. In the early days, the house was moved from another nearby location; it now has additions, including the ell at the right and offices at the rear.

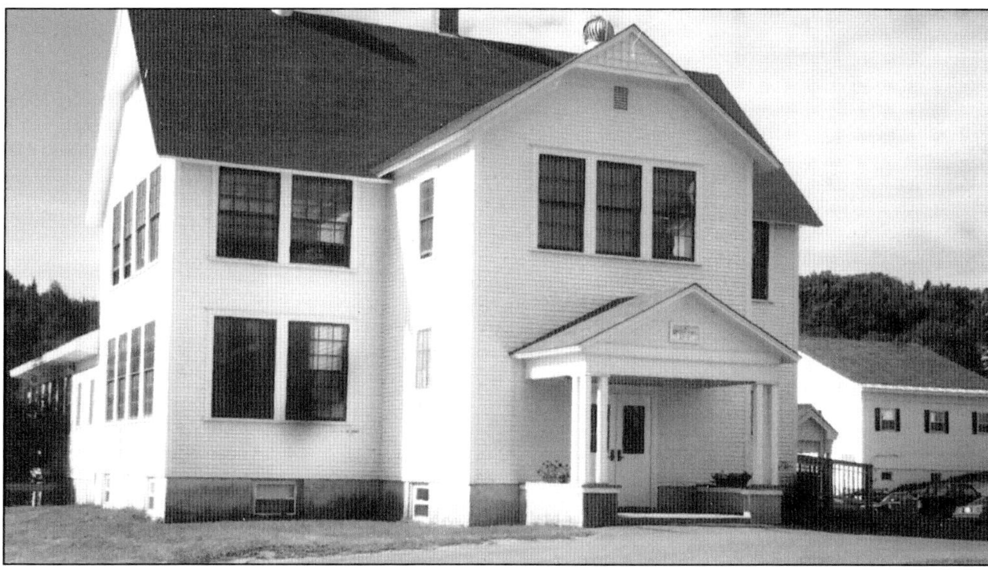

**THE CAMPUS SCHOOL.** Built in 1900, the campus school replaced the old Lyndon Center graded school that was located by the cemetery. When the new Lyndon Town School was built to accommodate all pupils in kindergarten through grade eight, this school building was acquired by Lyndon Institute. It had been one of the practice schools for Lyndon Normal School students. It is now the Elizabeth Harris Brown Commercial Center for the Lyndon Institute business education and the Lyndon Institute financial business offices. (See page 25.)

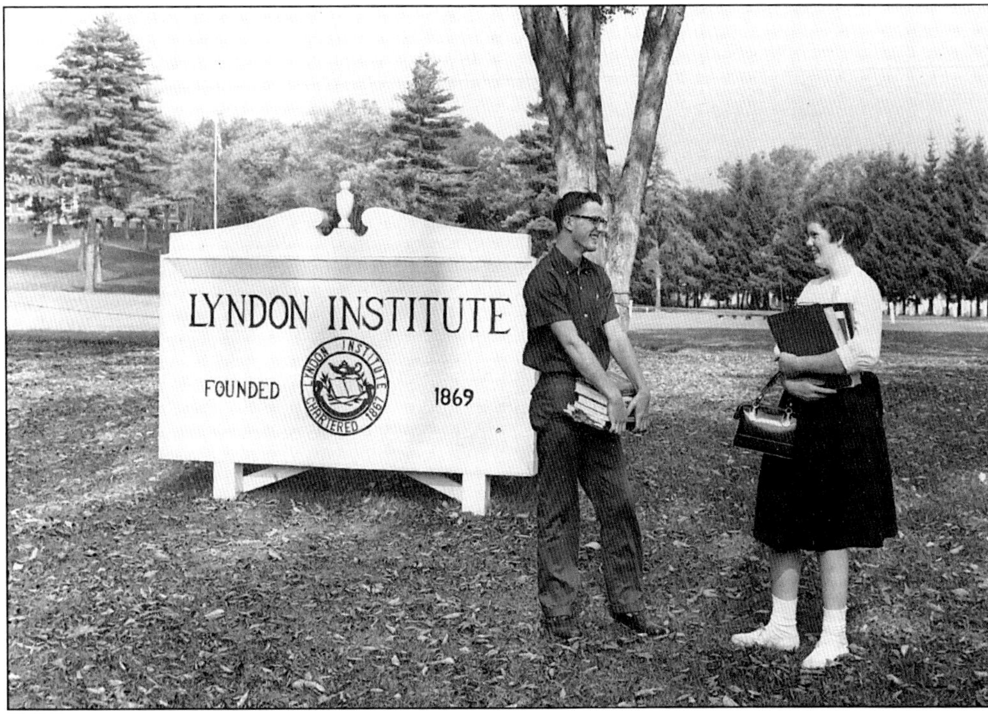


**CHATTING ON THE CAMPUS.** These studious classmates—if we can judge by the books they are carrying—stop to talk by the Lyndon Institute sign. They are Wilder Simpson '60 and Margaret Jardine '60. As the sign states, Lyndon Institute was chartered in 1867 and founded in 1869.

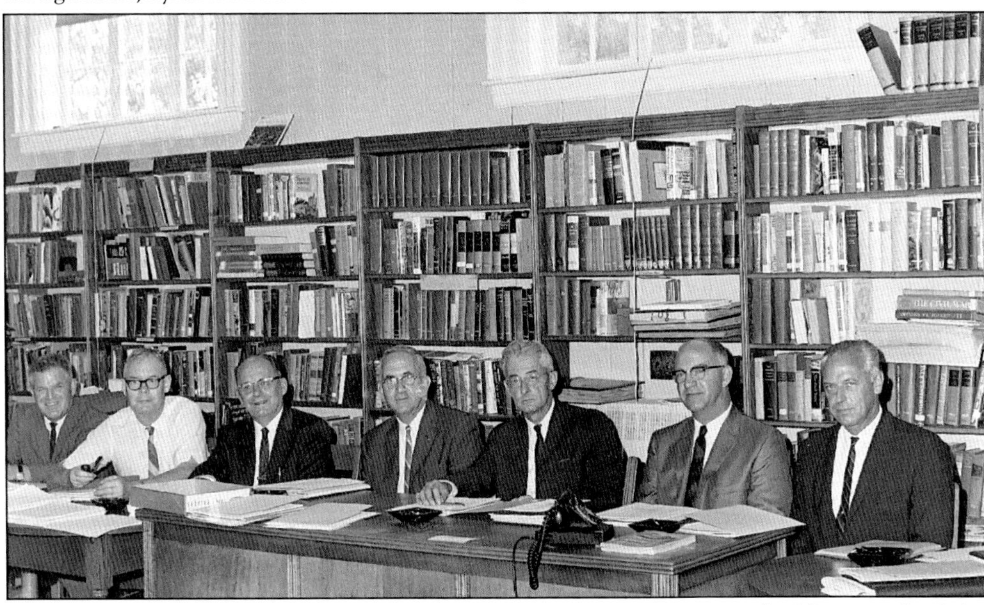

**RESPONSIBILITY.** Members of the Executive-Finance Committee meet at the library in the Baker Building in 1966. They are, from left to right, Archie Mallon, headmaster; Dr. Ralph Jardine; Robert F. Pierce; Maurice Hill; John Norris Jr.; Hazen Russell; and Clarence Akley. Designated by the Board of Trustees, the committee meets monthly and is responsible for the overall operation of the school.

**ENVISIONING THE FUTURE.** Albert Forrest, assistant headmaster, left, and Archie Mallon, headmaster, have a picture in their minds of just how the new Alumni Auditorium and Gymnasium wing will look when these plans are carried out.

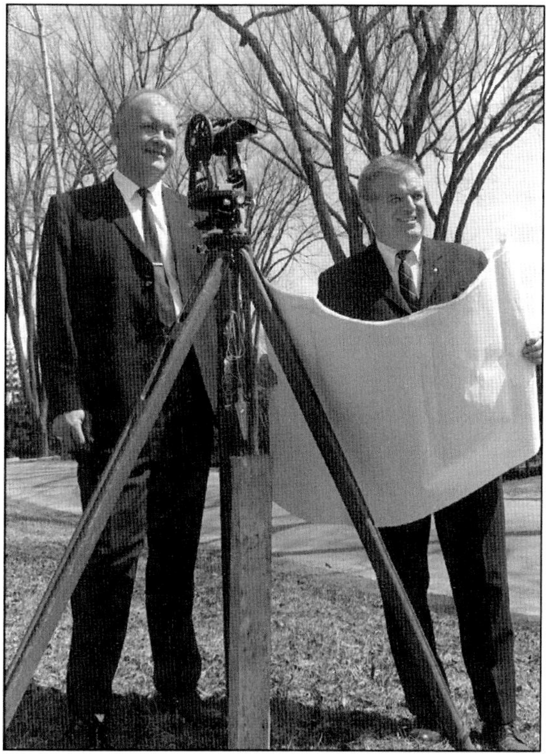

**A BIG DAY FOR LYNDON INSTITUTE.** John L. Norris Jr., Lyndon Institute president, and Maurice Hill, left, lift the first shovelful of earth for the new Alumni Auditorium and Gymnasium wing foundation on April 15, 1964. Building committee members and other trustees looking on are, from left to right, Donald Beattie, Robert K. Lewis, Curtis Sargent, Fr. Aime Trahan, Leon E. Hopkins, W. Arthur Simpson, Urban Wakefield, Everett King, and Robert F. Pierce. Archie Mallon, headmaster, is the man directly behind Norris.

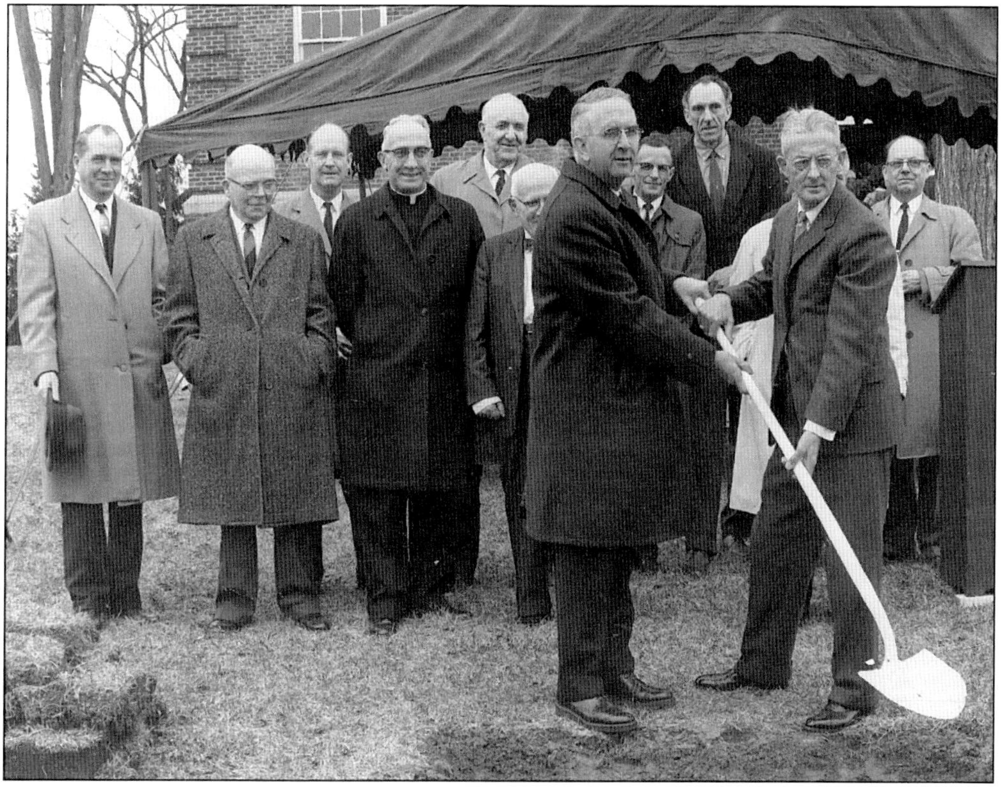

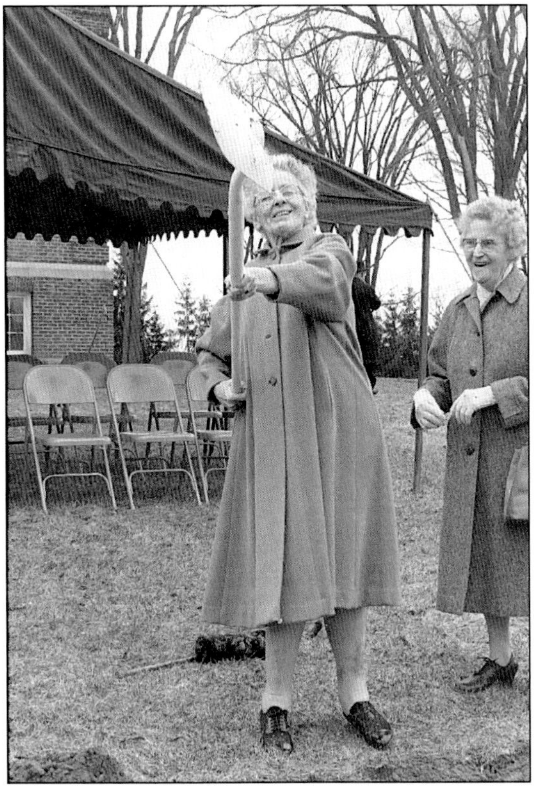

**A Happy Occasion in 1964.** May Campbell, '06, a retired teacher, tosses a shovelful of earth while Ethel Conner cheers her on during the ground breaking ceremony for the new addition.

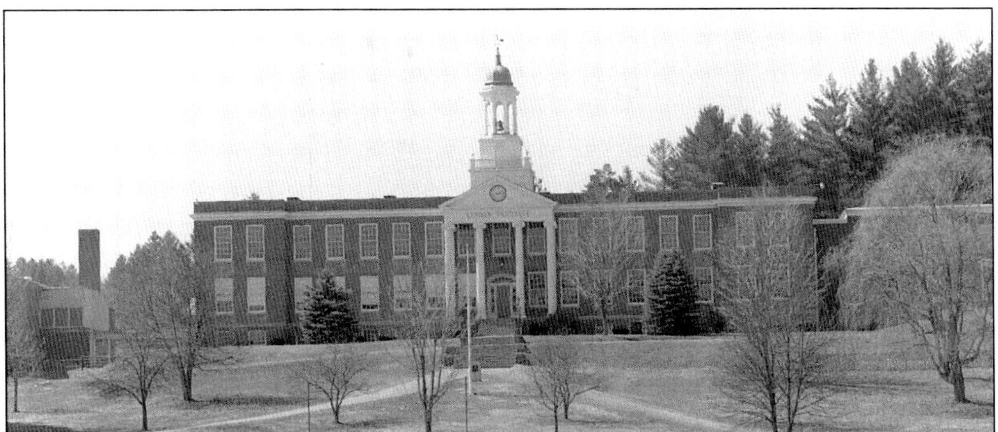

**Classic Lines.** The wings on each side of the institute building were well planned and do not detract from the original classical style and appearance. The left wing is the Alumni Auditorium and Gymnasium, built in 1965. It is separated from the main building by a covered passageway. The right wing, built in 1976, includes the cafeteria and classrooms; it was named for Robert F. Pierce, a longtime Lyndon Institute treasurer.

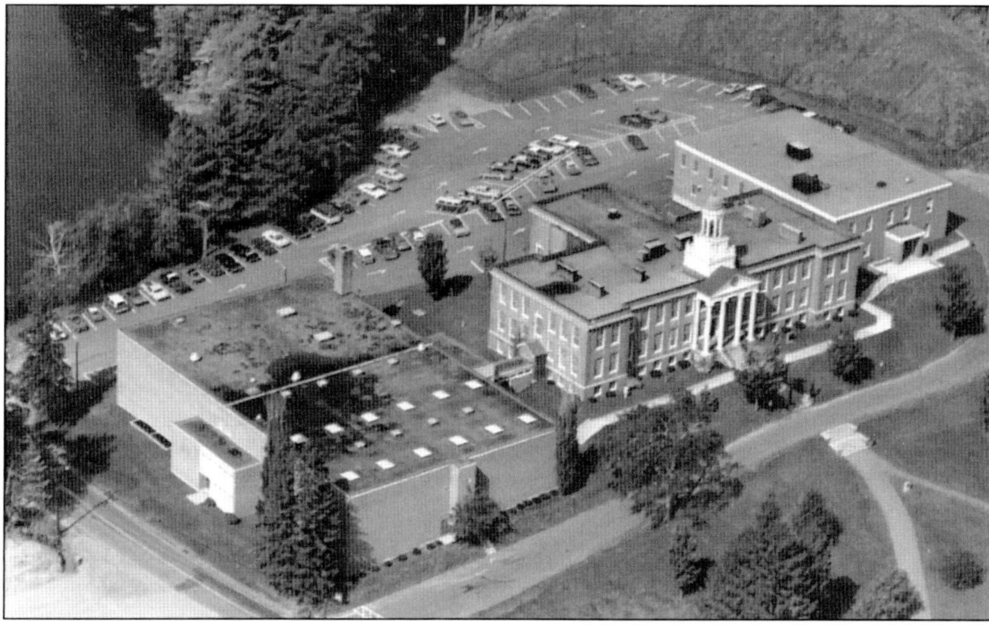

**AN OVERHEAD VIEW.** This image shows how the institute maintains its original look, even with the wings on each side. After the elms died, other trees were planted to replace them.

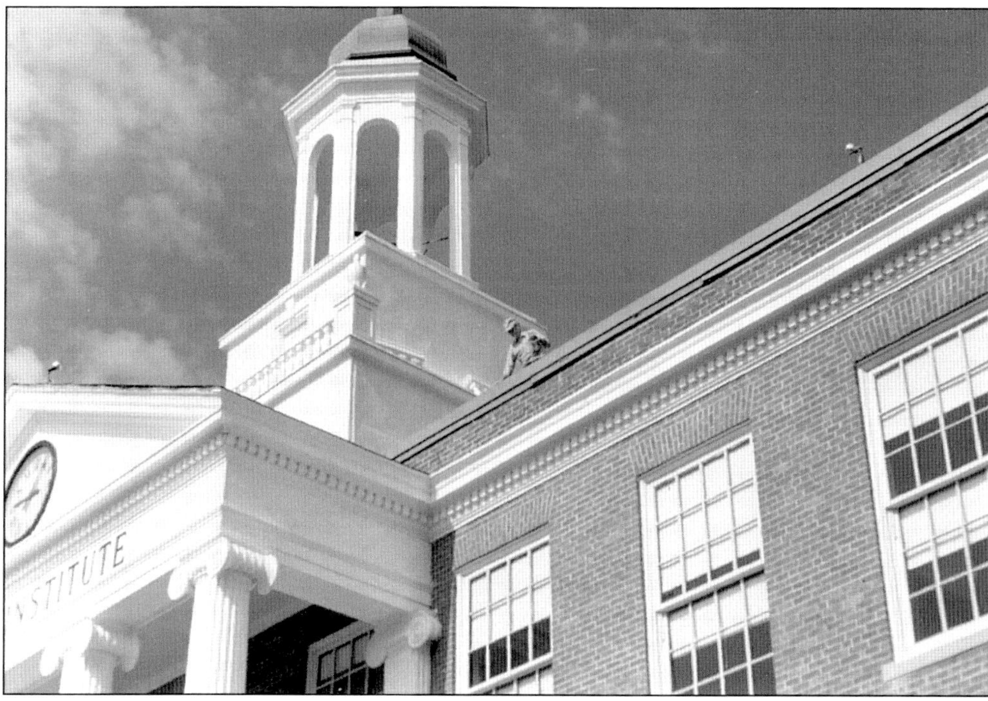


**ANGLES.** A worker peers down from the roof, near one of the many different angles that make up the institute facade. In 1997, the clock underwent repairs. Funds for the costly clock and bell repairs was a gift of the Class of 1957, given in memory of Milburn "Red" Nutting '34, who served for years on the Lyndon Institute maintenance crew. Funds from the Classes of 1937, 1943, and 1982 enabled the tower to be restored, as well.

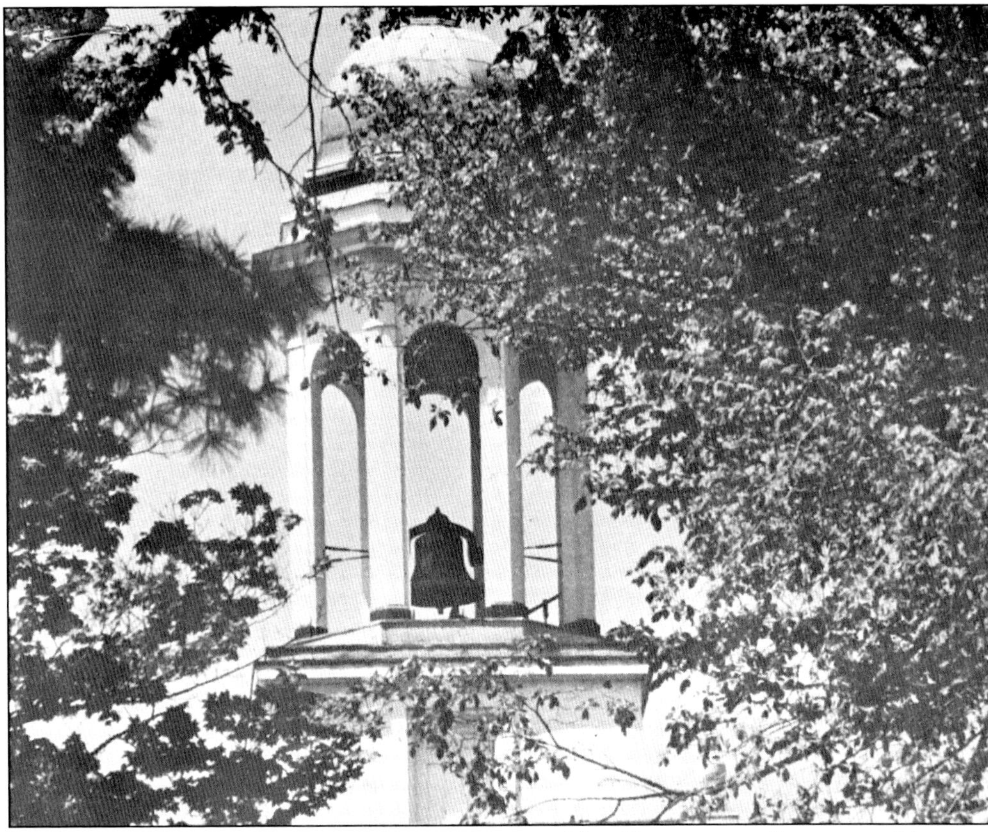

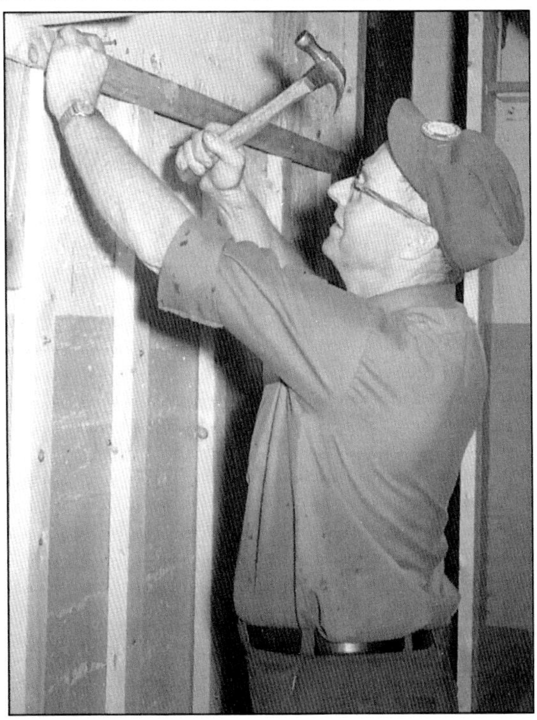

**THE VOICE OF THE INSTITUTE.** The bell for the new institute was a gift of John L. Norris Sr., whose son John L. Norris Jr. was a trustee for a number of years. The new building was erected in 1922, after the destruction of Thompson Hall by fire. The ringing of the new bell was a welcome sound after several years of silence.

**MORE THAN A HANDY MAN.** Custodian Milburn "Red" Nutting '34 really could hit the nail on the head. For years, Nutting managed the teenage dances that were sponsored by the American Legion. The young people respected him at the dances and at the school. If teens acted up at a dance, Nutting asked them to leave, but they were always welcomed back the next time and given another chance. Nutting worked at Lyndon Institute for some 26 years.

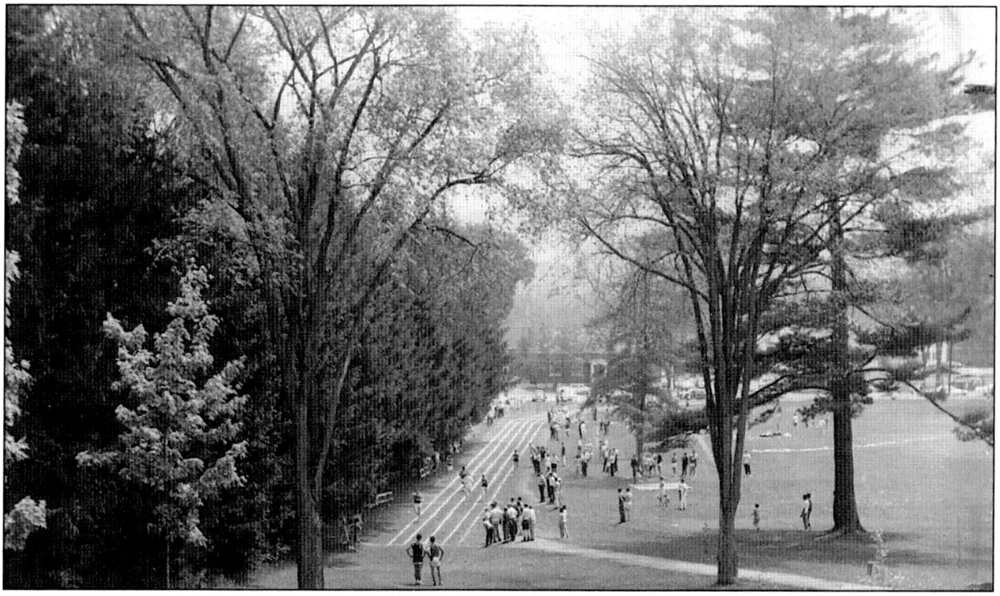

**The Town Green of the Olden Days.** A few elms left were still left when this photograph was taken in 1976. The campus has many different uses, which change with the seasons, including football, track, soccer, field hockey, and outdoor graduations.

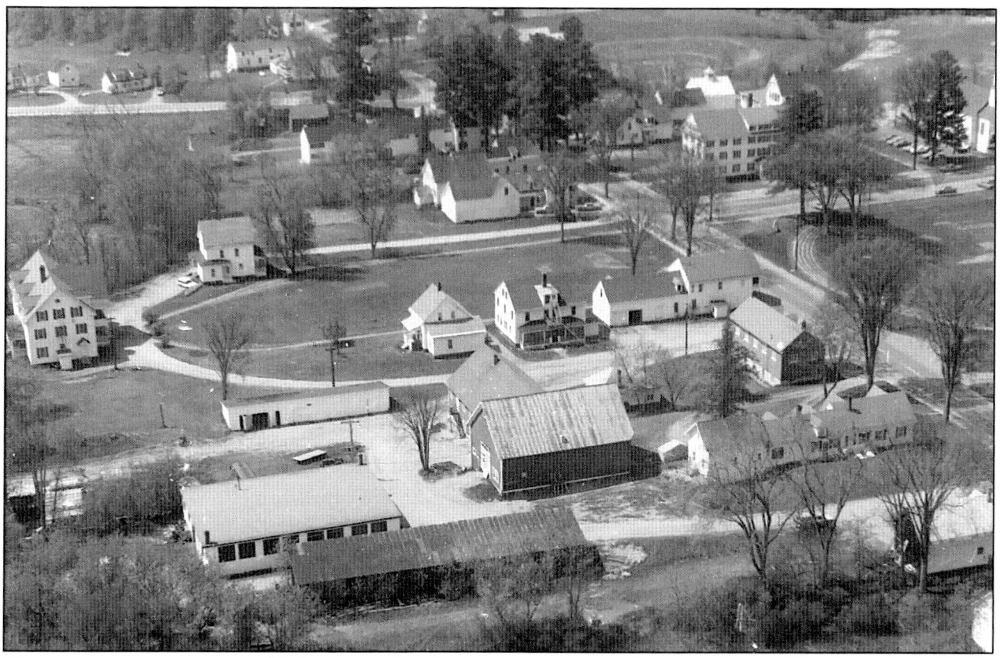

**The Lower Campus.** Clockwise around the loop, from the far left, stand the Mathewson House; the Collison Cottage; the Willey House; the Family and Consumer Science Building, which was converted from a barn; the post office and former store, facing the street; the Old Tavern; the Smith Cottage; and a storage shed. In the foreground, from left to right, are the Auto Mechanics Building; the Agricultural Barn; the Baker Building, on the street; and the Jeremy Pearl House. At the upper right are the Sanborn House and the campus school, both owned by Lyndon Institute, and the Baptist church.

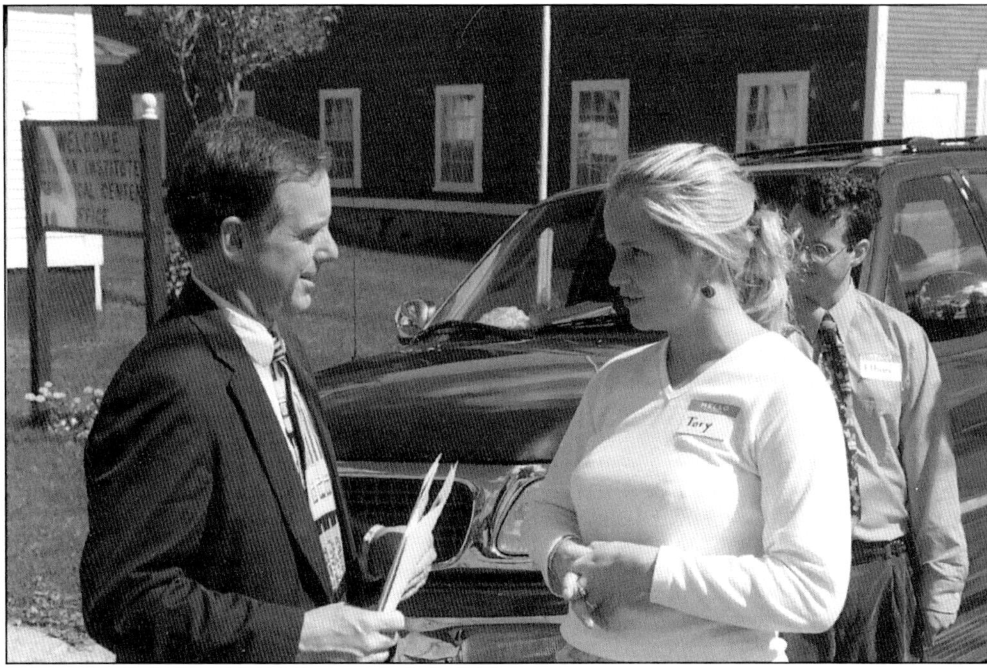


**THE GOVERNOR'S VISIT.** Tory Oliver was one of the student guides who escorted Gov. Howard Dean when he visited Lyndon Institute on September 11, 1998. Dean called the school a "hidden gem," and added that it is a good example of what his educational plan is aimed at achieving statewide. According to David Stahler '65, a Lyndon Institute trustee, Dean reacted the same way that many people do: they assume that Lyndon Institute is a small school with meager means until they visit the sprawling campus.

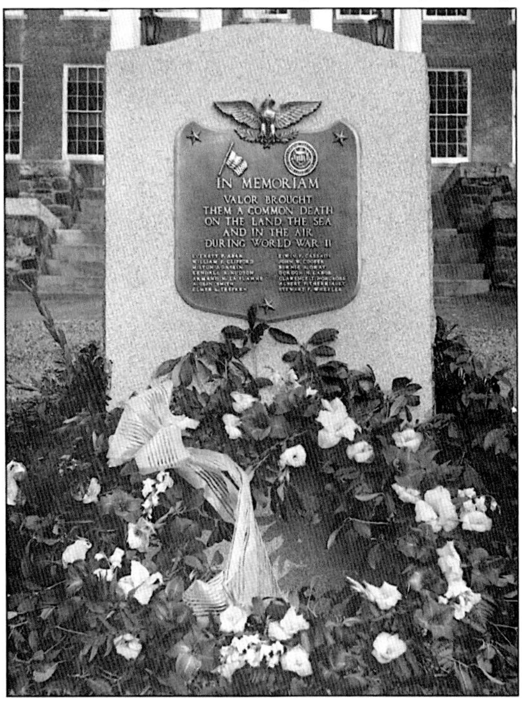


**FOR VALOR.** The highlight of Alumni Day, June 3, 1948, was the dedication of this memorial. It says: "In Memoriam. Valor brought them a common death on the land, the sea and in the air during World War II." The names are: Everett P. Abar, William P. Clifford, Milton J. Gaskin, Kendall A Hudson, Armand N. LaFlamme, A. Olin Smith, Elmer L. Trefren, Elwin F. Cassady, John W. Cooper, Burnie A. Gray, Gordon H. Labor, Clarence T. Norcross, Albert F. Therriault, and Stewart F. Wheeler.

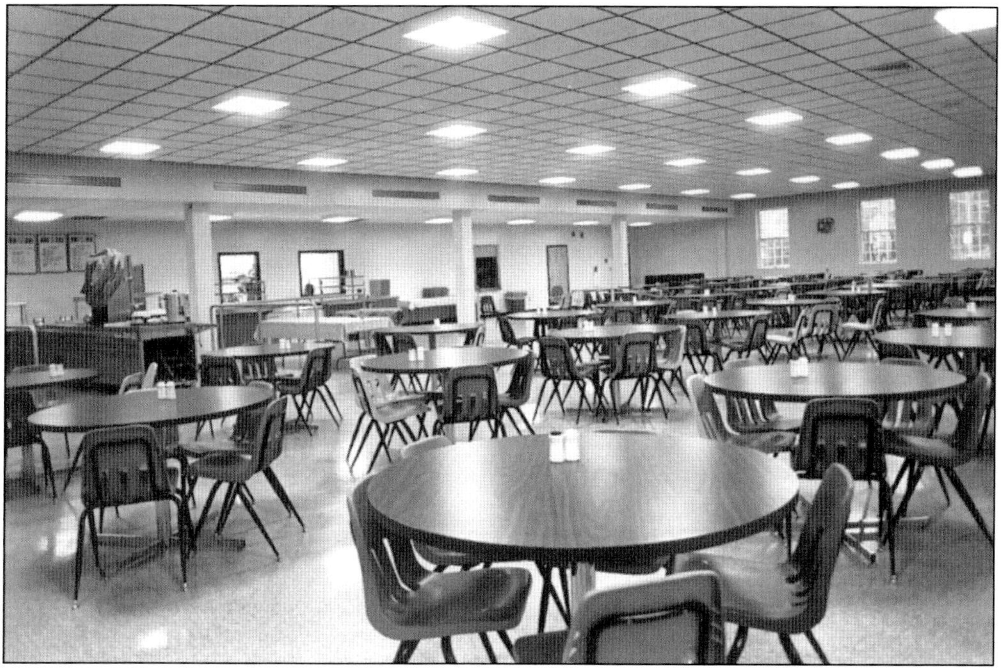

**The Cafeteria.** When the cafeteria wing was added in 1976, with classrooms above, it was named for Robert F. Pierce, longtime treasurer of Lyndon Institute. Besides serving as a student lunchroom, it is a place for special events, such as student gatherings, annual meetings of the institute corporators, the annual alumni class secretaries' supper, and other special occasions.

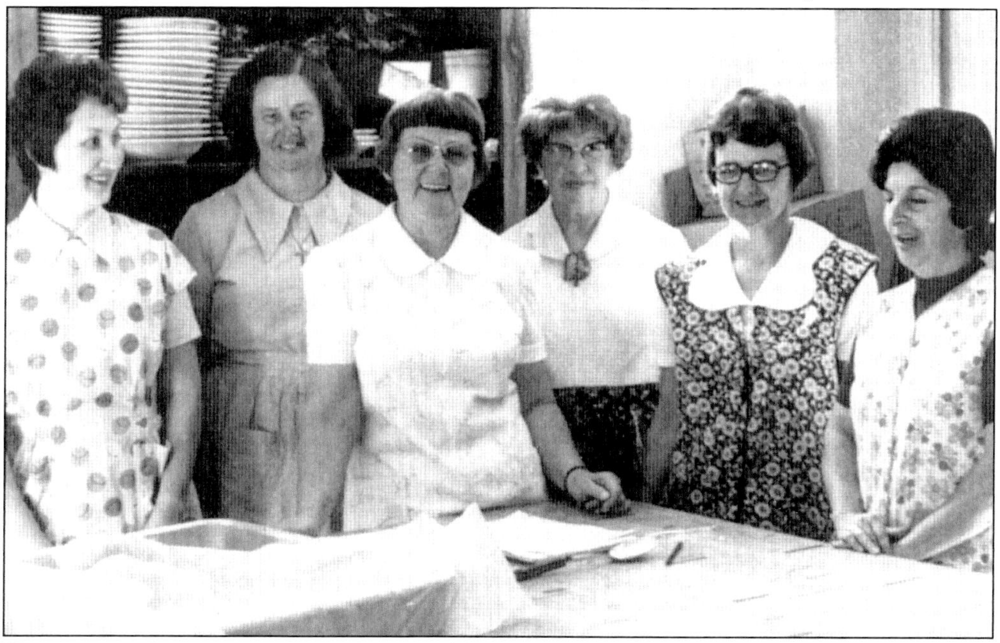

**Keeping the Students Fed.** Students and faculty who do not bring their own lunches have a choice each day of two or three different main dishes, prepared in the Lyndon Institute kitchen. The cooks on duty in 1976 are, from left to right, Mrs. Bishop, Mrs. Goodwin, Mrs. John, Mrs. Hardie, Mrs. Gardner, and Mrs. Taylor.

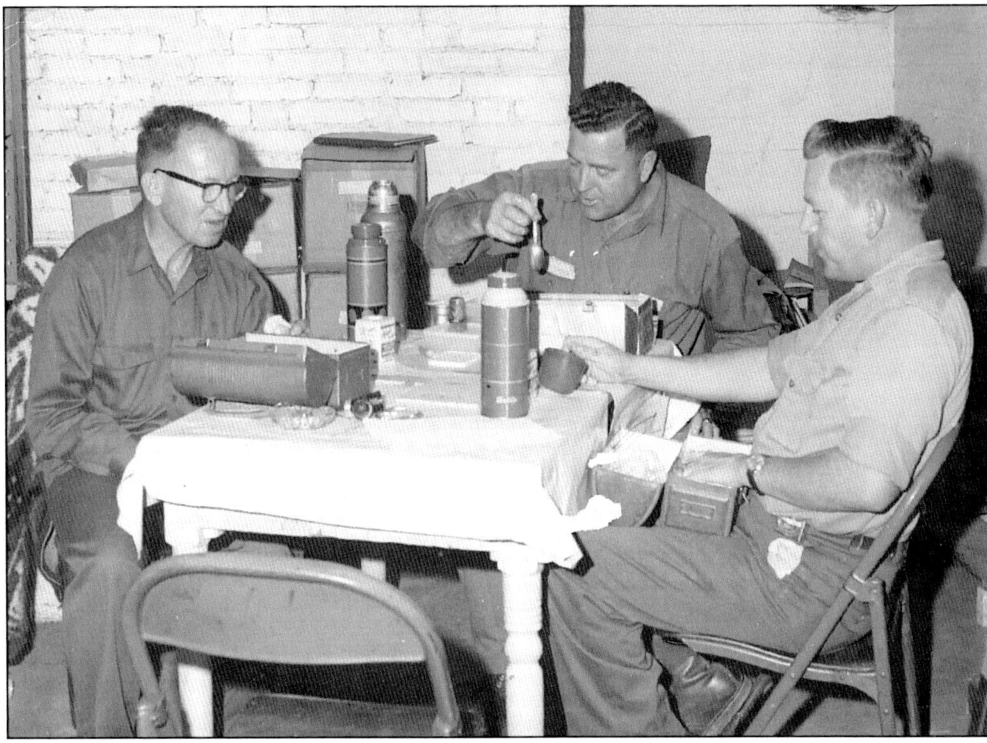

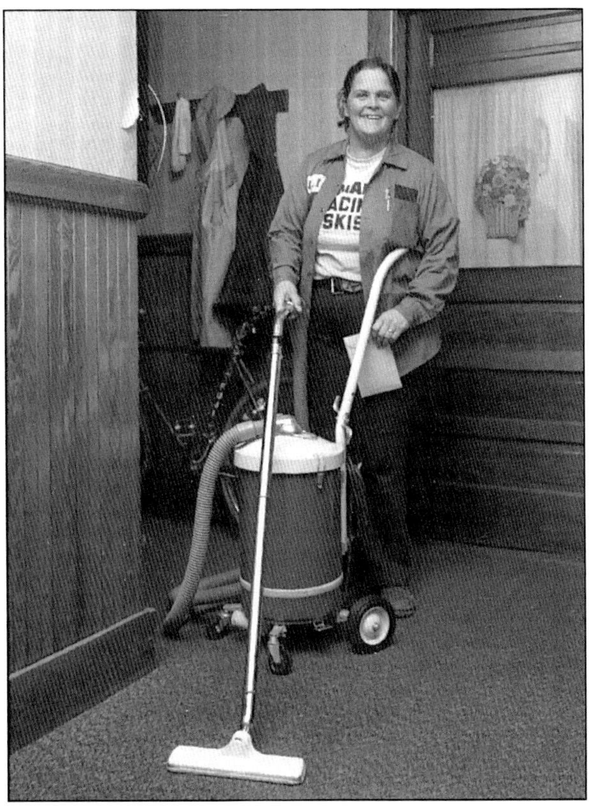

**Time Out for Lunch.** Three of the maintenance workers stop for lunch during their busy schedule of keeping the Lyndon Institute facilities in good order. They are, from left to right, Mr. Heath, Mr. Cote, and Mr. Brill.

**Sweeping Up.** Shirley Brill smiles as she wields the vacuum cleaner. She is one of many who have helped keep Lyndon Institute spick-and-span.

# *Six*

# Academics

Tuition for courses offered at the opening of the Lyndon Literary and Biblical Institution in 1870 was as low as $1.50 for penmanship and as high as $10 for piano, with an additional $3 charge for use of a piano. Classes were to be held in temporary quarters, but the advertisement said that the Seminary Building was to be ready for the winter term. Students either boarded with families for $3.25 per term—which covered room and washing—and took care of their own meals, or they roomed in clubs for reasonable rates.

Changes have been made to keep in step with the times; however Lyndon Institute has always taken pride in offering small classes; a well-maintained campus; a clean and safe environment; respect for individuals; a friendly atmosphere; award-winning academic, art, and technology programs; strong and varied educational, cultural, and athletic opportunities; well-educated, student-oriented faculty; close proximity to other resources; a supportive community; and equal opportunity for all students.

Included in this chapter are a few longtime teachers who meant much to the school. Many other teachers did also—probably almost all of them—but these are some of the great teachers who have been a vital part of Lyndon Institute. The headmasters included here are the ones who have served the longest terms in some of the more recent years. Rather than a list of qualifications, the information on the headmasters contains a more personal view of their terms on campus. The following headmasters who came after Archie Mallon are not included in this chapter: David Leavitt (1973–74), Gerald Dennis (1975–81), Cyrus Benson (1981–87), and Paul Johnson (1987–1988).

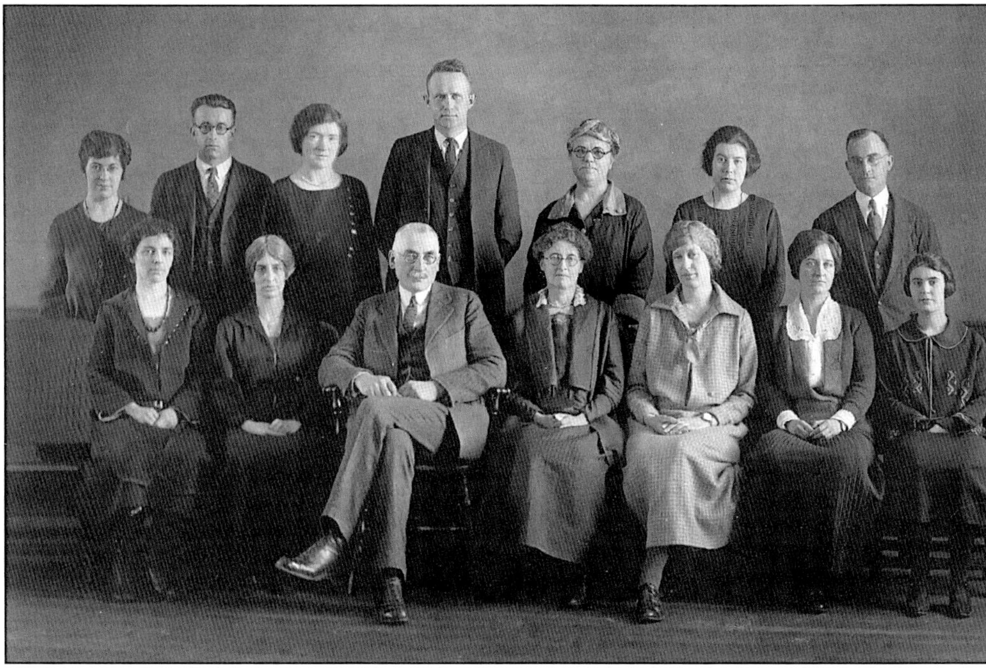

**The 1924 Faculty.** Faculty members, from left to right, are as follows: (front row) May Campbell; Clara Eastman; O.D. Mathewson, principal; Mabel Hayes; Evelyn Fuller; Theta Baker; and unidentified; (back row) Grace Gould; Eugene Robinson; Mary Root; Clayton Fisher; Bessie Verder; Lois Alger; and Amory Seaver.

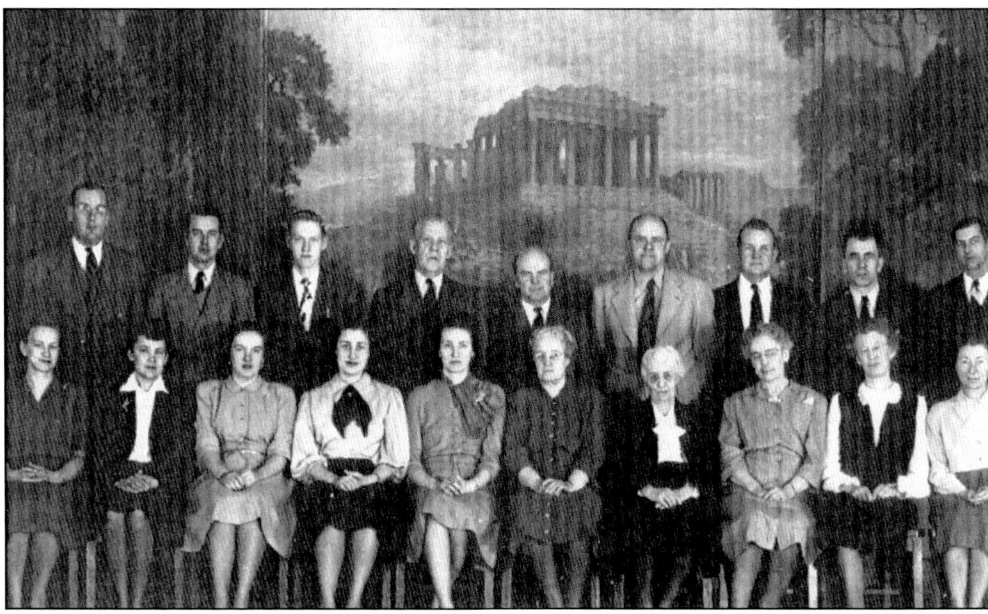

**The Faculty of 1948.** More than 20 years later, many of the fine teachers above were still inspiring students. Seen here, from left to right, are the following: (front row) H. Michalowski, secretary; M. Peck; H. Thissen; D. Goss; G. Wilcox; T. Baker; C. Eastman; M. Campbell; E. Fuller; and R. Emerson; (second row) J. Goss; J. King; R. Phillips; Mr. True, headmaster; R. Lewis, assistant headmaster; C. Wright; A. Forrest; H. Ross; and A. Pratt.

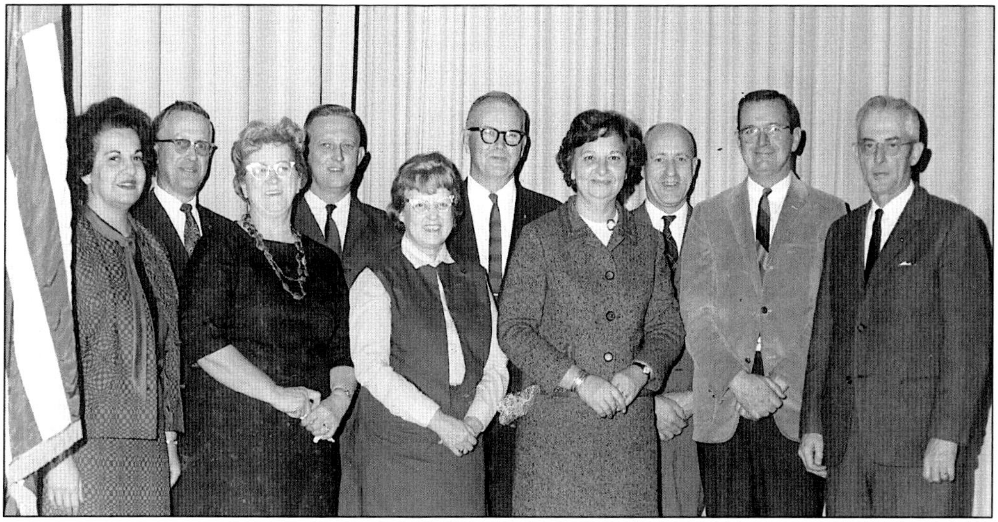

**LATER FACULTY.** This group includes Bertha Koury, Gerald Aubin, Marion Wakefield, Norris Elliott, school librarian Clara Aubin, Albert Forrest, Winnie King, Arthur Lord, Jack King, and John Norris, trustee president.

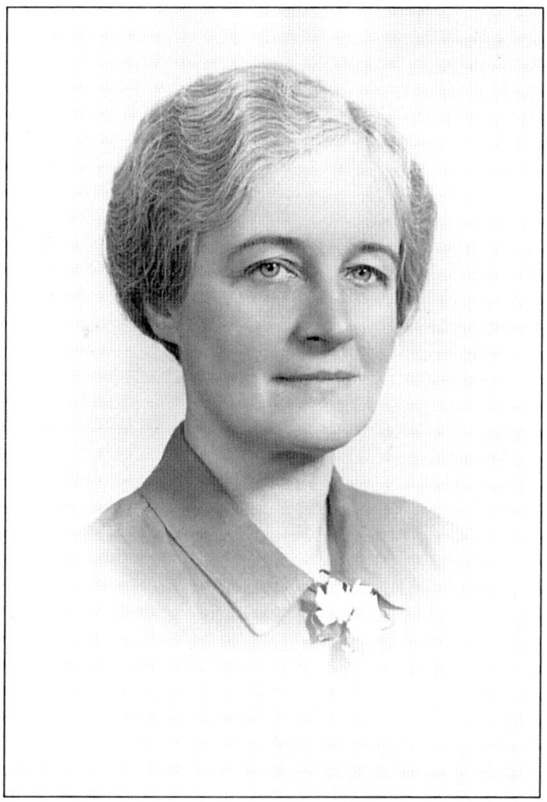

**THETA HELEN BAKER.** Theta Baker came to Lyndon Institute from Maine in February 1919 to substitute for Miss Eastman, who was ill with flu; she remained for 37 years. She taught English and Latin, was the senior class adviser, introduced Class Day for seniors, was a faculty sponsor for establishing a chapter of the National Honor Society at Lyndon Institute, and was one of the originators of the *Cynosure*, the school yearbook, in 1924. The brick library was named in her honor. She retired in 1956 and made her home in Lyndonville.

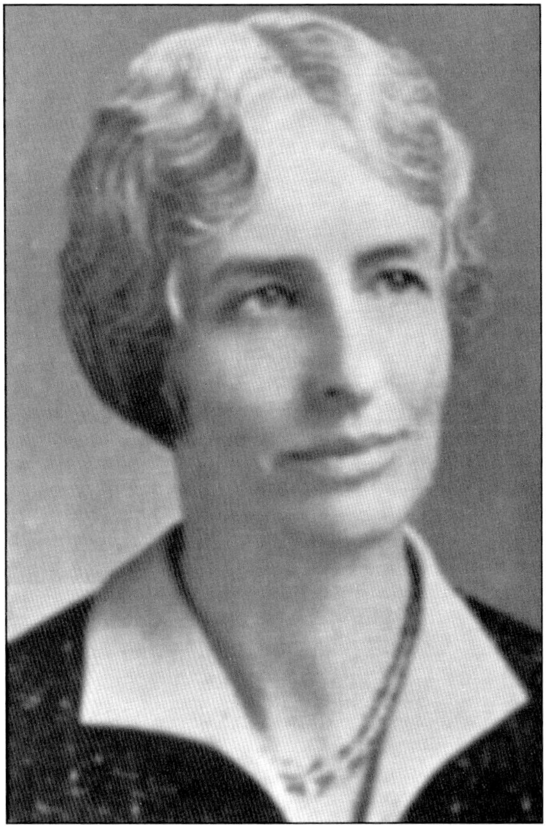

**Clara Eastman.** Clara Eastman came to Lyndon Institute in 1912 and for more than four decades taught English I and English Literature IV. The Class of 1937 dedicated the *Cynosure* to her for her "cheery smile, and inexhaustible patience. She gave us confidence as freshmen, and incentive as seniors. She greets us upon our entrance and four years later, upon our graduation, lingers to wish us 'God speed.'" She retired in 1954.

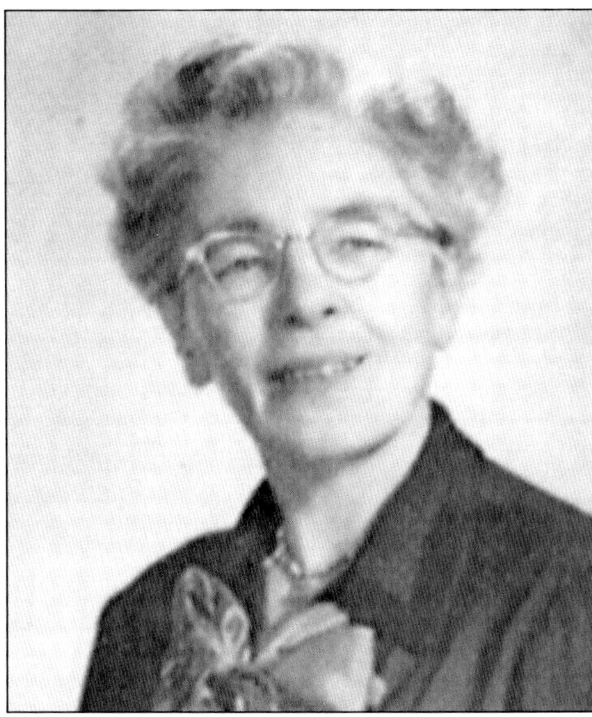

**May A. Campbell, 1888–1979.** May Campbell graduated from Lyndon Institute in 1906. From the University of Vermont, she received an M.A. in education in 1911 and a Ph.D. cum laude. In 1918, she came to Lyndon Institute, where she taught Latin, history, English III, biology, and business English. She was a senior adviser, a dramatic coach, and a Student Council adviser. In 1957, she received a Master Teacher Certificate at Lyndon Teachers College. She was also active in several clubs and organizations in Lyndonville. She retired in 1958.

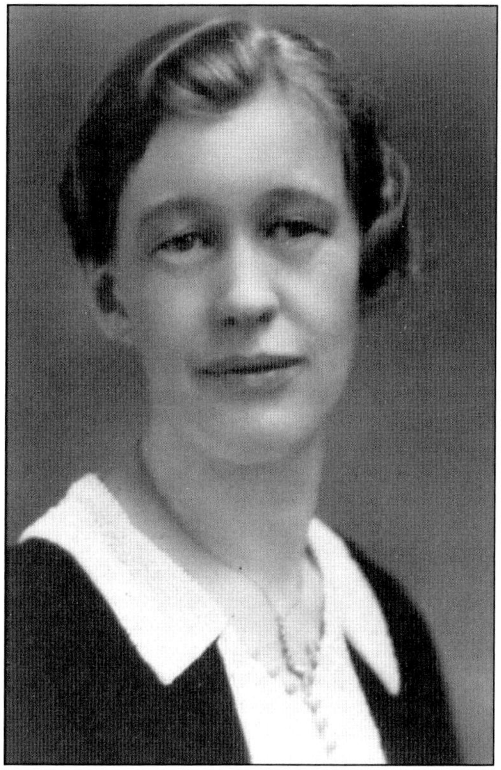

**EVELYN FULLER.** A 1916 graduate of Radcliffe College, with an A.B. degree and distinction in Romance languages and literature, and an M.A. in French from Middlebury College, Evelyn Fuller came to Lyndon Institute in 1921 to teach French. She became junior class adviser, assistant dramatic coach, assistant senior class adviser, and winter carnival coordinator. She retired in 1958.

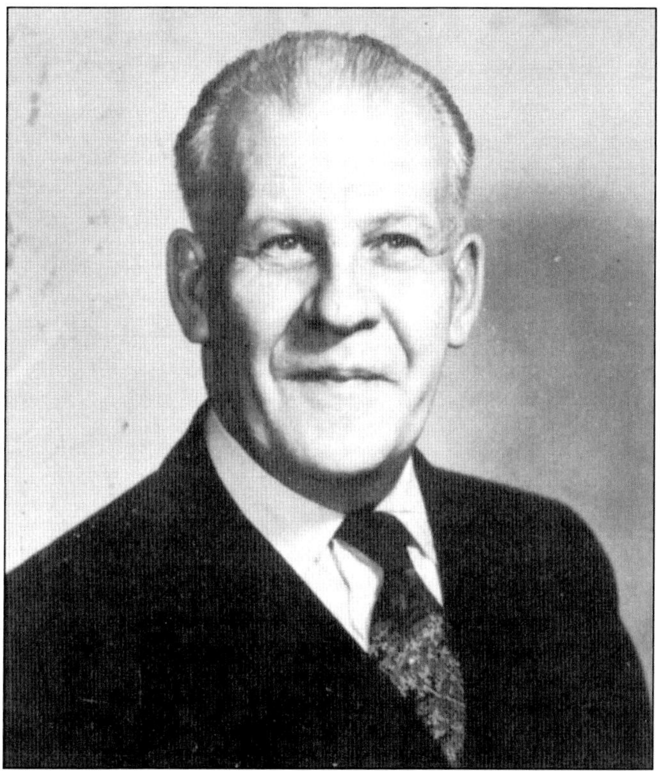

**WALTER F. TRUE.** Walter True added the agricultural course in 1946, auto mechanics in 1947, and building trades in 1955, making Lyndon Institute a school that could fill the needs of every student. He taught several years at Lyndon Institute before becoming headmaster from 1943 to 1957.

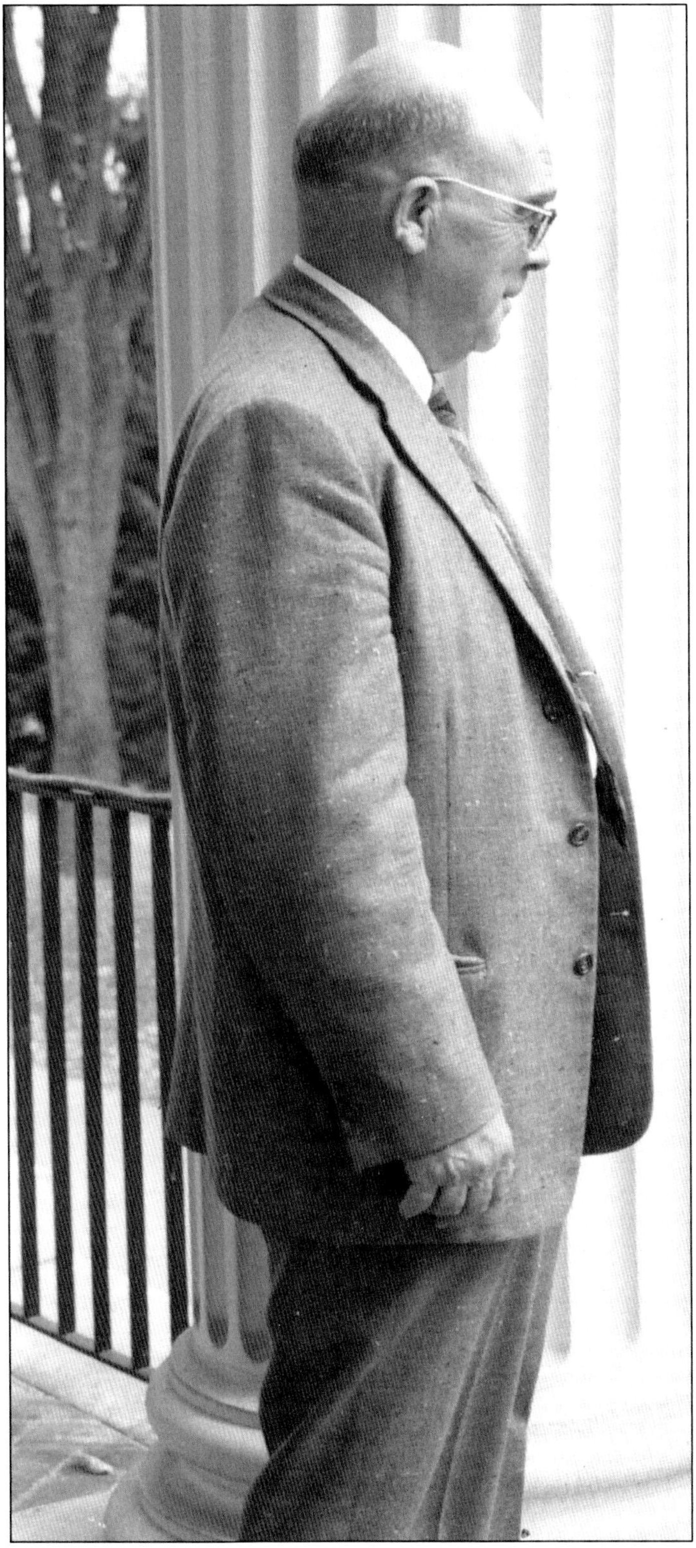

A MAN OF MANY TALENTS. Robert K. Lewis (1898–1966) was born in Honey Brook, Pennsylvania. In 1924, he came to Lyndon Institute, where he taught ancient, medieval, and modern history and coached football and track. He was in charge of the boys' dormitory with Arthur Elliott. In 1930, he married Eleanor Huer, the home economics teacher. He introduced competitive skiing into the athletic program. He was a charter member of the Lyndon Outing Club and served on the board of directors for 26 years. He was named headmaster in 1957. When he retired in 1963, the Lyndon Institute Board of Trustees recognized his love of the school, his willingness to work, and his desire to keep the school at its high level, and named him to head a fund drive for badly needed additions and building improvements. The result of this drive was the new Alumni Auditorium and Gymnasium that was completed in 1965. The Lewises purchased a retirement home on Skyline Drive that was built by the Lyndon Institute building trades students.

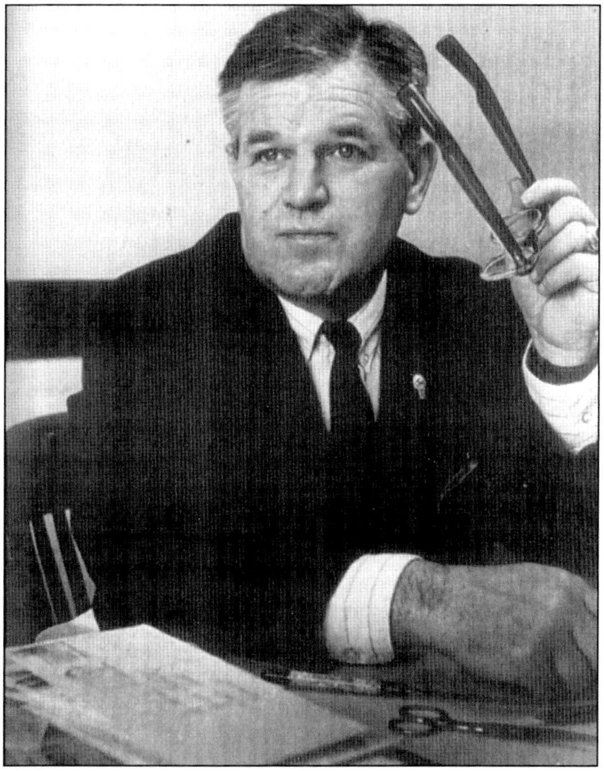

**ARCHIE P. MALLON, 1918–1999.** Archie Mallon, a graduate of Dartmouth College and an enlistee in the U.S. Air Force in World War II, held teaching and educational administrative positions before coming to the Lyndon Institute as headmaster in 1963. In 1973, he returned to Chatham, New York, where he resumed teaching mathematics. He spent his final years in Lyndonville, where he attended and enjoyed many Lyndon Institute functions, rooting avidly for the athletic teams. He also took part in the band concerts at the park, playing the saxophone in the Lyndonville Band.

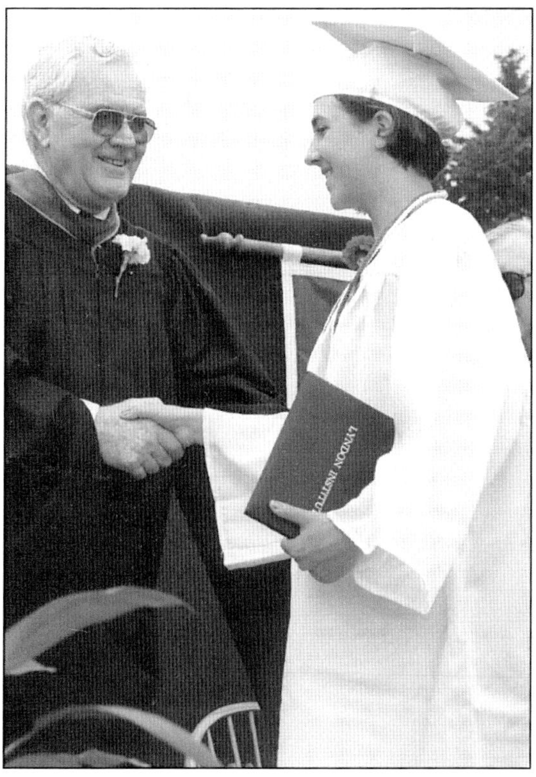

**DWIGHT DAVIS.** Dwight Davis '50, seen here congratulating 1999 graduate Mona Lowandoski, was the first development director and was made headmaster six months later in 1988. He continued to pursue development opportunities for the school and worked hard on the capital campaign at the same time. He is currently president of the Alumni Association and the first executive director of the Vermont Independent Schools Association.

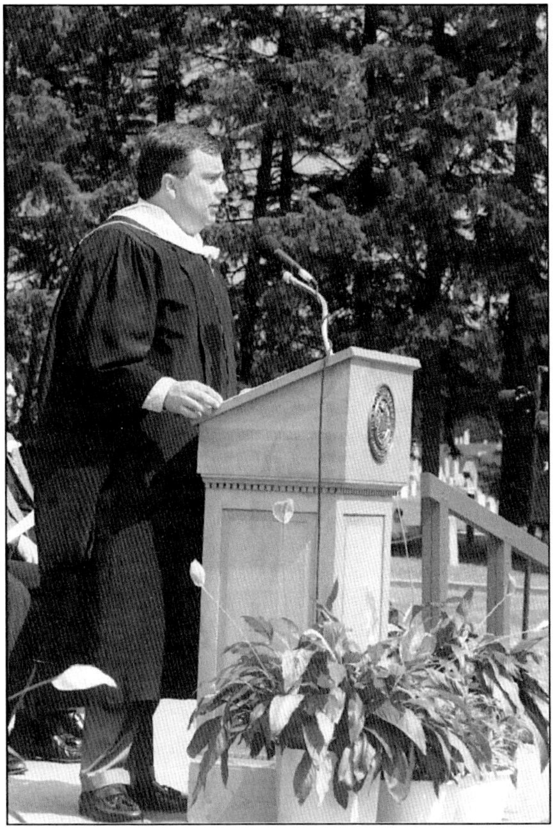

**A New Headmaster.** In July 1999, Richard D. Hilton arrived from Pennsylvania to become Lyndon Institute's new headmaster. He graduated from Notre Dame and received his master of arts in English from Villanova University. Among the qualities of Lyndon Institute that he appreciates is the fact that although an independent institution, it is an *inclusive* school, serving all kinds of students and involving the whole community in its work.

**What's Cooking?** Something flambé no doubt, judging by the flames. Whatever it was, science teachers Rick Eliot, Bud Courser, Rick Cameron, and Timothy Simpson seem pretty pleased with the results—or is that surprise on their faces?

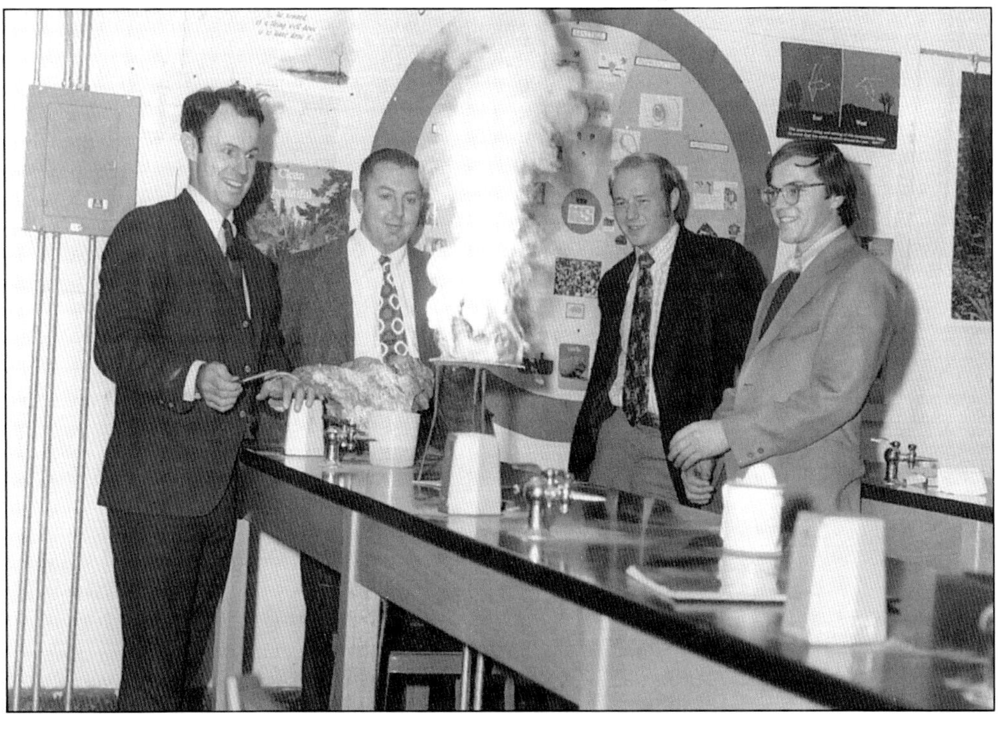

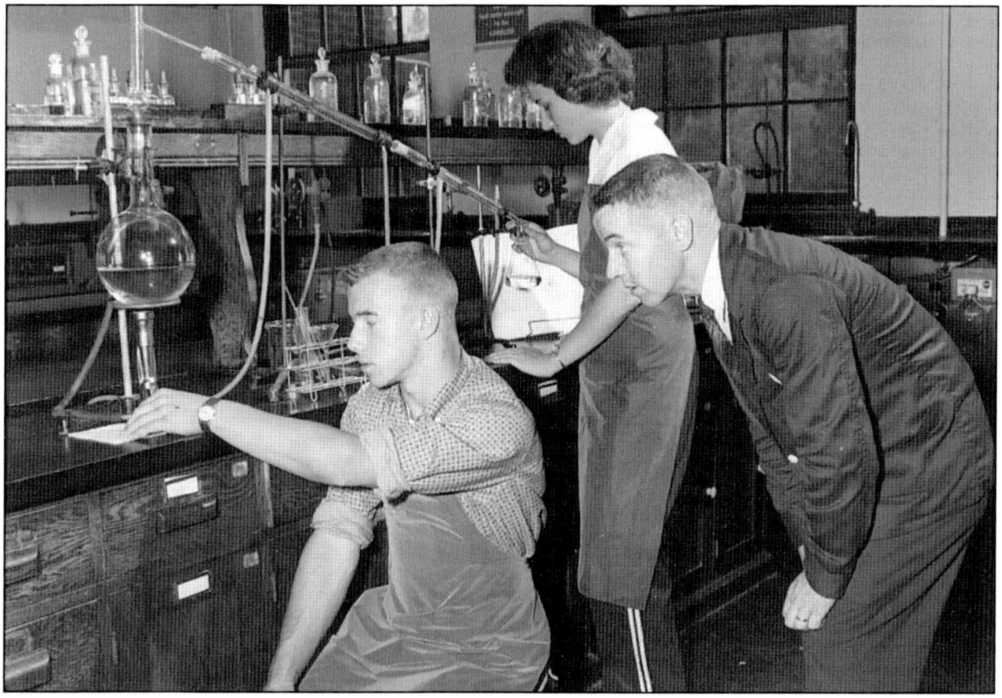

**NO FLAMES HERE.** Whatever students David Beattie '61 and Judy Vantine '60 were working on in the chemistry lab, it was under the instructions of teacher Donald Erskine (right).

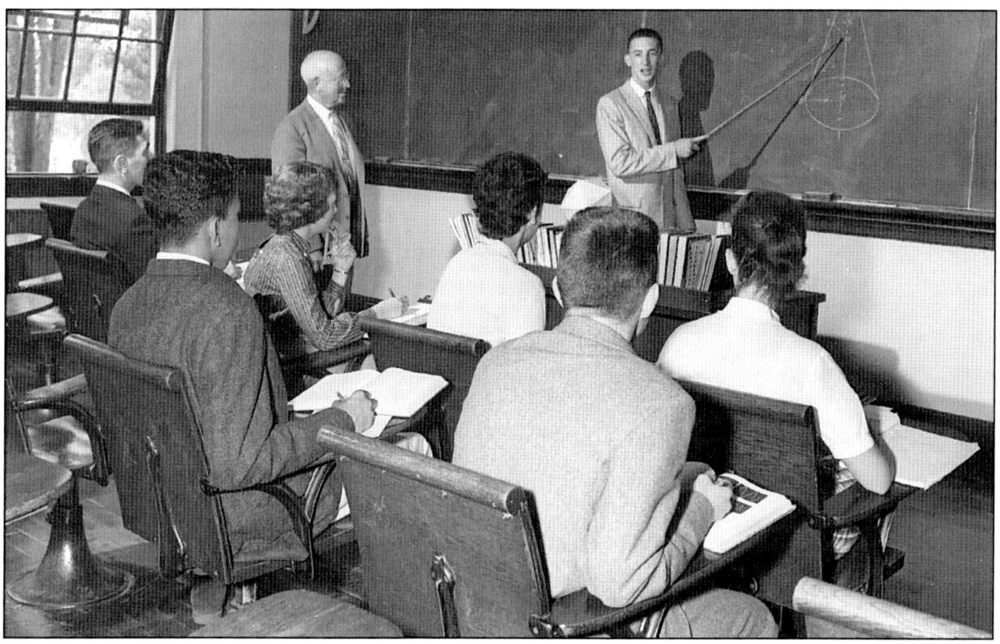

**GEOMETRY CLASS.** Math and geometry teacher Amory Seaver watches a student, identified as Richard Ashton '61, as he points out the steps of the problem on the board. Seaver taught at Lyndon Institute for many years. Later, Ashton also taught geometry at Lyndon Institute and went on to become an actuary at the National Life Insurance Company.

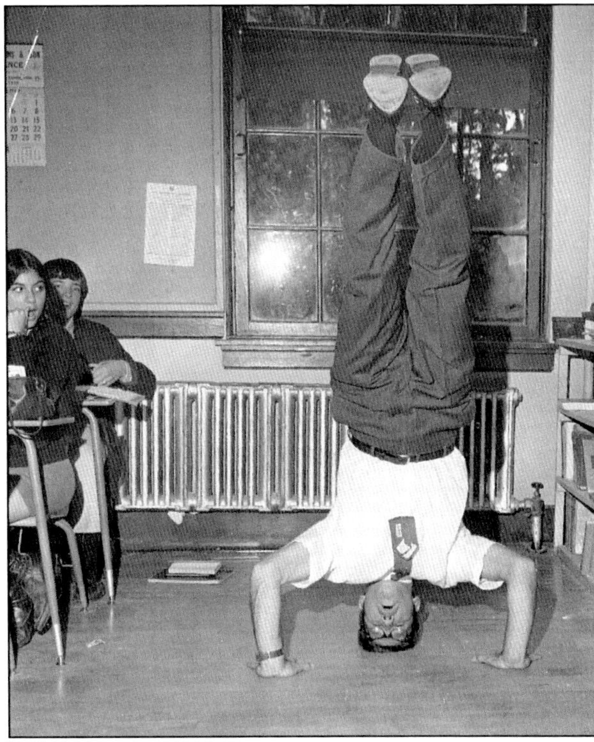

**Don't Forget to Invert the Denominator.** Why not stand on your head to make a point, thought math teacher Ronald Prinn in 1970. He evidently surprised the students, judging from the astonished looks on their faces. They probably got the message.

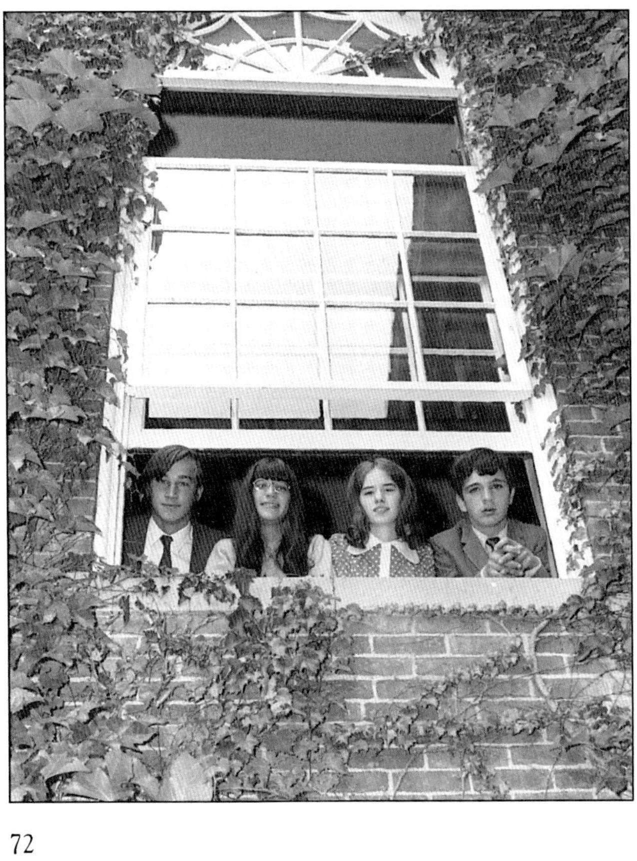

**Looking into the Future.** Glenn Laplant, Raelene St. Hilaire, Judy Cameron, and Tim Ruggles appear to be contemplating their future, as they look out the window from the ivied walls of Lyndon Institute. What will we learn here before we graduate in 1973? (Photographed in 1971.)

# *Seven*

# Fine Arts

Music, both instrumental and vocal, has been an important part of the Lyndon Institute curriculum ever since the beginning. When Walter Ranger was principal, his wife, Mabel Bemis Ranger, was instructor of instrumental music and Joseph Humphrey was instructor of vocal music. Music courses changed through the years. Today, there is a stage band, a marching band, a jazz band, a girls' chorus, a boys' chorus, and other smaller groups. Music teachers of later years have included Ruby Blaine, Celia Teis, Roy Christophersen, and currently John Padden, with a few others in between, along with the teachers who instructed the vocal groups. The Lyndon Institute often brings back awards and trophies from music festivals and competitions.

Every year, the graduating class puts on a senior play. The drama club enters the one-act play competition and has won many awards. The institute's auditorium has the largest stage in the area, and Catamount Arts sometimes uses this facility for the productions they book because of the size and excellence of equipment.

A publication called the *Janus* includes students' literary work and is sold in local bookstores. In 1997, 1998, and 1999, the publication won the All New England Honors in the New England Scholastic Press Association competition at Boston University College of Communication. Students also have won poster awards and other commendations for their artwork, their photographic work in the camera club, and their work in forensics.

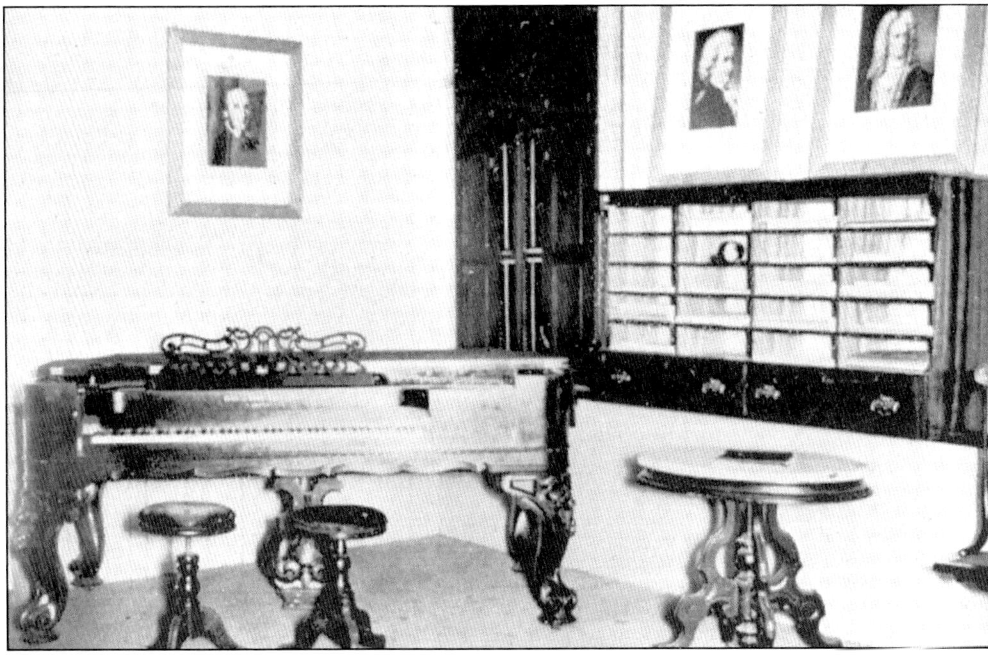

**THE MUSIC ROOM.** In the early days, there were several music rooms in Thompson Hall, the first main building that burned in 1922. Each room had a piano so that students could set up practice hours or vocal lessons. "The advantages of the course is enhanced by frequent public recitals," stated the catalogues of those early days. Today, music students still make many public appearances.

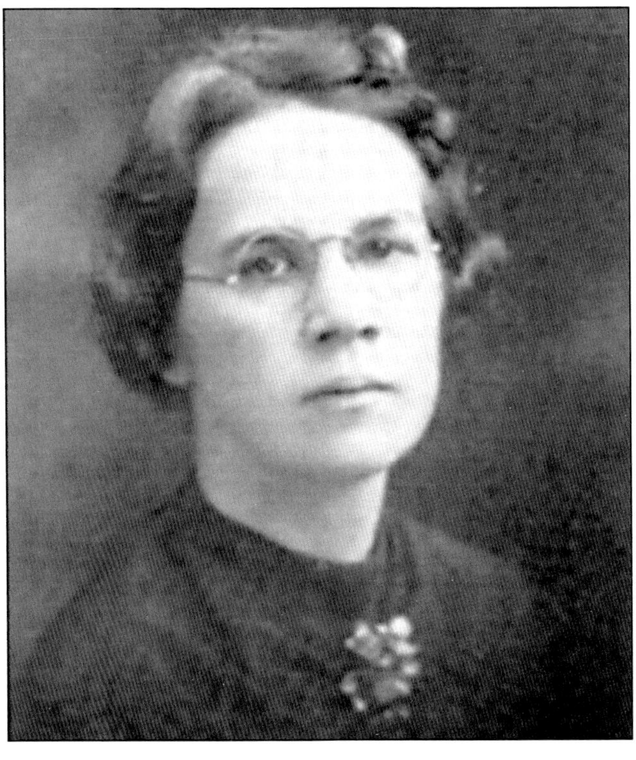

**RUBY BLAINE.** Besides directing the Lyndon Institute orchestra and the glee club from 1930 to 1941, Ruby Blaine also taught a course in civics. At the same time, she was teaching music to grades one through eight in the Lyndonville Graded School and the Lyndon Center Campus School, as well as method and music appreciation to the Lyndon Normal School students. After retirement, even as late as in her 90s, she loved traveling and taking or auditing courses at Lyndon State College.

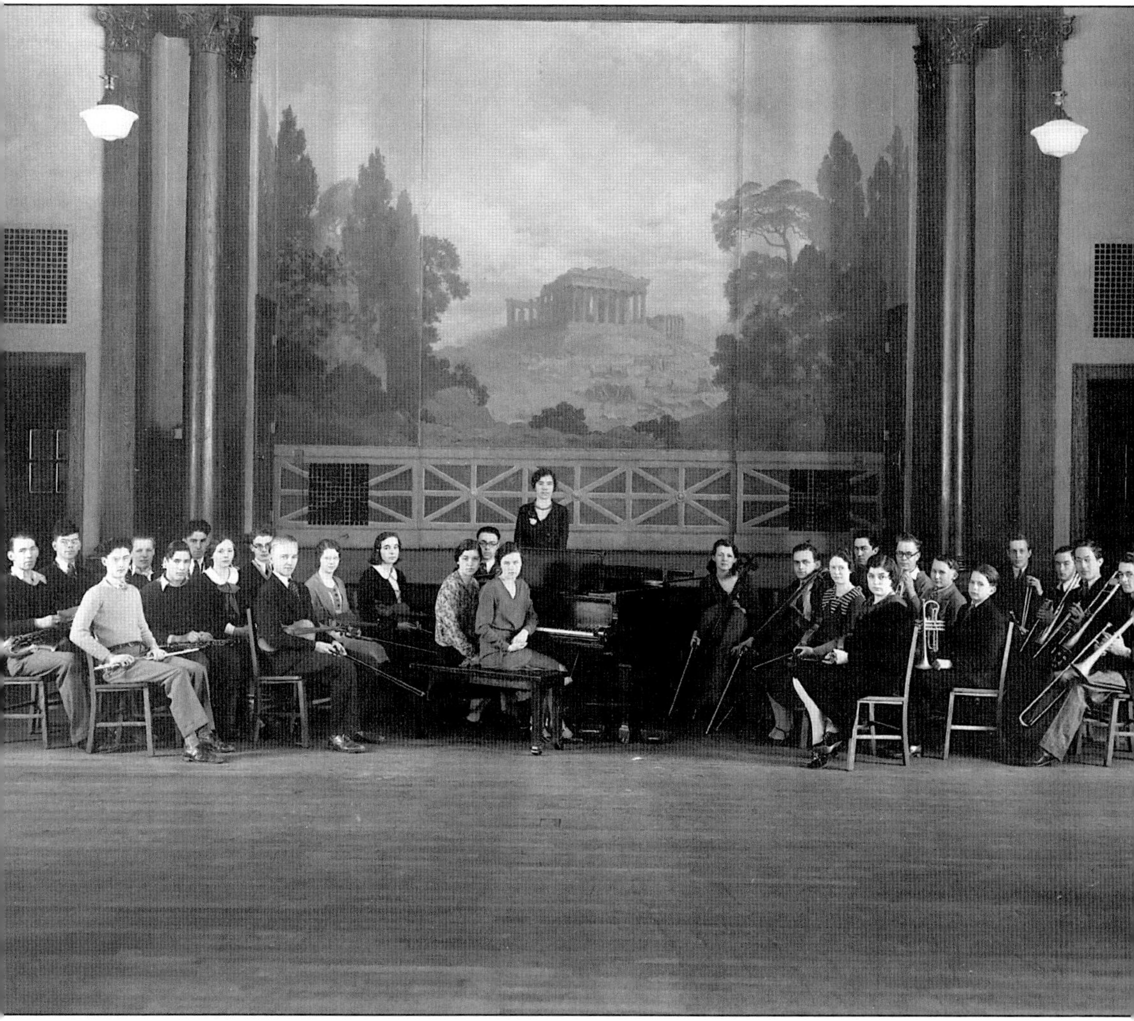

**INSPIRATIONAL PAINTINGS AND MUSIC.** The painting of the Parthenon in the chapel-assembly hall was an inspirational background for the Lyndon Institute orchestra and glee clubs, which were under the direction of Ruby Blaine from 1930 to 1941. In 1941, Ruby Blaine left to go to Columbia Teachers College in New York City for her master's degree in music education. To quote Alice (Fisher) Cook Bassett '42, "I think we all developed a love of good music under the competent direction of Ruby Blaine." When the new classic-style Lyndon Institute building replaced the burned Thompson Hall in 1922, an unknown benefactor commissioned the 15-foot by 20-foot painting of the Parthenon for the new chapel. The painting, symbolizing the classical roots of Lyndon Institute, underwent restoration in 1983. When the new auditorium wing was built in 1965, the chapel became the dining hall. After the dining hall wing was added in 1976, the old chapel then became, appropriately and perhaps inspirationally, the arts studio.

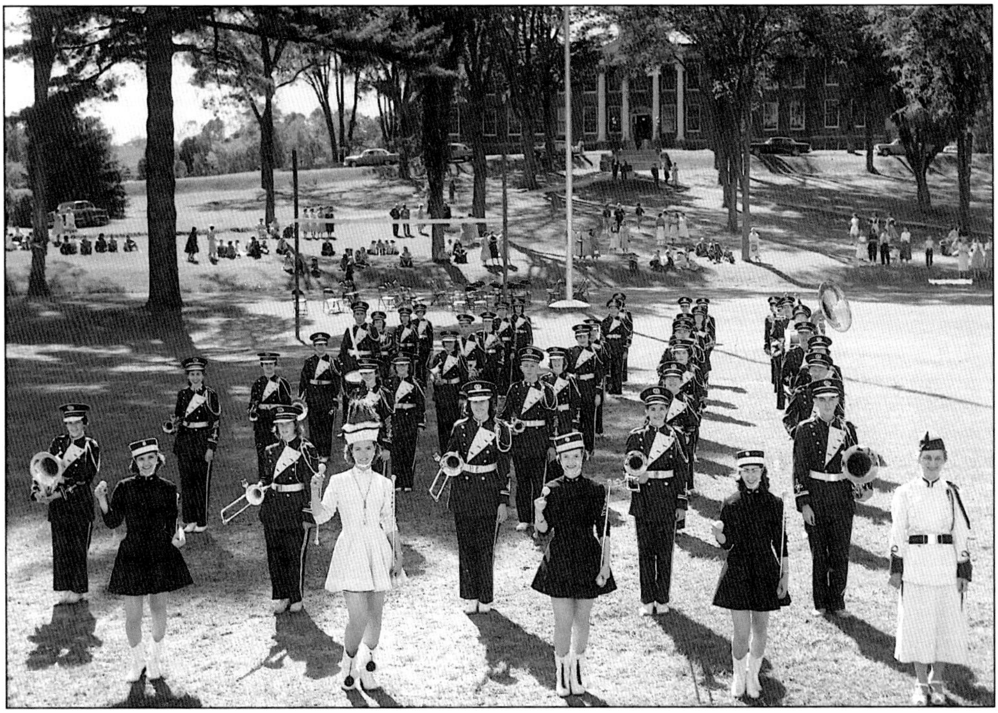

**MARCHING AT HOME.** Celia Teis was the music teacher when this image was taken, showing the band ready to strut their stuff at halftime during a football game. She taught music at Lyndon Institute during the 1950s.

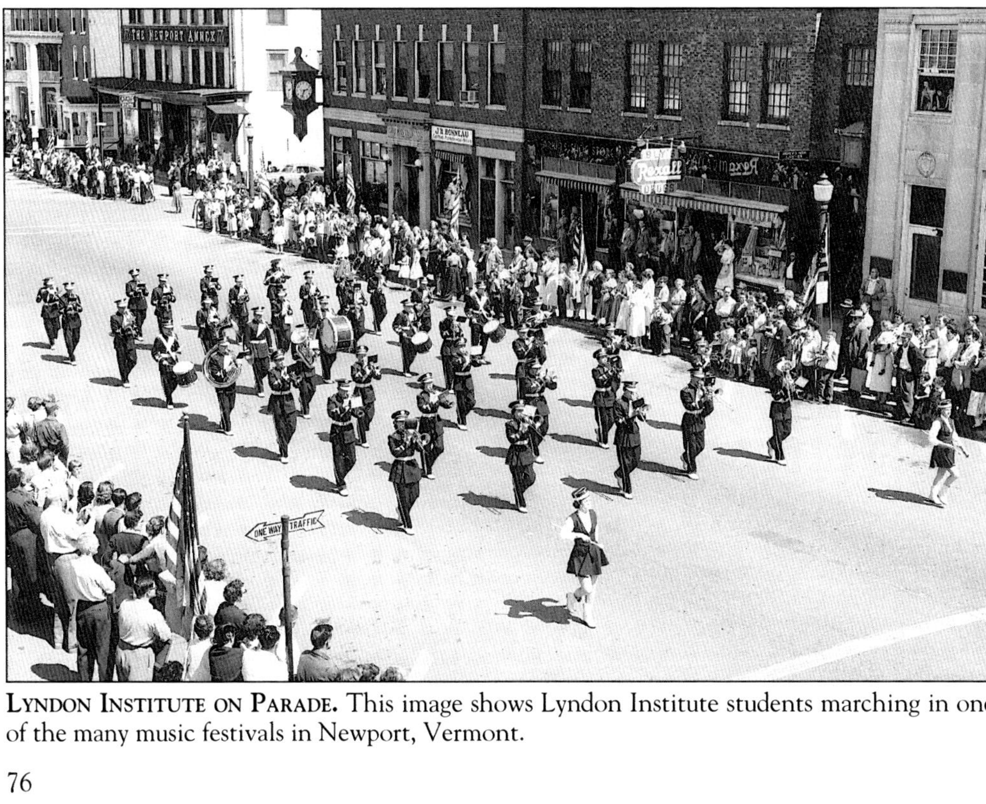


**LYNDON INSTITUTE ON PARADE.** This image shows Lyndon Institute students marching in one of the many music festivals in Newport, Vermont.

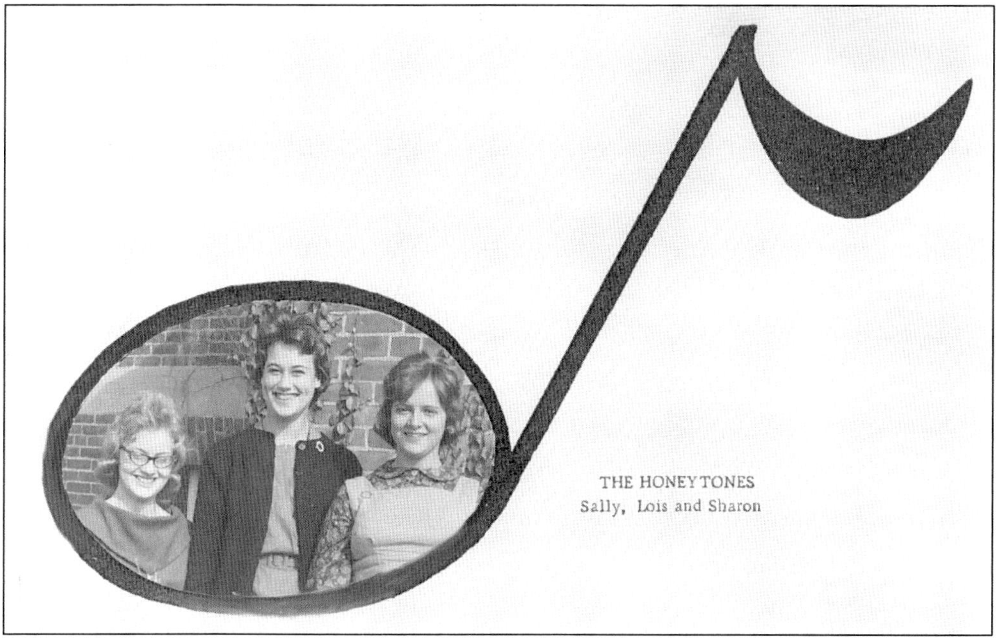


**THE HONEYTONES.** This was the name of a trio from the music department. All from the Class of 1962, Sally Leonard, Lois Fisher, and Sharon Hill were pictured in this manner in the *Cynosure*.

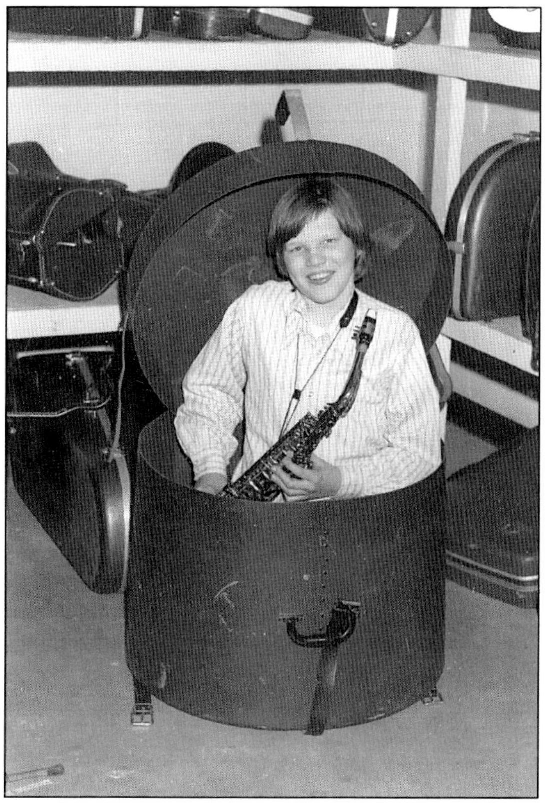

**MUSIC BOX.** William McKnight '75 pops out of a drum case with his saxophone, no doubt surprising his classmates.

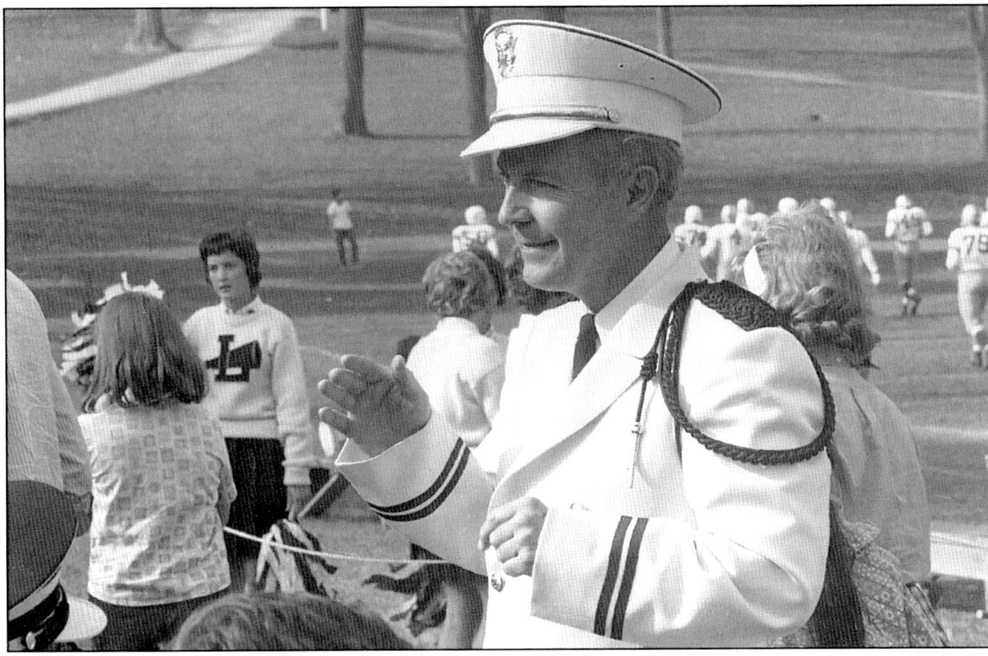

**MR. CHRIS.** Affectionately called Mr. Chris by his students, Roy Christophersen led the marching band, the stage band, and the orchestra through their musical paces for many years at Lyndon Institute. He also gave private music lessons and taught music in the elementary schools. He was a member of the Lyndonville Military Band, which played summer outdoor concerts at Bandstand Park in Lyndonville. Here, he is directing the Lyndon Institute band at a football game.

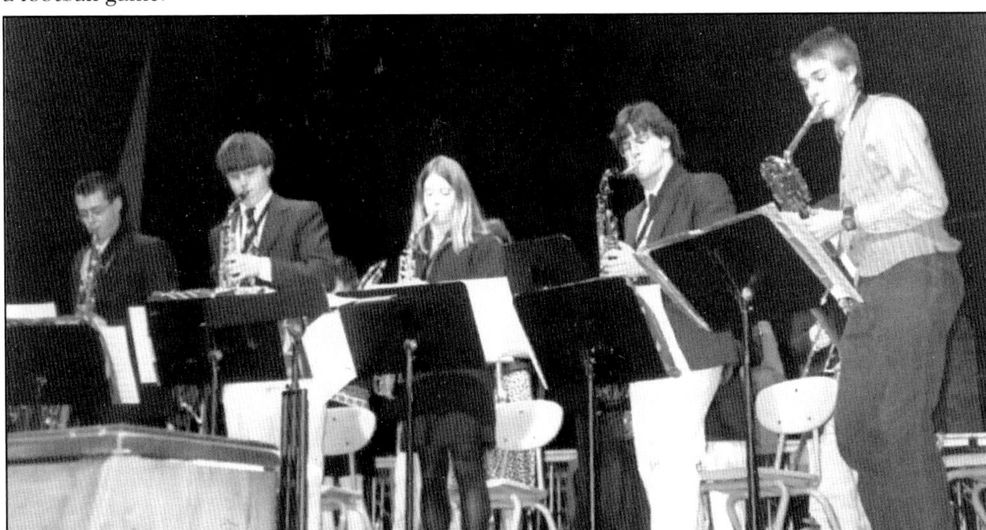

**THE JAZZ BAND.** Music teacher John Padden conducts a marching band, a stage band, and the very popular jazz band. He also started an alumni band of former music students, who give a lively concert in the auditorium Saturday evening as part of Alumni Day activities. Lyndon Institute often wins awards and trophies in music, and Padden himself, who came to Lyndon Institute in 1979, has received awards and honors. The jazz group here, from left to right, consists of Ethan Croteau, Nicholas Emery, Michelle Lane, Jason Harris, and Lucas Laplant.

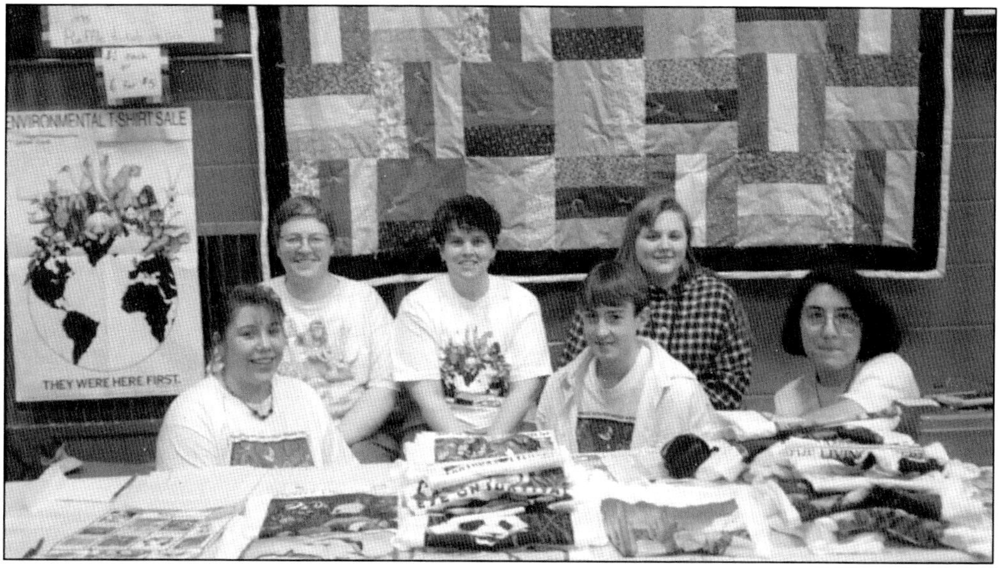


**EARNING A TRIP.** The Latin club raised funds with car washes and a food and craft sale in April 1994 for a trip to Rome. Other people with crafts could, for a fee, exhibit their wares also. Helping at their own table, offering T-shirts and a raffle quilt made by the club members, are, from left to right: (front row) Stephanie Smith, Scott Donaghy, and Meg (Hemond) Gregory; (back row) teacher Jean Thompson, Cheri (True) Goldrick, and Hannah Temple.

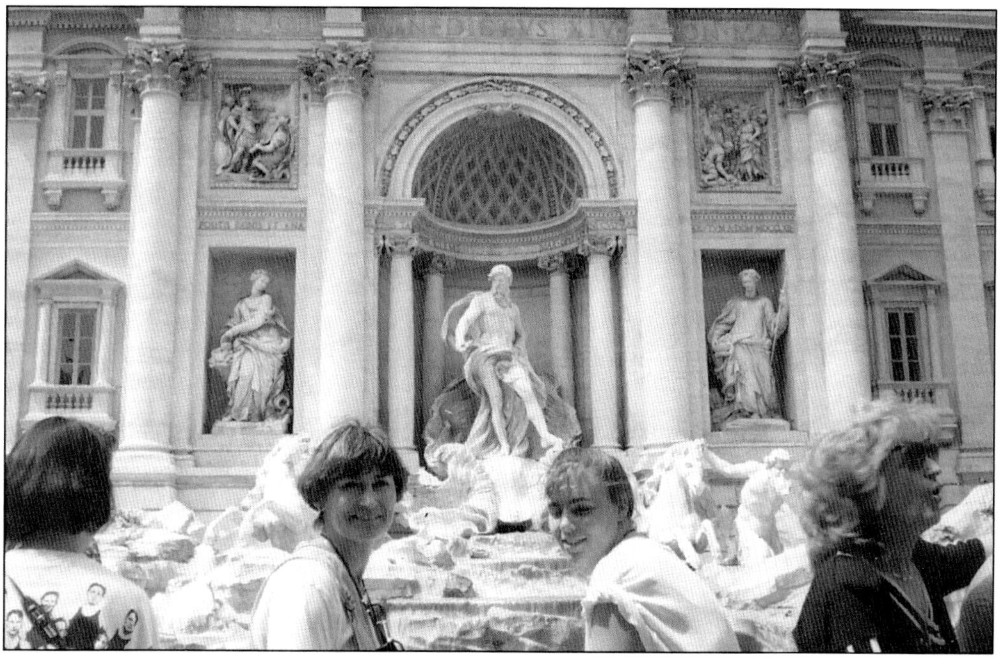

**IT'S AWESOME!** The trip finally happened in 1995. Teacher Cisi Flynn and student Marci Laramee turn from the Trevi Fountain for a photograph by Latin teacher Jean Thompson. The other two were not part of the Latin club group. According to legend, visitors who throw coins into this famous fountain will someday return to the city. On a trip like this one, students see for themselves the city of the classics they study at Lyndon Institute.

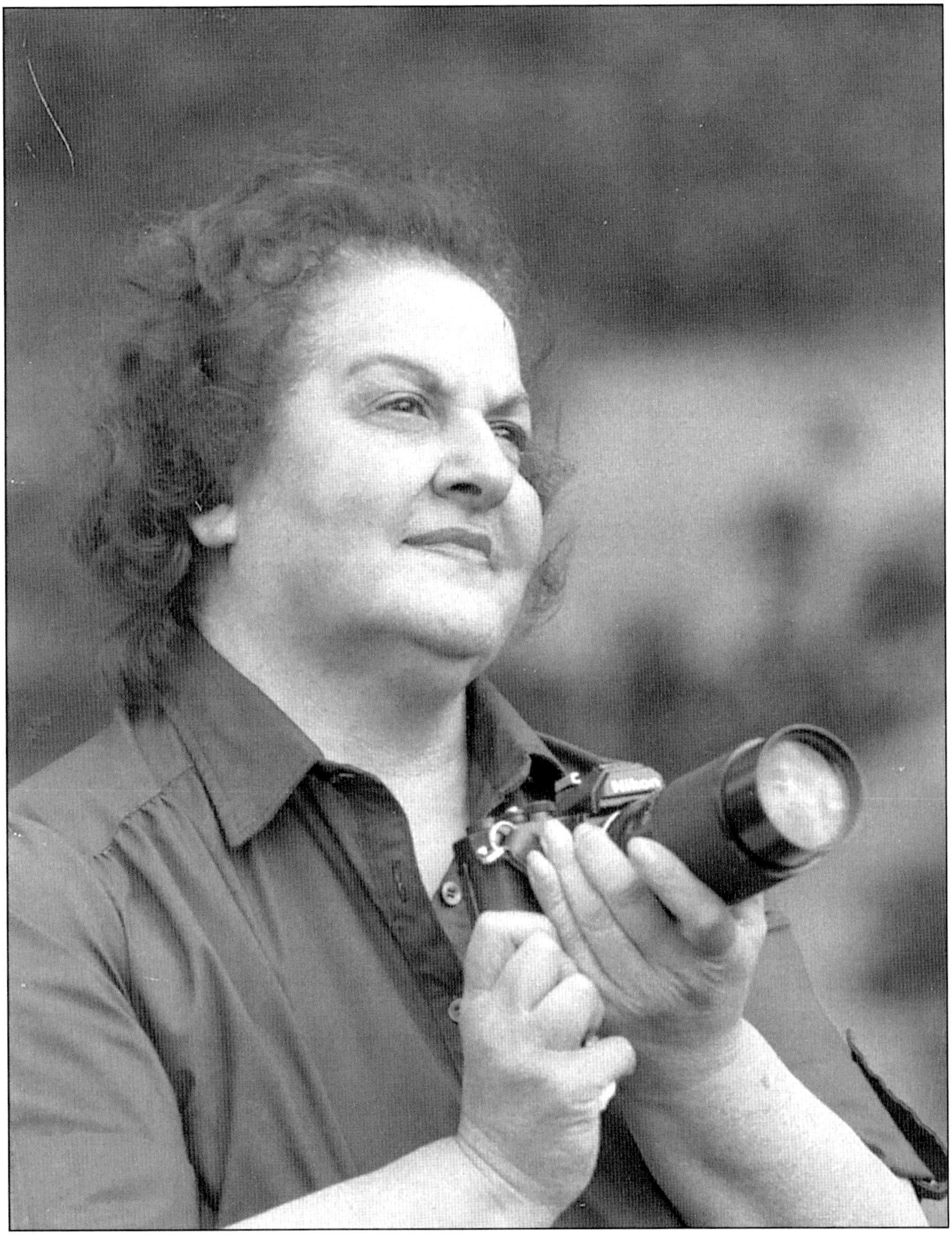

**A Lady with a Camera.** Bertha Koury came from Greenville, South Carolina, in 1951 to visit her sister and found an opening to teach at Lyndon Institute. She taught American government and art for 12 years and then devoted her time to teaching art. She inspired her students with, "Good, better, best, never let it rest till your good is better and your better, best!" She was both a forensic and a drama coach; her students often won awards for performances in both these programs. She is an excellent photographer with a flair for depth and for capturing beauty in the simplest subjects. When she retired in 1990, a plaque was placed in the institute's art studio, naming it in her honor.

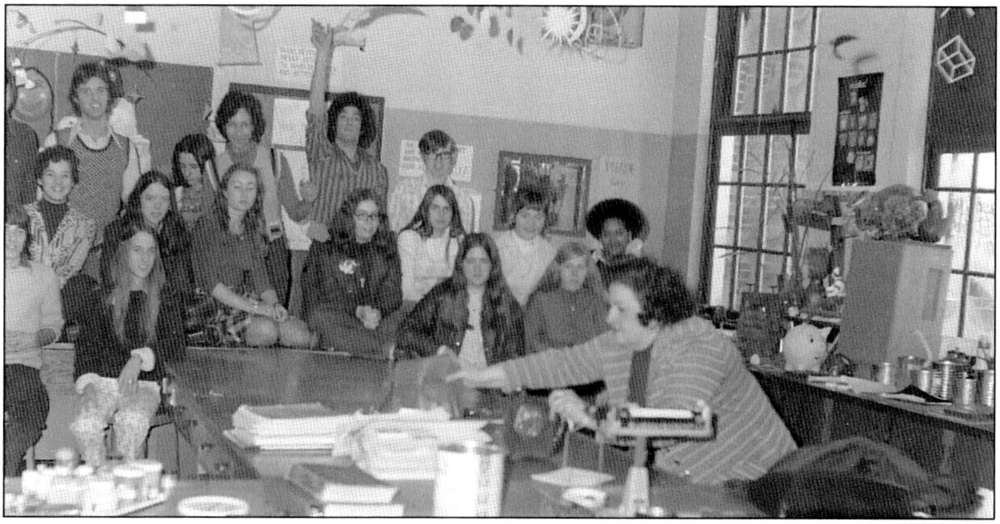

**The Art Club.** Bertha Koury, right, works with the art club in the Lyndon Institute art studio. She always encouraged her students to try different art media, not only for the adventure of it, but also to give students a chance to see where their talent might lie.

**In the Limelight.** Matthew Elliott and Nathan Hartswick perform in *Murder II*, a student-written musical production. A new dimmer switch was purchased by the Lyndon Institute Loyalty Fund in 1986 and was first used by the Catamount Arts production of Trisha Brown Dance Company. The new system upgraded the alumni auditorium facilities and serves to enhance the quality of stage productions.

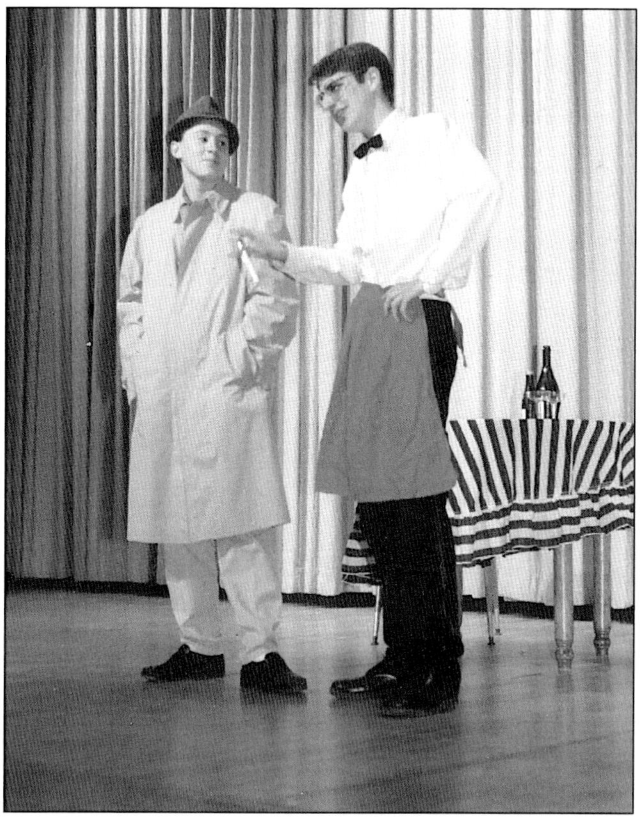

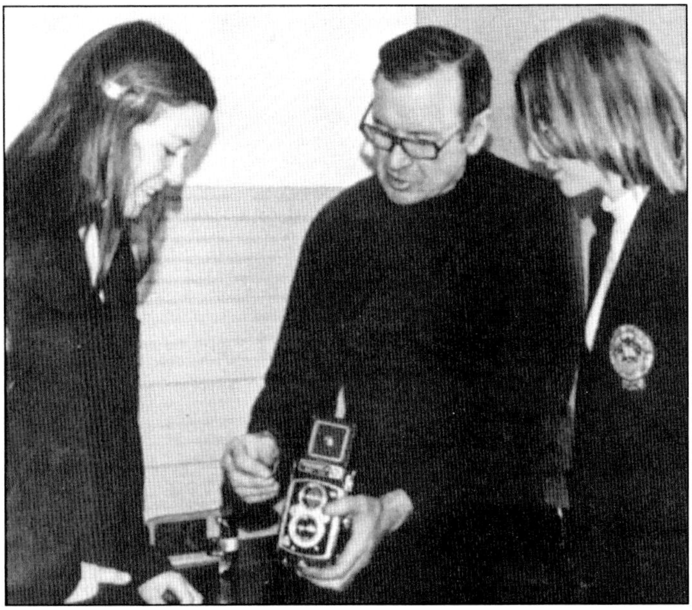

**The Camera Club.** Tina Christophersen and Betsy McKay listen intently to John King, who besides working with the camera club also taught auto mechanics. Photographed in 1976, they were learning important points about taking pictures and developing and printing film. Over the years, club members have taken photographs for the *Cynosure*, the yearbook. "Watch out, when you least expect it you may be the next victim of the Camera Club!"

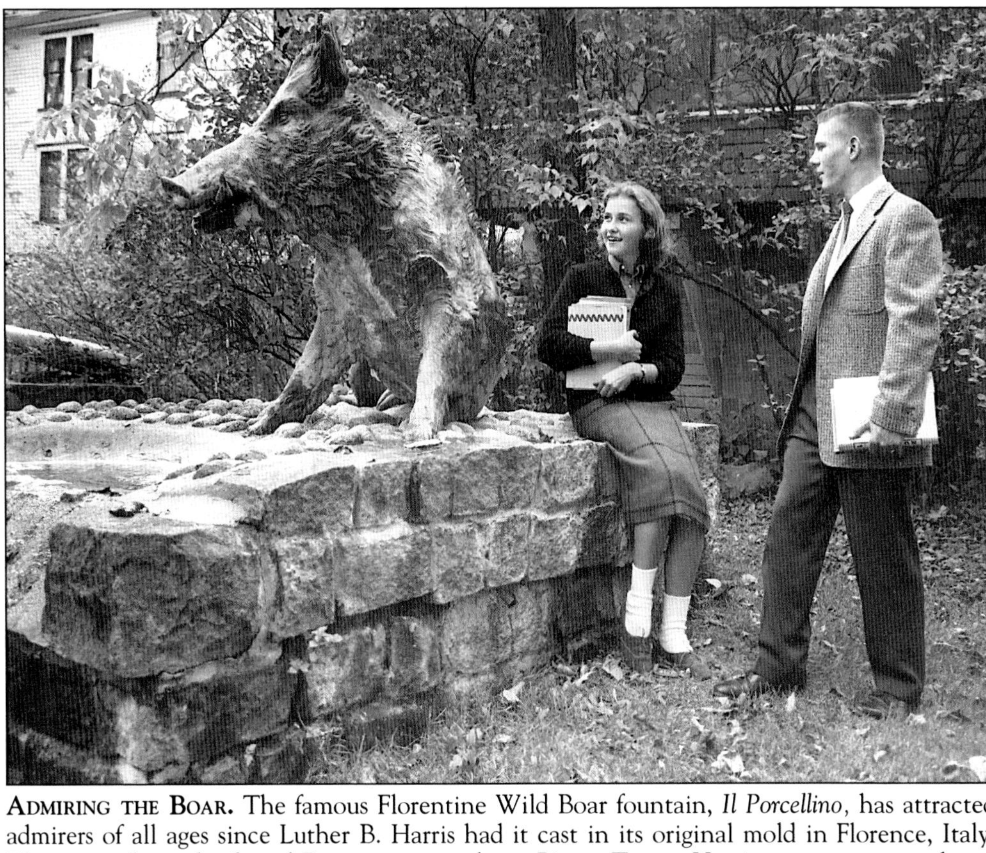

**Admiring the Boar.** The famous Florentine Wild Boar fountain, *Il Porcellino*, has attracted admirers of all ages since Luther B. Harris had it cast in its original mold in Florence, Italy. The original was by famed Renaissance sculptor Pietro Tacca. Harris, an amateur sculptor, made the base for the boar in the Lyndon Center park in 1912. Lyndon Institute students Roberta (Thorpe) Hagar '62 and Jim Pape '61 pay their respects to the famous sculpture.

# *Eight*

# Domestic Science and Vocational Technology

The department of household economics was organized in 1912. All girls were required to take work in this department. Home economics is now called family and consumer science, and there is a human services careers program for students who are preparing for careers in childcare, elder services, and nursing. When T.N. Vail took over the management of Lyndon Institute and created the quadrangle (see Chapter 1, page 20), one building that moved was the Ruggles Hotel, originally built in 1831. It was remodeled for advanced home economics for girls who had a high school diploma or its equivalent.

When the state gave up the Agricultural School after Mr. Vail died in 1920, it reverted to Lyndon Institute and the Speedwell properties were sold (See Chapter 3). Then, in 1923, vocational agriculture began at Lyndon Institute. A Lyndon chapter of the Future Farmers of America (FFA) was organized and continued until around 1990, when farming was dropping off in Vermont and there was no longer enough interest to sustain the agricultural courses.

In earlier times, these courses were generally for students who were not going on to higher education but might be planning to join family farms or industry. Over time, technical courses have been established, such as automotive technology, building trades, welding/metals fabrication, human services careers, drafting, small boat building, family and consumer science, driver education, and adult technical education classes. The once creamery building, later the Alumni Museum and office, today houses the Technology Center offices.

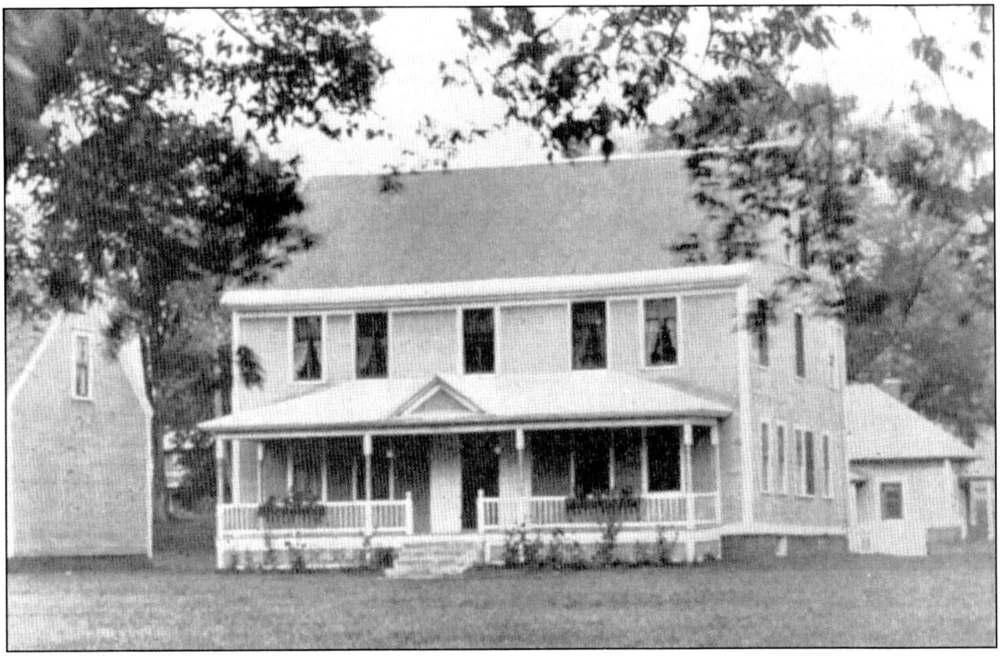

**The Tavern on the Green.** This tavern had been remodeled to contain kitchens and sewing rooms for home economics classes. Lyndon Institute catalogues advertised it as a "Brief course cottage facing a large green lawn, with living quarters for girls taking a one-year home economics course." A two-year course was added later. Girls taking this course were already graduates of a secondary school or the equivalent and lived in the Tavern with teacher supervisors. Later in 1919, Ye Olde Tavern served as a boys' dormitory. The Tavern is now a Lyndon Institute rental property.

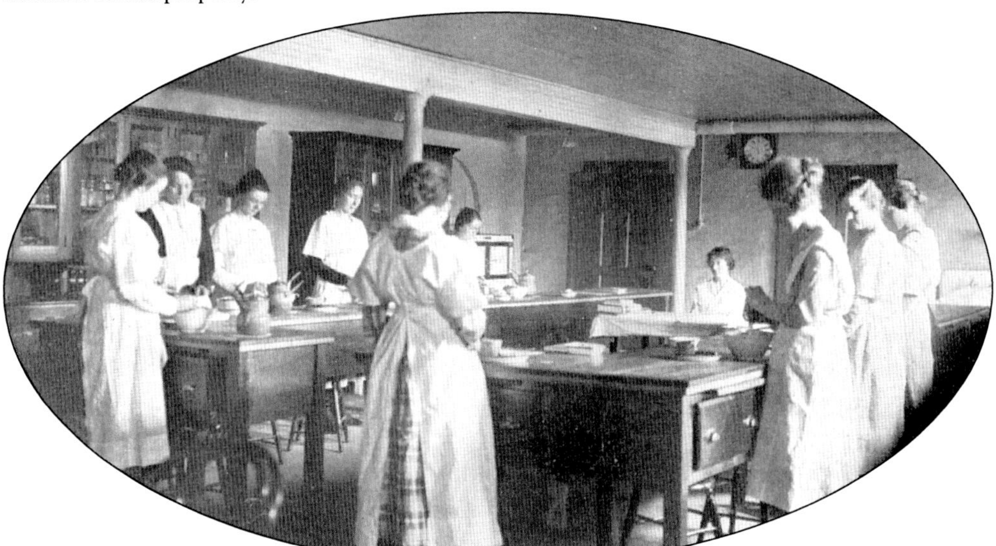

**Home Economics.** The first mention of preparation in home economics appeared in the 1912–13 catalogue. It said, "Courses in cooking and sewing will be arranged. All girls will be required to take work in this department." The remodeling in Thompson Hall created a well-equipped kitchen and an equally well-equipped sewing room.

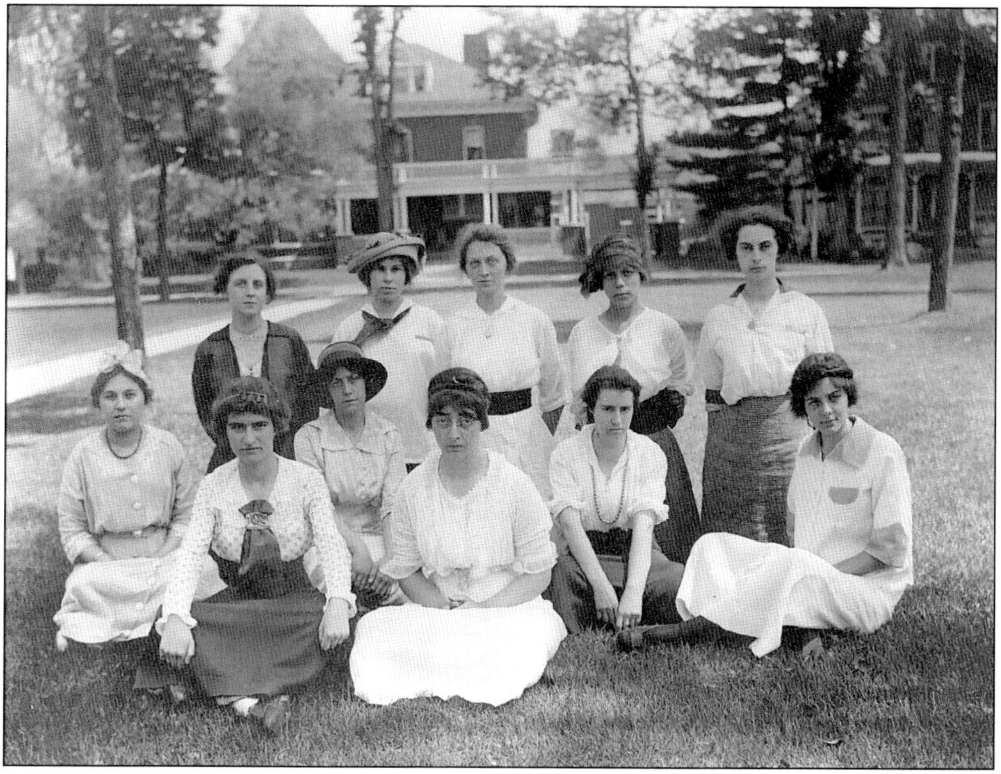

**THE FIRST COOKING CLASS AT LYNDON INSTITUTE.** Posing on the Main Street park in Lyndonville, this 1914 cooking class is identified as, from left to right, as follows: (front row) Laura (Whipple) Eastman, Georgia McDonald, Blanche Cusson, Florence Cushman, Anna Hoffman, and Belle Chayer; (back row) Gladys Mayo, Marion Gorham, Marjorie Post, Edith (Hazelton) Fitch, and Lillia (Gilman) Carter.

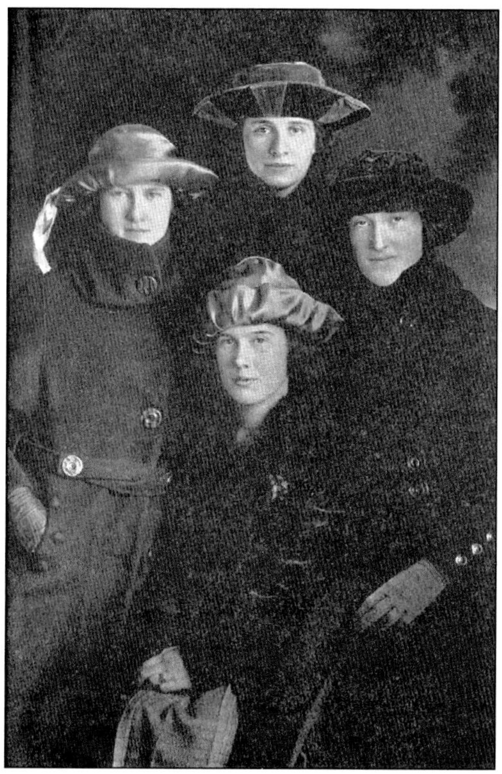

**THE LATEST IN HATS.** The Lyndon Institute offered thorough and practical courses in sewing, cooking, and household management for girls as part of training youth for rural life and occupations. Even girls who pursued the classical course of study were required to take sewing and cooking three hours a week. In 1924, these girls modeled the hats they had made or remodeled in sewing class.

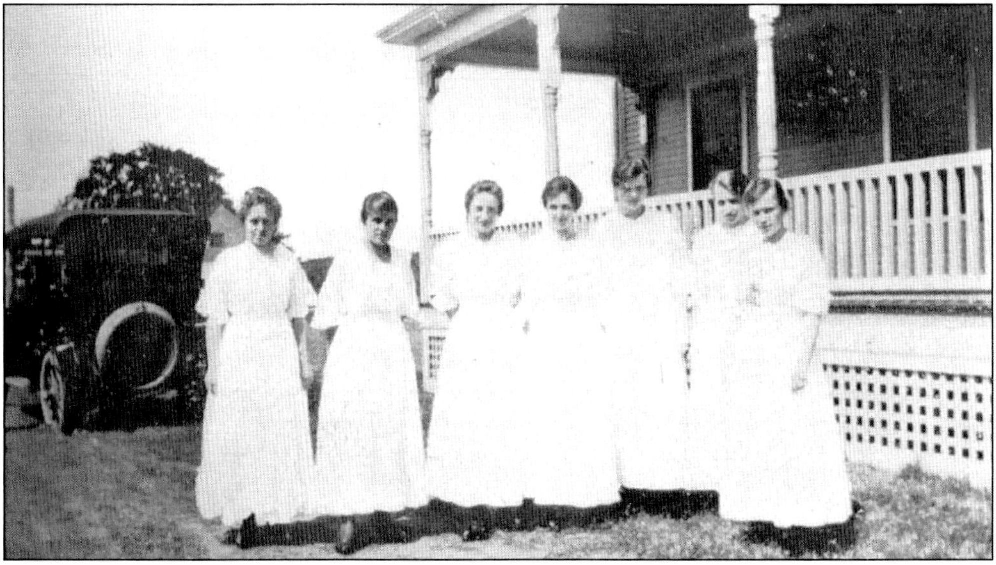

**SPECIAL DRESSES.** Senior girls were expected to make their own graduation dresses "which must be inexpensive and of simple design." This practice continued until caps and gowns became the graduation attire.

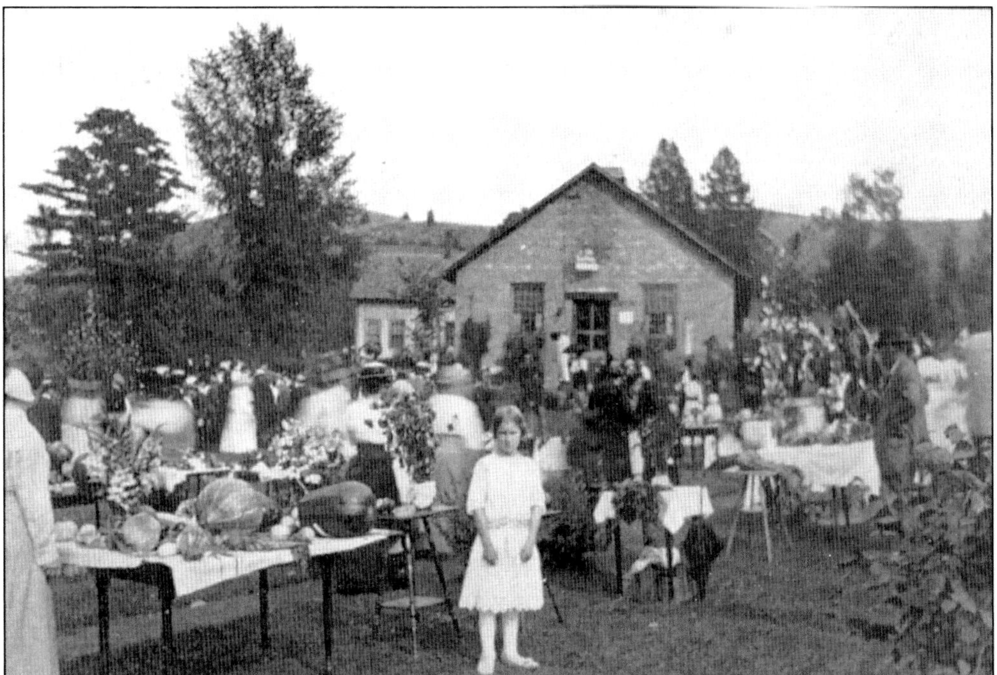

**THE HOME PROJECT CLUB FAIR.** Important extension work of the Lyndon Institute years ago included the home projects club, with boys and girls ages 5 to 19. Field expert Gertrude Newton, working with Elisabeth Chase, used kitchen and sewing rooms at Lyndon Institute when needed. Boys and girls learned skills in gardening, canning fruits and vegetables, maple sugaring, forestry, and working with animals. A fair held annually showed their work. These projects organizations preceded 4-H Clubs.

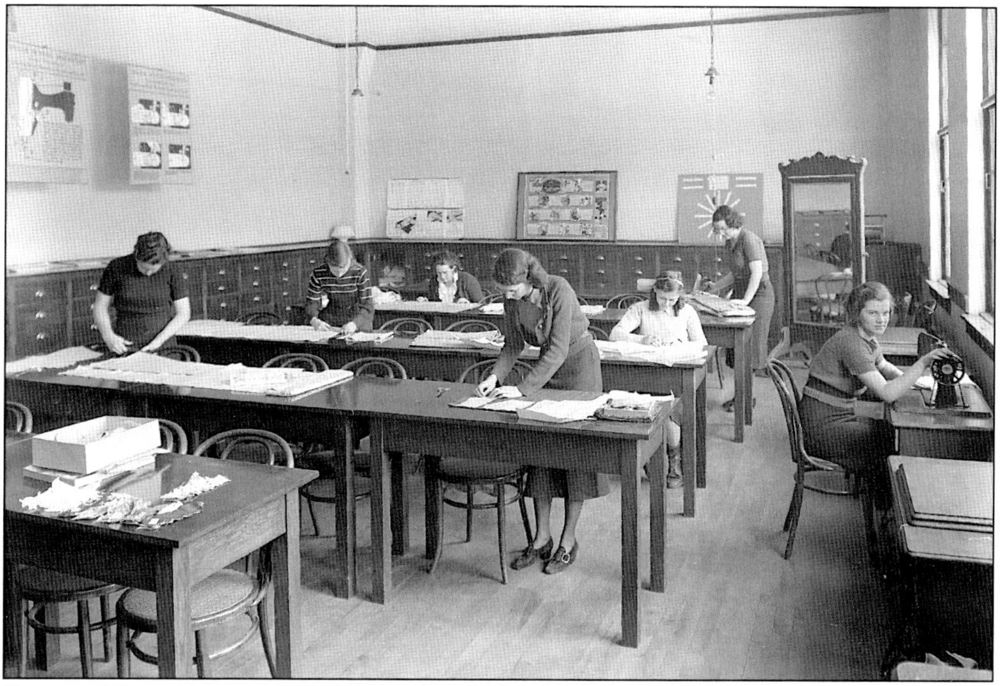

CUTTING UP AT LYNDON INSTITUTE. These girls in 1937 get credit, not detention, for cutting up in sewing class in the Lyndon Institute's main building. Freshmen and seniors had clothing classes twice a week all year, and sophomores had classes for half a year. During commencement week activities, the clothing classes gave a fashion show on the attractively arranged stage in assembly hall. There was also a kitchen for cooking classes in the main building.

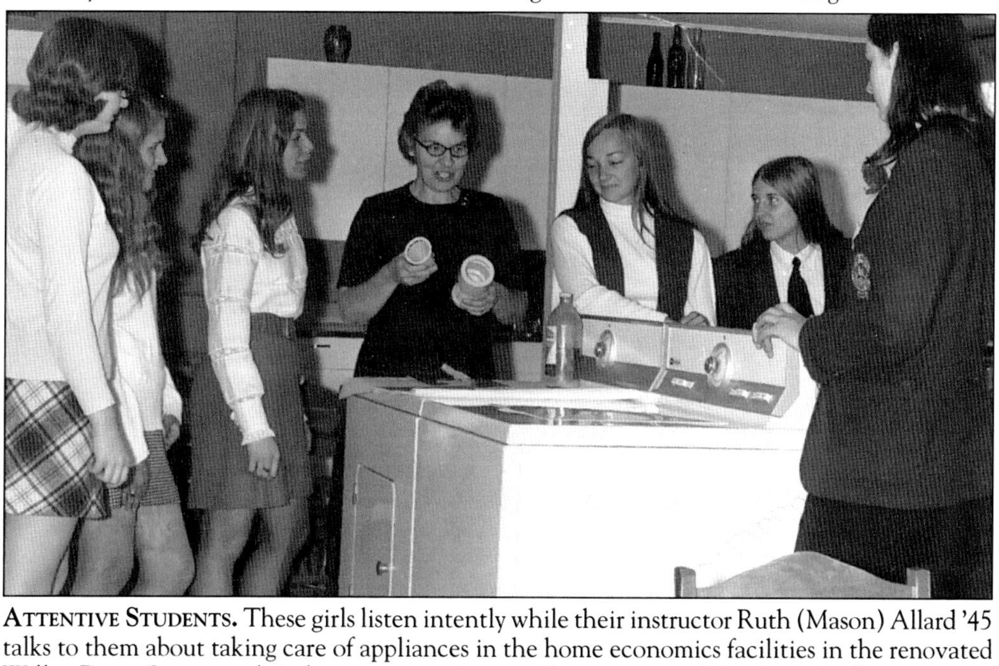

ATTENTIVE STUDENTS. These girls listen intently while their instructor Ruth (Mason) Allard '45 talks to them about taking care of appliances in the home economics facilities in the renovated Willey Barn. Coursework in home economics is no longer required. Today, this department is known as the family science center.

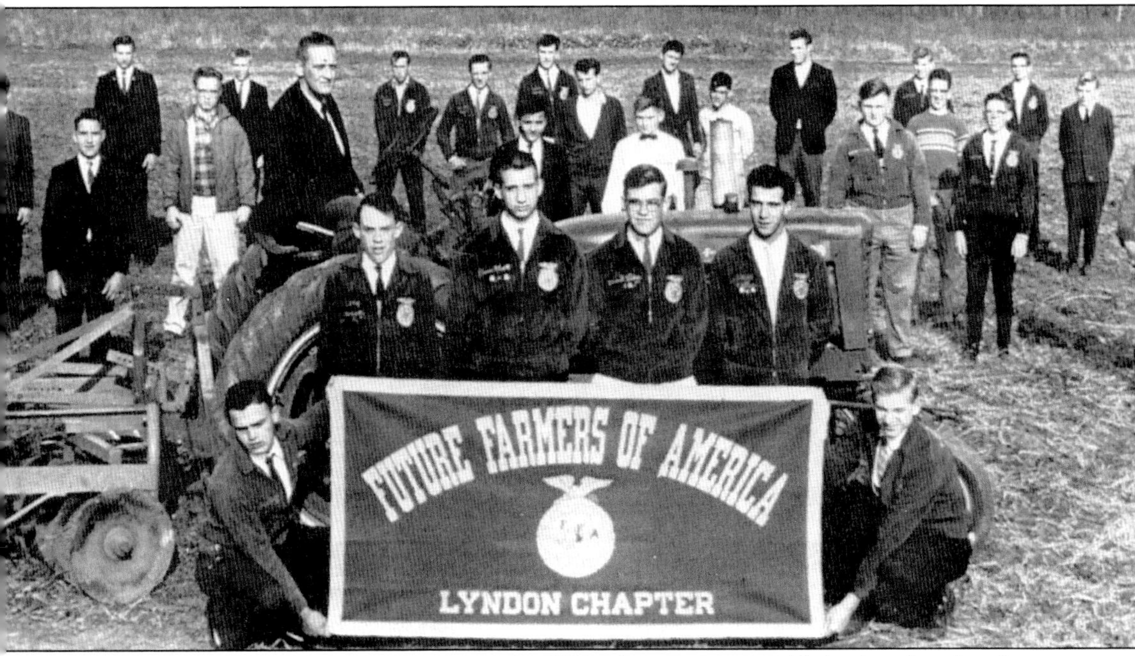


**The Future Farmers of America.** An FFA chapter was established at Lyndon Institute, and FFA students learned many things besides agriculture which could lead to other careers besides farming. The motto was "Learning to do, doing to learn; earning to live and living to serve." Each year, FFA delegates went to the convention in Kansas City. The students had to be neat when attending meetings and had to wear the regulation jacket of blue with the golden corn emblem and lettering. FFA chapters were self-supporting, raised food for the Lyndon Institute dormitories, and processed meat for the freezers. In this 1961 image are, from left to right around the sign, Wayland Brill, reporter; Tony Rossier, sentinel; Glenn Olcott, secretary; Kermit Fisher, president; David Patten, treasurer; Raymond Wheeler, vice-president; and Norris Elliott, adviser, "in the driver's seat." Other members of the chapter are gathered in the background. There is no longer a chapter at Lyndon Institute, as vocational agriculture was discontinued *c.* 1991.

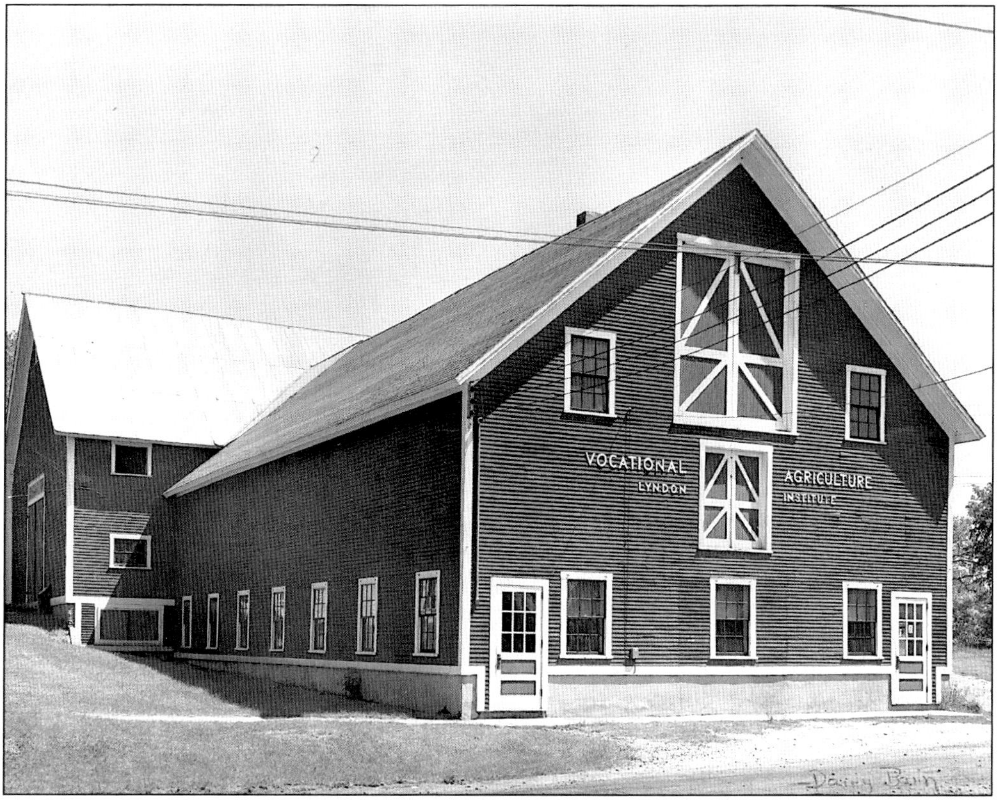


**The Dairy Barn.** In summer, the cows were pastured on the meadow by the river. After dairying was discontinued at Lyndon Institute, FFA students raised cattle at home, with periodic visits and reports from the instructor. The words, "vocational agriculture" have been removed from the barn, which is now used for work in several technology courses, including small boat building. The big meadow is now the Albert Forrest Athletic Field.

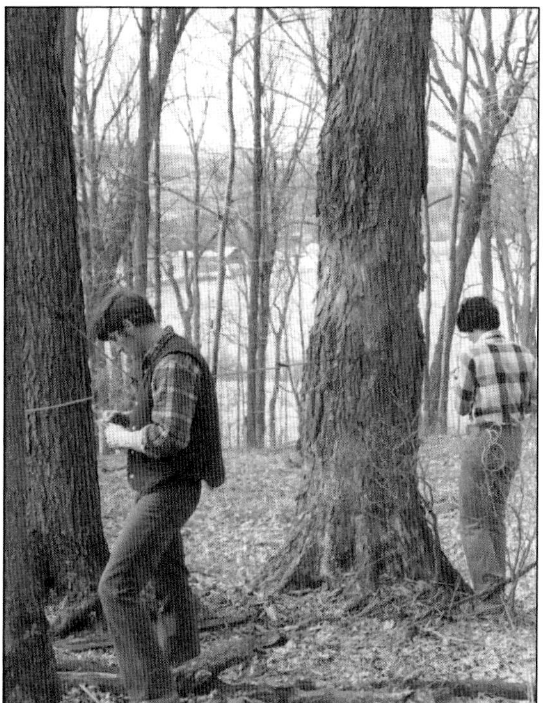

**Tapping the Trees.** For several years, forestry students tapped trees in the Fletcher Farm sugar woods, owned by Harriet (Fletcher) Fisher '37, only two miles from the campus. The side hill location adapted well to a pipeline setup. The Lyndon Institute pickup with a gathering tank drove to the site to gather the sap from the line and then transported it to the campus sugarhouse.

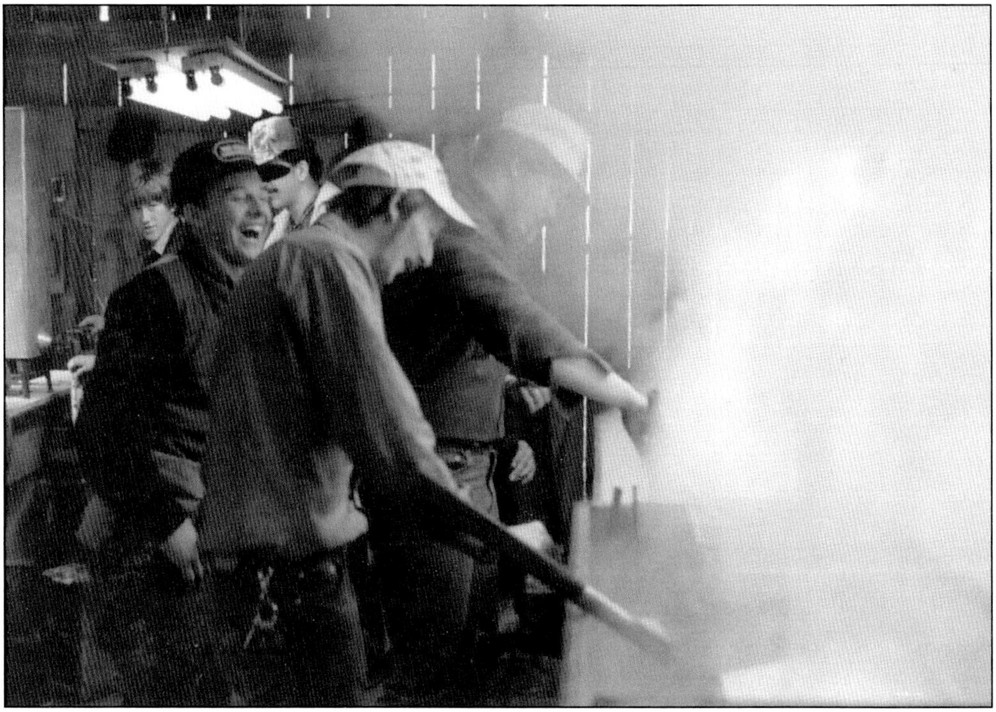

**Production Practices Bring Results.** Tom Winans and forestry students boil sap in the Lyndon Institute vocational campus sugarhouse, *c.* 1979. At the end of the season each year, the general public was invited to a sugaring-off party, where everyone enjoyed sugar on snow. At the same time, an open house was held so that visitors could tour the shops and see what the students were working on in the various departments. Forestry has also been dropped from the curriculum due to lack of interest.

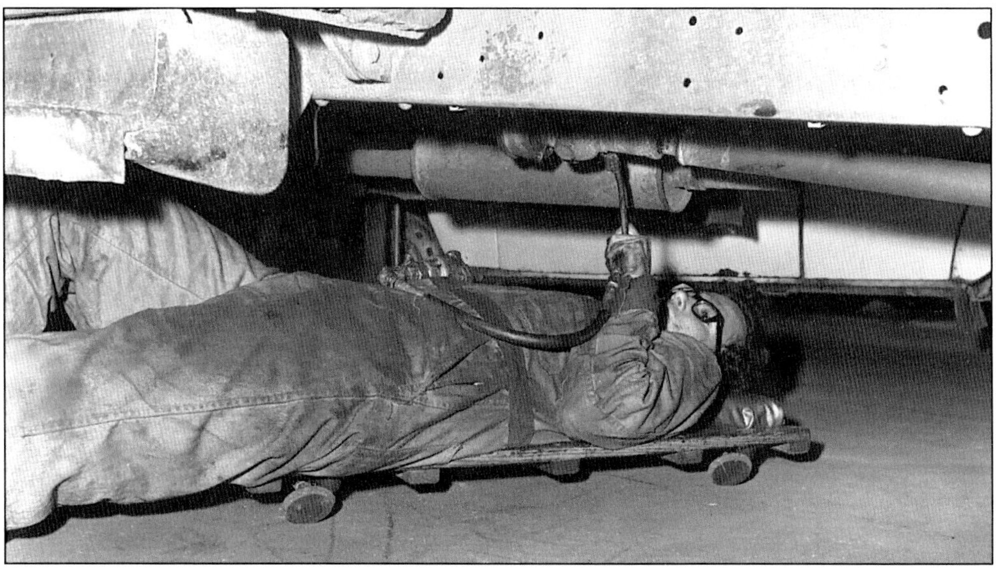

**Looking Up.** Sometimes you have to get on top of a problem by starting at the bottom. This is what Jim Sears '71 is doing in his auto mechanics class. Auto mechanics was started in 1947 and is still a popular class today.

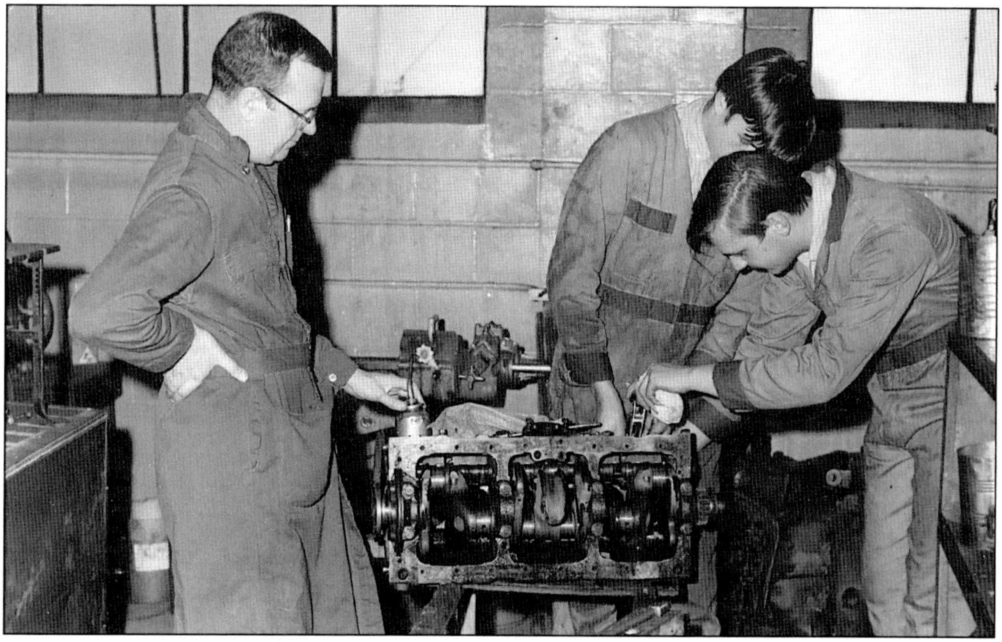

**LEARNING BY DOING.** Richard Gorham '69 and another auto mechanics student work on an engine under the supervision of instructor John King, left. Over the years, local vehicle owners have brought in their cars or tractors for the class to work on for real practice.

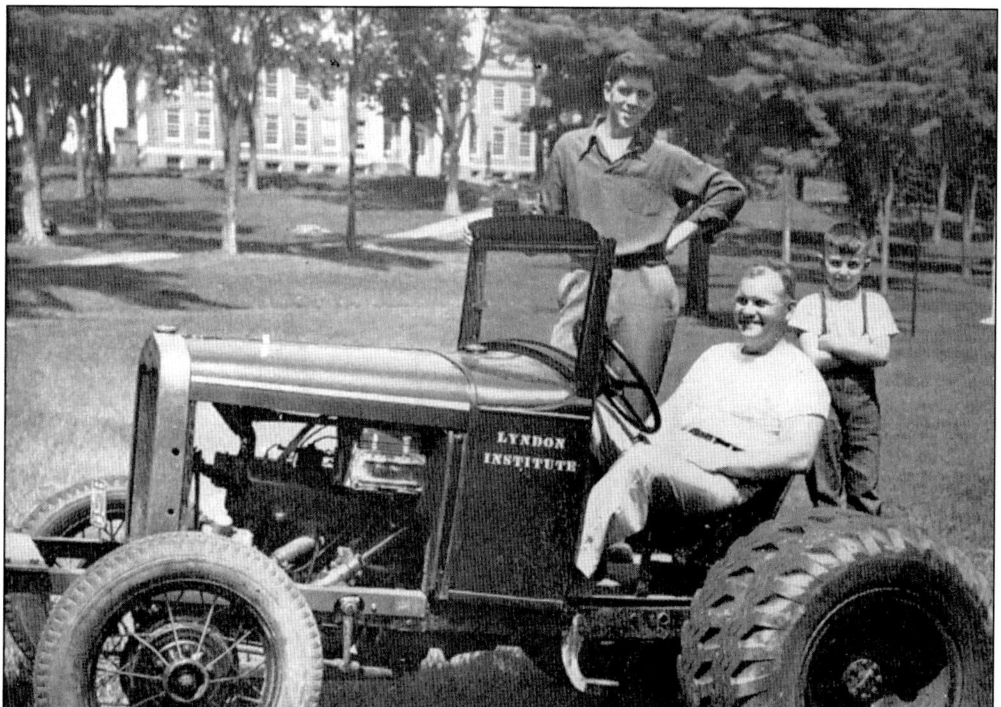


**DOODLE BUG.** Coach Albert "Pop" Forrest looks happy with this doodlebug made by students in the auto mechanics shop. Looking on is a little boy, who may be Forrest's son John. This handy vehicle did a lot work on the Lyndon Institute grounds.

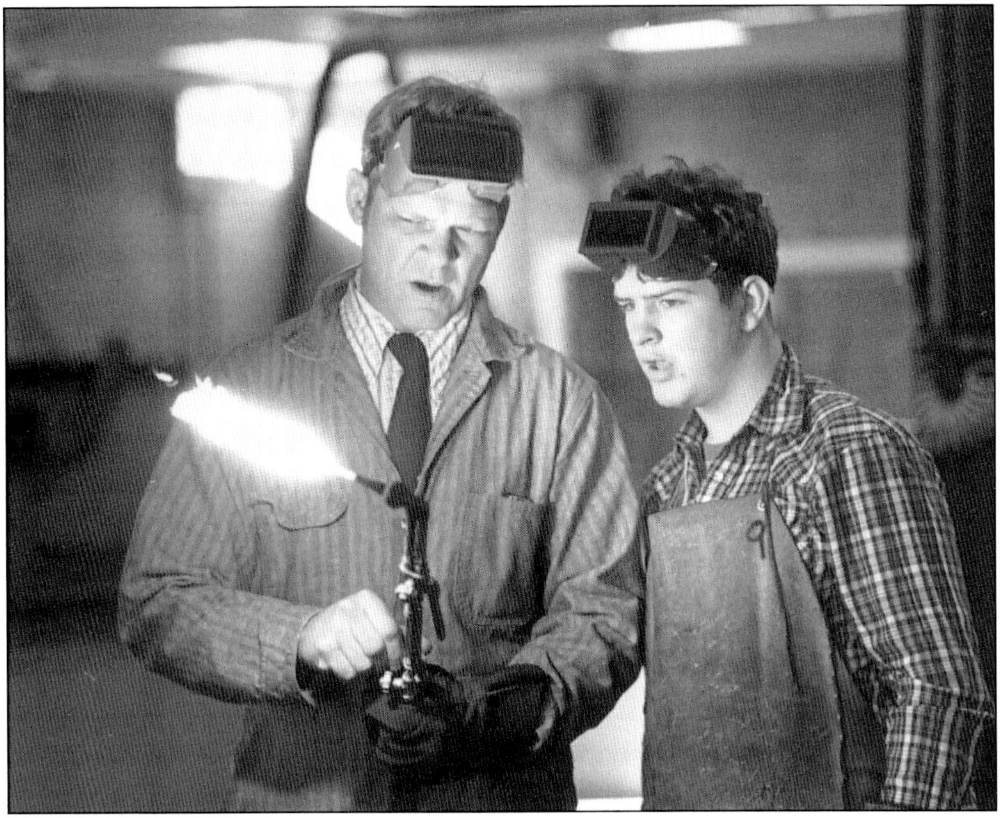

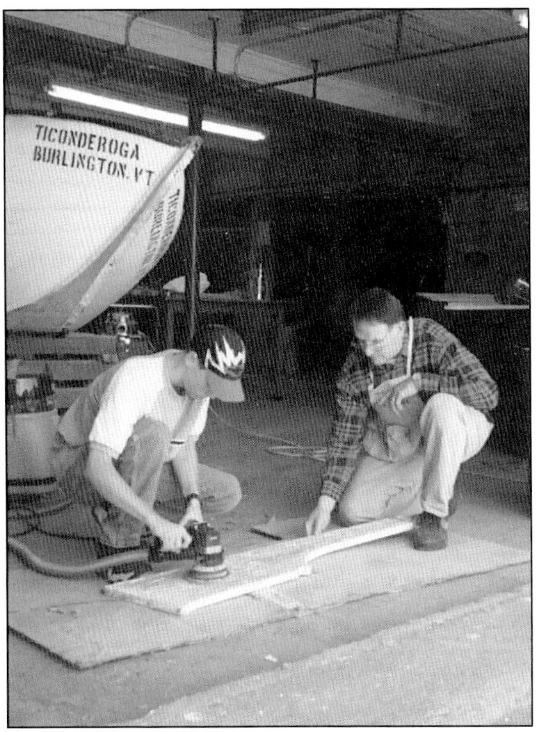


**THE TORCH.** Welding instructor Larry Kirchoff shows a student how to adjust the welding torch. The photograph was taken *c.* the early 1980s.

**THE LIFEBOAT.** Instructor Paul Hillard, right, is proud of the work his 14 students, including Troy Ranney, left, did in the Lyndon Institute boat building shop in 1998 to restore a lifeboat for the *Ticonderoga*, once a popular passenger steamboat on Lake Champlain but now a permanent attraction at Shelburne Museum. Canoes and other boats are built by boys and girls in this class. Men and women in adult evening classes have enjoyed building canoes in the shop.

# *Nine*

# SPORTS

Lyndon Institute believes that the activities of students outside of school should be directed as carefully as the work within the school. As far as is consistent with satisfactory schoolwork, "students are encouraged to participate in some form of athletics to develop a strong body, an alert mind, and a spirit of fair play"—Lyndon Institute catalogues. Home basketball games were played in the Music Hall in Lyndonville. Both boys' and girls' teams played other schools, such as Barton, Newport, and Bradford, and traveled there by train. For some years, tennis courts were provided for girls. There was an elective organized out-of-door club for both boys and girls. Activities included "many delightful walks" and during the winter, country tramps on snowshoes.

Sports today include, in the fall, freshman, junior varsity, and varsity football; freshman, junior varsity, and varsity field hockey; junior varsity and varsity boys' and girls' soccer; girls' cross-country running; and cheerleading. Winter sports include freshman, junior varsity, and varsity boys' and girls' basketball; boys' and girls' Alpine skiing; boys' and girls' Nordic skiing; boys' ice hockey; and girls' cheerleading. Spring sports include boys' and girls' track and field; junior varsity and varsity softball; junior varsity and varsity baseball; and boys' and girls' golf. All these sports activities keep hundreds of students busy practicing on Forrest Field, the old meadow by the river, after school. The home of the Vikings Ice Hockey is the nearby indoor rink named for Fenton Chester '37, which opened in 1979 with Kermit Fisher '65 as the first manager. The cabinets in the auditorium that are filled with trophies show the dedication of Lyndon Institute teams.

The images in this chapter are just a sampling of Lyndon Institute sports.

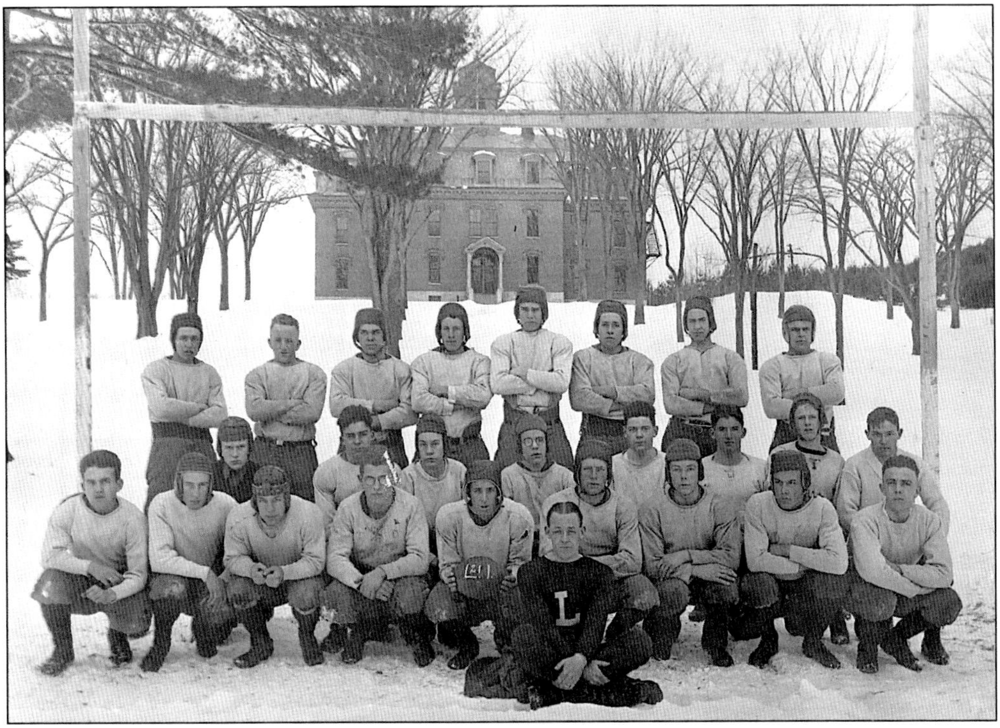

**Football, 1921.** These players pose under the goalpost in front of Thompson Hall in a snowstorm. There have been times when football has been played in the snow. The coach seated in front is Cecil "Peanut" Burns. There is a great difference in the pants, jerseys, helmets, shoes, and shoulder pads, compared with today's well-dressed and better-protected players.

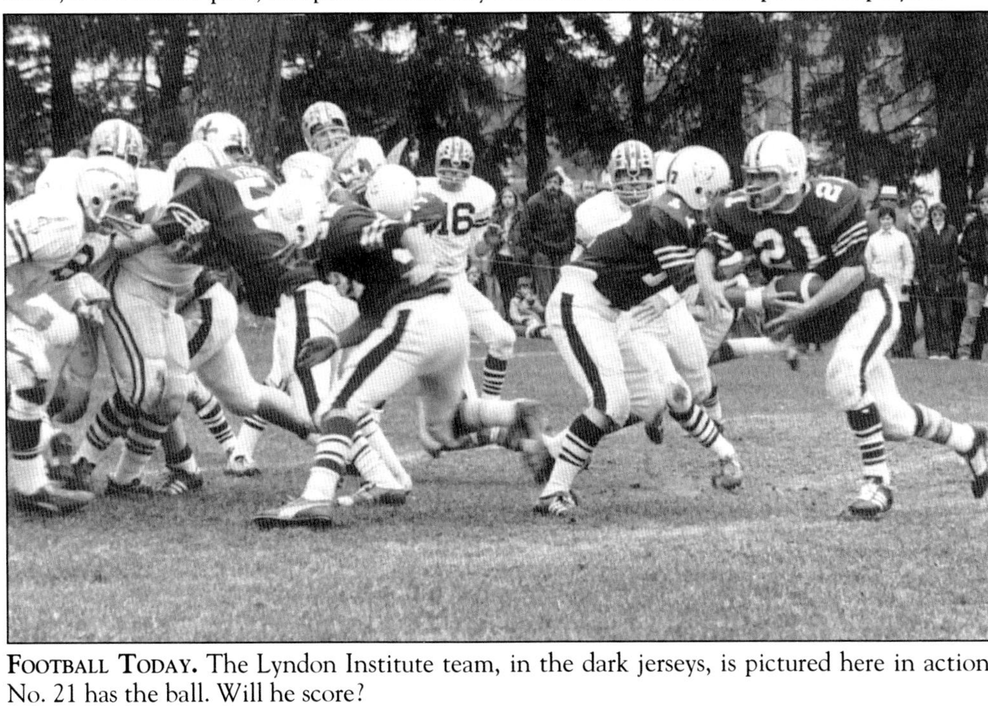

**Football Today.** The Lyndon Institute team, in the dark jerseys, is pictured here in action. No. 21 has the ball. Will he score?

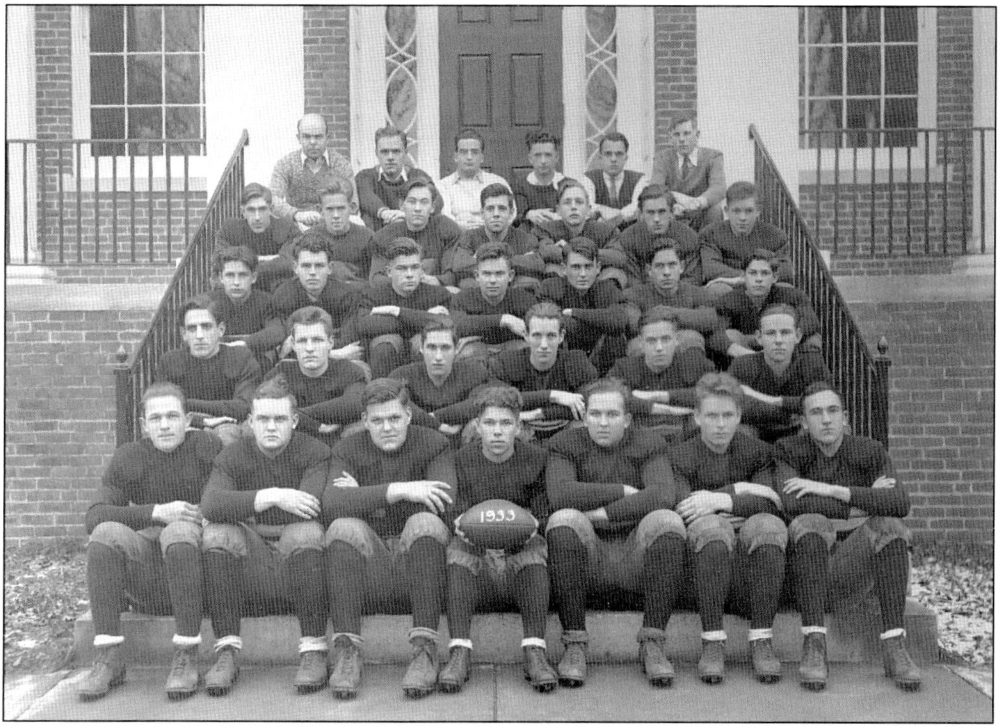


**THE 1933 CHAMPIONSHIP TEAM.** Seen here, from left to right, are as follows: (first row) Laplant, Forrest, Goulding, Emery, Eaton, Wishart, and Magill; (second row) Andross, Carter, Squires, Gour, Akley, and Lynch; (third row) Fairchild, Sylce, Perrault, Whitcomb, Lang, Edmunds, and Gale; (fourth row) C. Wheeler, Allard, Smith, Gray, Elliott, W. Wheeler, and Boardman; (fifth row) head coach Lewis, line coach Wright, assistant coach Brown, freshman coach Butterfield, Selby, and Watson.

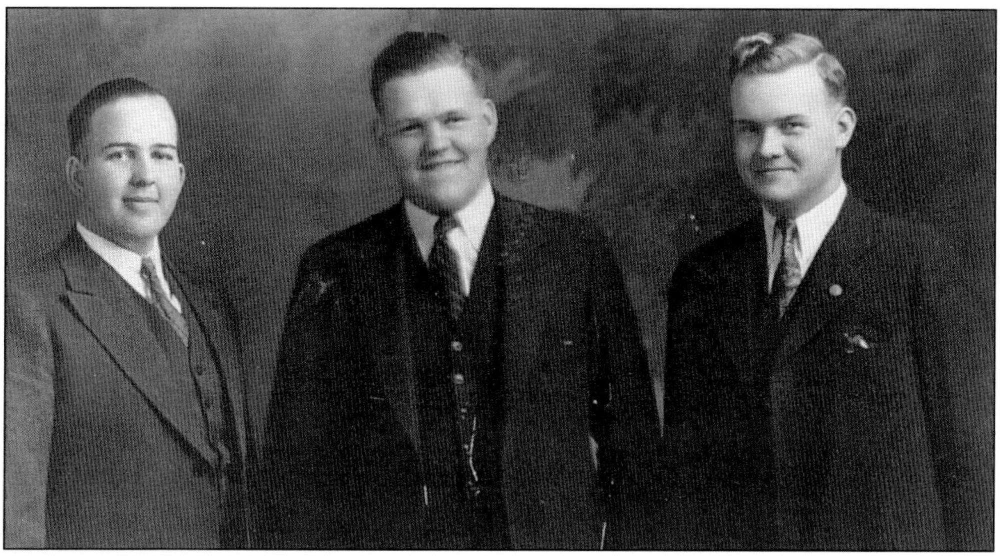

**THE BIG THREE.** That name was given to these football players when Lyndon Institute beat St. Johnsbury Academy after many years of defeat. The three rugged football players are, from left to right, Julius Eaton, Lloyd Goulding, and Albert Forrest, all graduates of 1934.

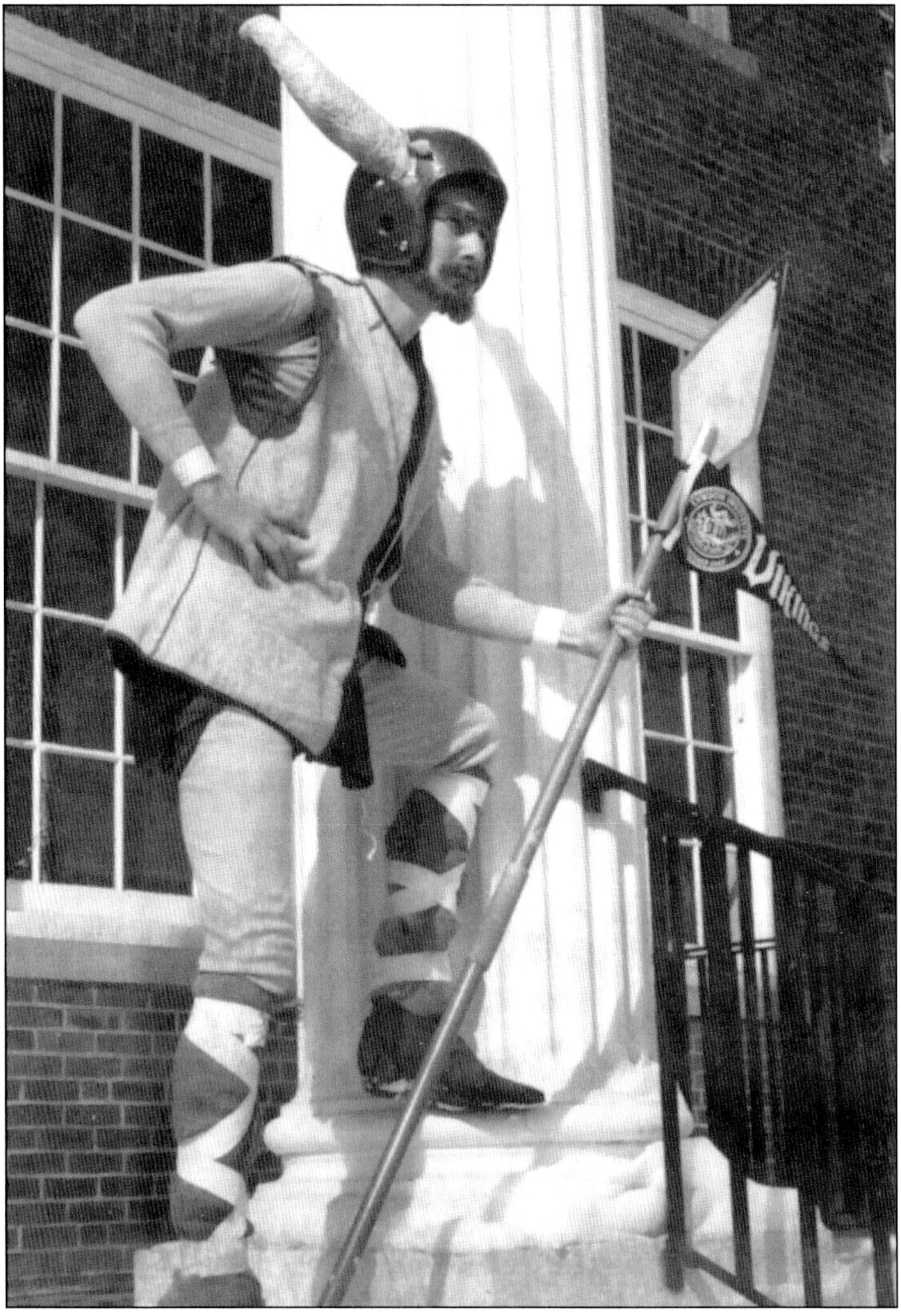


**They are Northmen and Proud of It.** "Vikings were Northmen, as we are at Lyndon Institute," said Al Forrest, the coach in 1961, when the name Vikings was chosen so that the sports teams would have a name instead of just calling them the "Maroon and White." The idea was to have the spirit of real people rather than of a shark or tiger. The original Vikings thirsted for adventure, discovery, and knowledge of what was over the horizon. If the Vikings were savage, Forrest said the LI Vikings would be savage only on the playing field. Andrew Wysmuller '67 was the first Viking and assumed this fierce pose, dressed in the costume designed and made by art teacher Bertha Koury, who took this photograph.

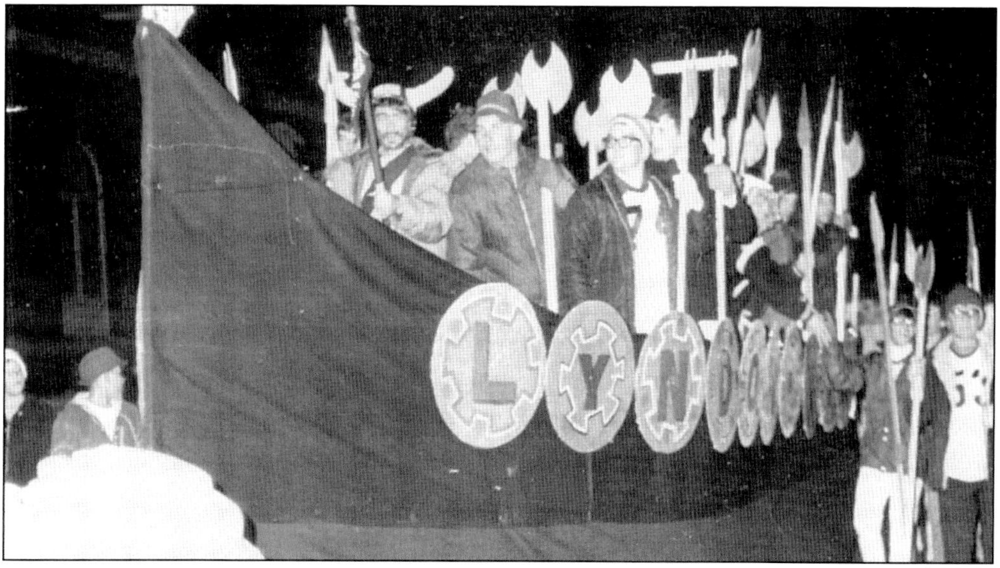


**The Big Pep Rally.** The Friday night before the big LI-St. Jay game, the Vikings "sailed" through Lyndonville, pounding their spears and looking fierce. Their following included Lyndon Institute students, coaches, and many townspeople as well. "Go, Vikings!" was the cry heard through the town for this big event pep rally; the band played "When the Saints Go Marching In!" The evening included the crowning of a queen, a prince, and attendants, and a bonfire on the campus.

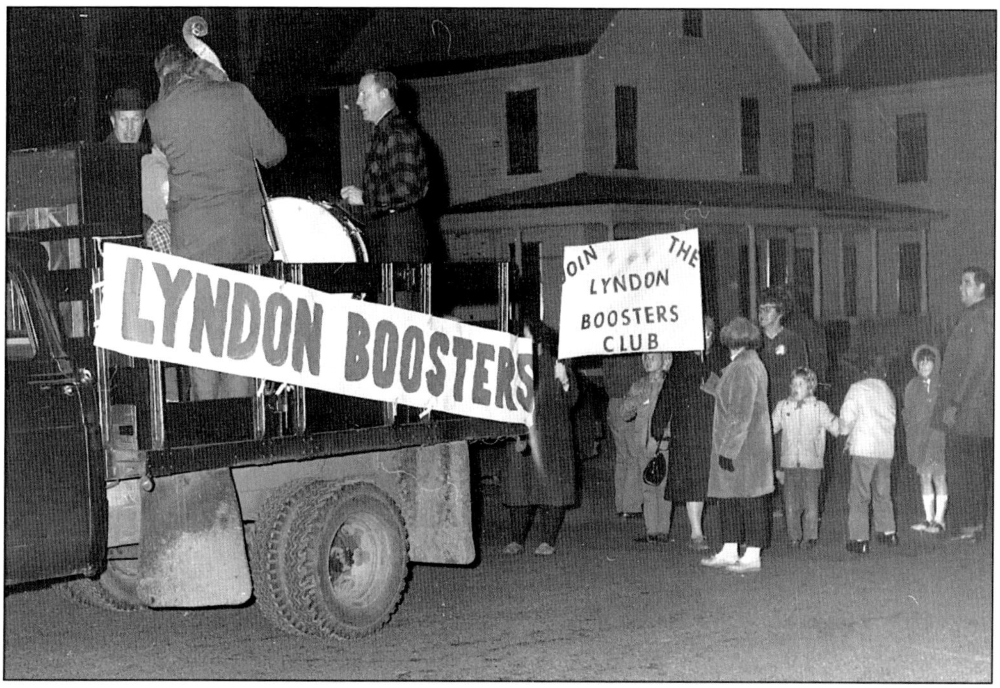


**The Lyndon Boosters.** The Lyndon Boosters Club was formed in 1965 to give support to the LI athletic teams. Here, getting ready to "boost" the big game rally, members of the Lyndonville Band, Paul Aubin '31 with trombone, and Jack Lynch '35 with drum, add to the singing, shouting, and cheering to excite the crowd always gathered to root lustily for the Vikings.

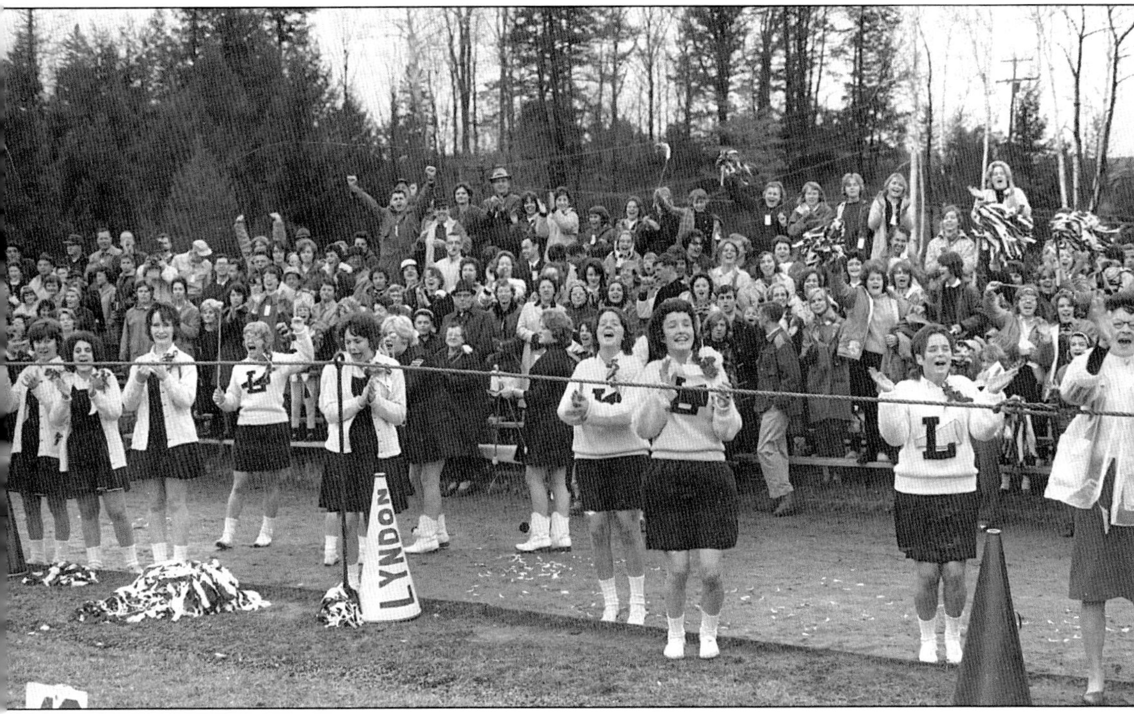


**EXCITEMENT ON THE 40-YARD LINE.** The traditional rivalry football game between St. Johnsbury Academy and Lyndon Institute is the sports highlight of the year. Cheerleaders and fans express their excitement as Lyndon Institute scores a touchdown at St. Jay's Hazen Field in 1963. It has been known that through the years, LI might lose most of the games in a given year and still beat St. Jay—or vice versa. No matter the standing of each team, the season's scores are irrelevant and the friendly rivalry between LI and STJA is the highlight that winds up the football season. This rivalry between these two neighboring towns has been going on since 1893.

**A Tough Decision.** Coach Robert "Bob" Heath is a good sport to allow this photograph to be taken of him with a tree on his head. But what is he cogitating about? Perhaps he is thinking, "I wonder if I've given the team the right play?" Heath '58 retired in 1998, after serving Lyndon Institute for 25 years as teacher and coach, and since 1974 as assistant headmaster.

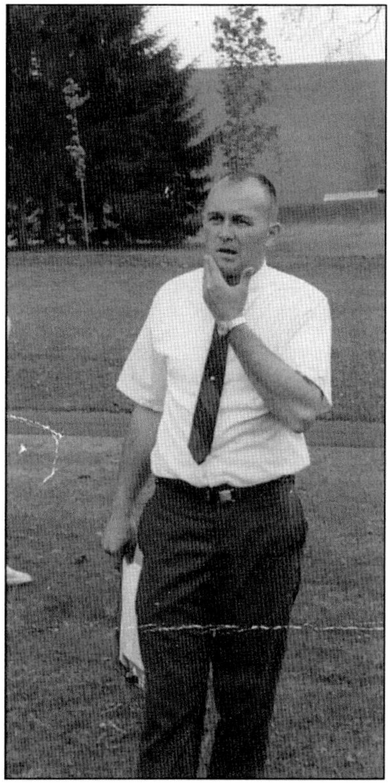

**Meet Bessie II.** Athletic coach Merlyn Courser shakes hands with the modern Bessie, plastic, not bones like Bessie I, but strangely enough the basic structure has not changed much from the first Bessie! (See page 23.) With the coach's help, Bessie II could show which bones need protection when an athlete is engaged in sports.

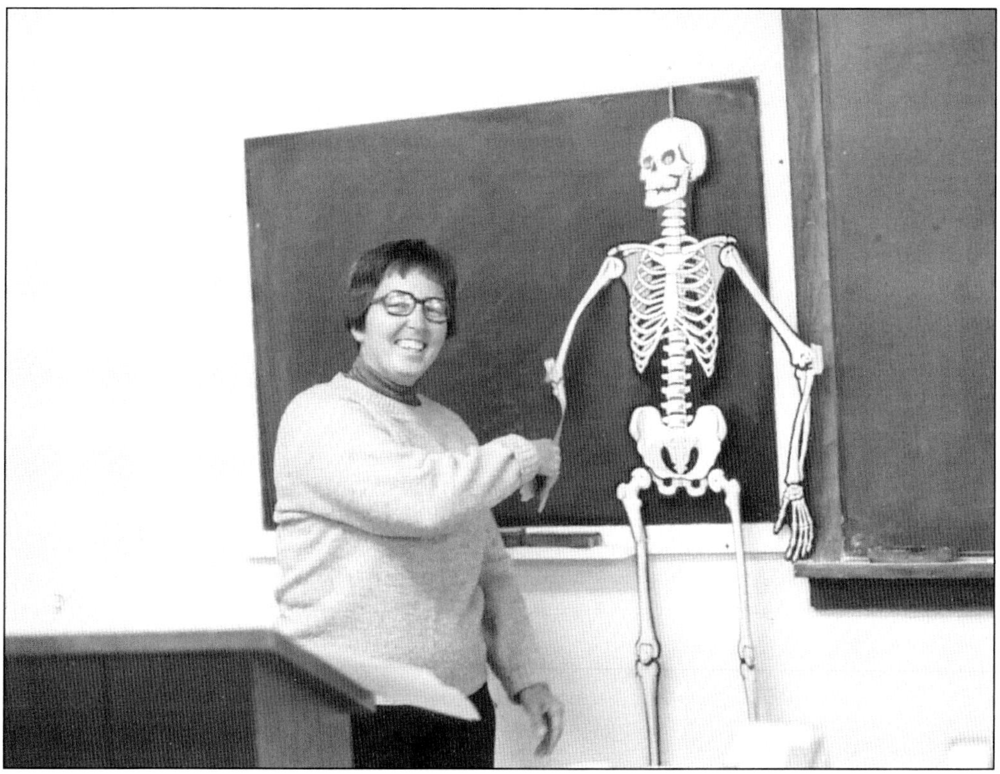

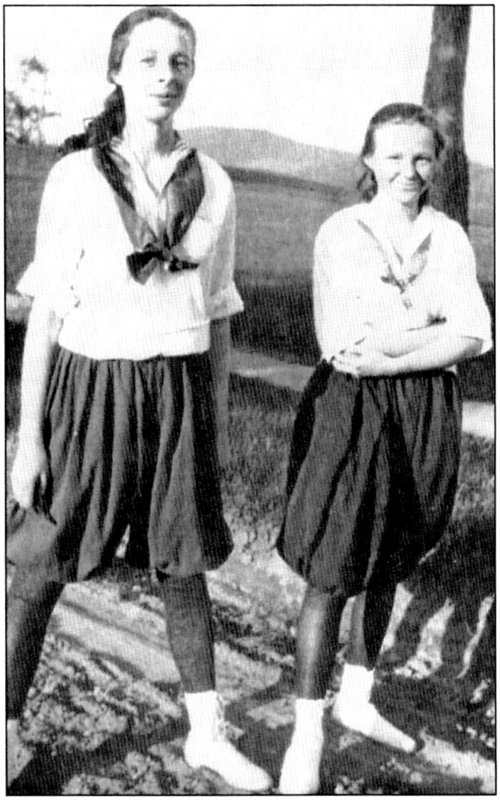

**The Girls' Sports Uniform.** In 1923, girls in sports, such as Louise (Morse) Wheeler '23 and Beda Gray '24, wore this standard uniform of a middy blouse with scarf, wool serge bloomers, long stockings, and high canvas shoes.

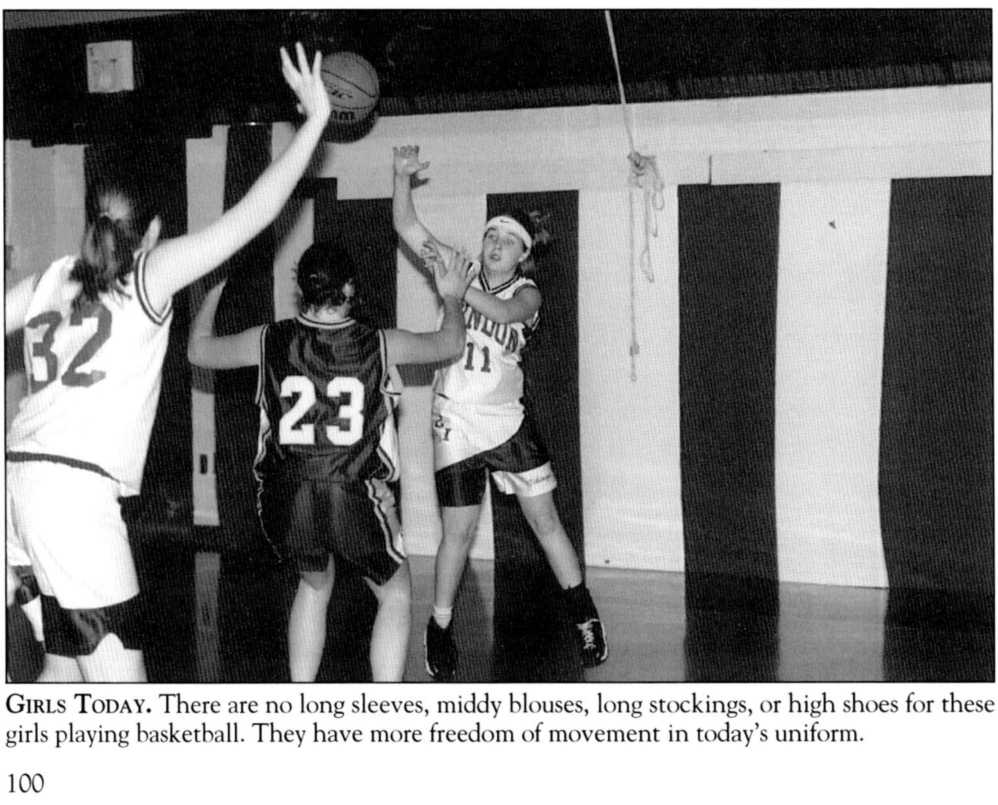


**Girls Today.** There are no long sleeves, middy blouses, long stockings, or high shoes for these girls playing basketball. They have more freedom of movement in today's uniform.

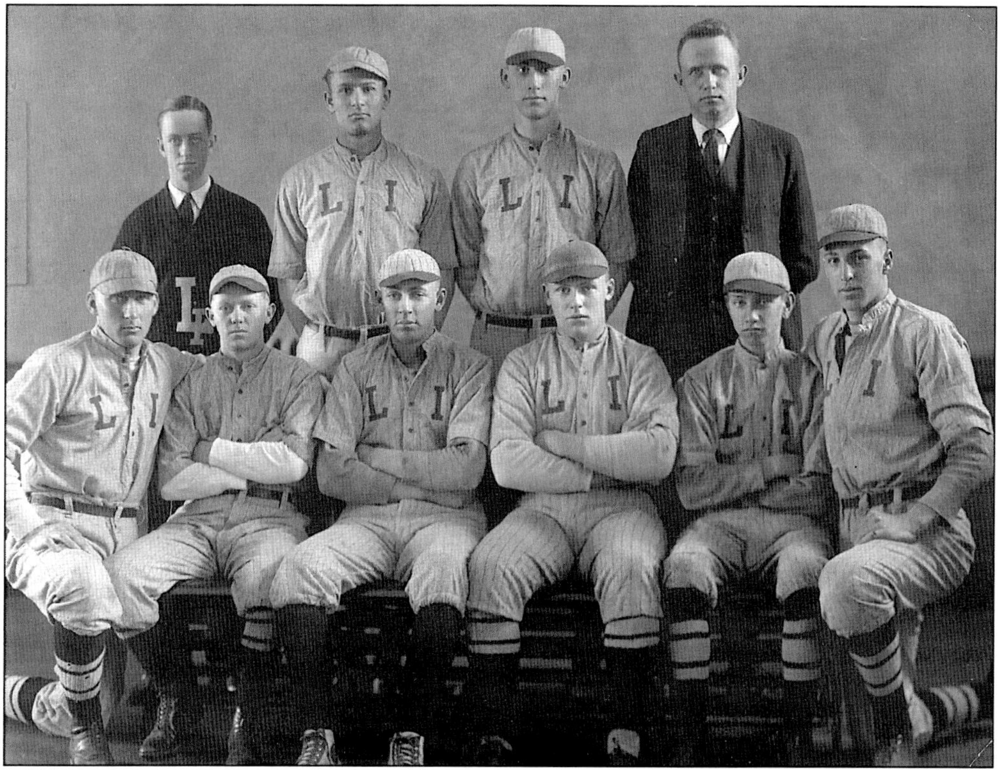

**The Baseball Team.** These young men look as though they mean business, posing for this photograph in 1924. They are, from right to left, as follows: (front row) Erton Brown, Harry Keniston, Charles Dwyer, Fay Bean, Raymond Kinney, and Nelson Wood; (back row) Manager Kenneth Whitney, Arthur Robinson, Wesley Emerson, and Coach Clayton Fisher.

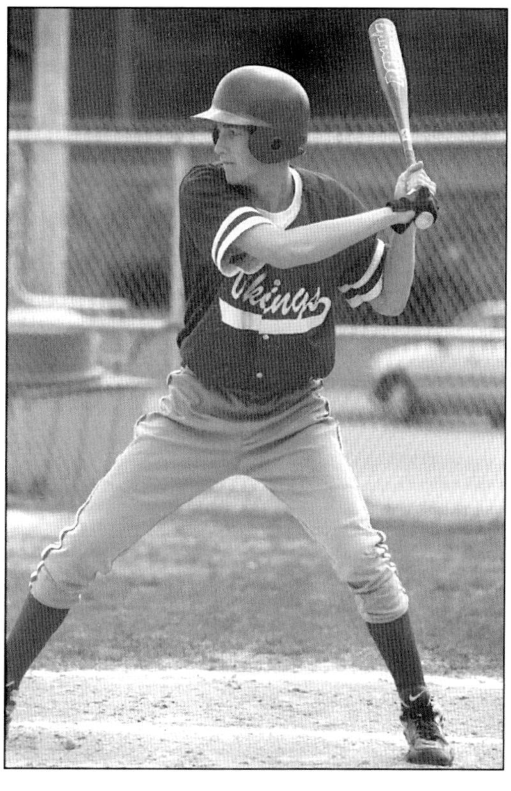

**Baseball Today.** Viking baseball team member Ryan McCaffrey is ready to swing in this 1999 photograph.

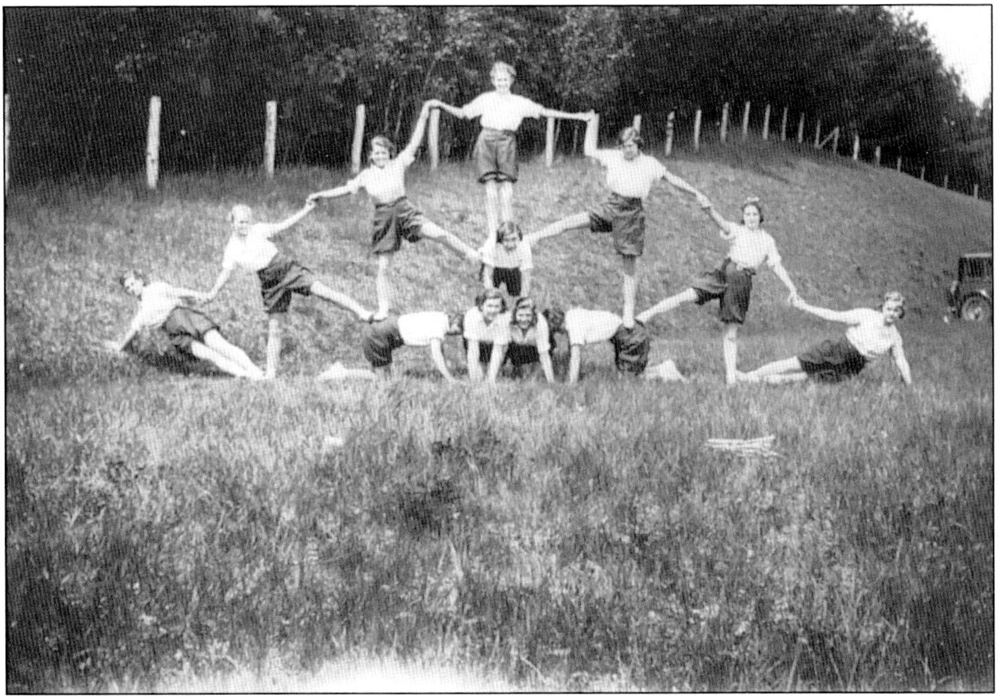

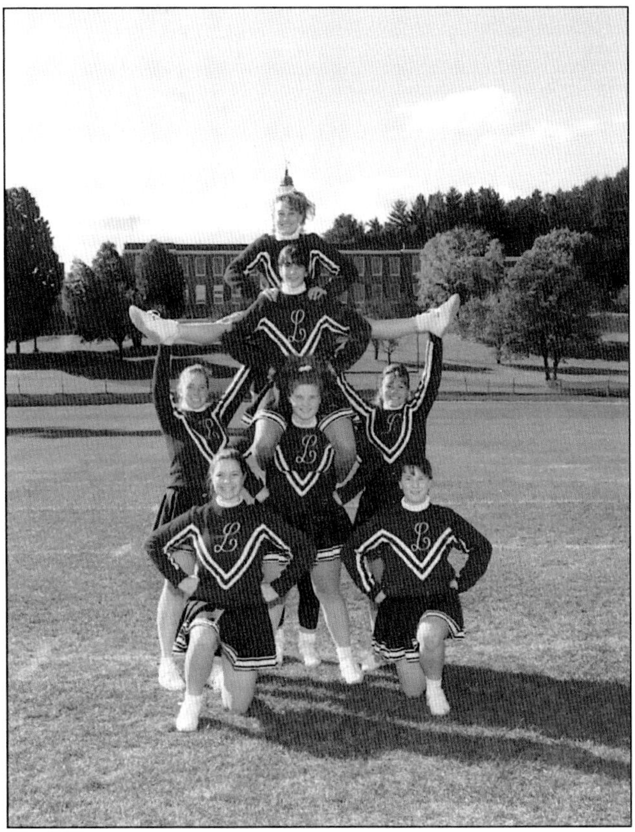

**The Pyramid.** These were not cheerleaders, but student from a c. 1935 physical education class. Physical education was required twice a week. Making the pyramid are, from left to right, as follows: (bottom row) Dorothy Webster, Hazel Smith, Zelda Cox, and Emma Barber; (center) Harriet (Fletcher) Fisher; (top row) Floy Smith, Jennie Gaskin, Angie Duford, Leona Hebert, Reta Howe, Dolores Allard, and Betty Nelson.

**A Modern Pyramid.** The cheerleaders try an interesting pose. Note that the Lyndon Institute tower happens to top off the picture, becoming the peak of the pyramid.

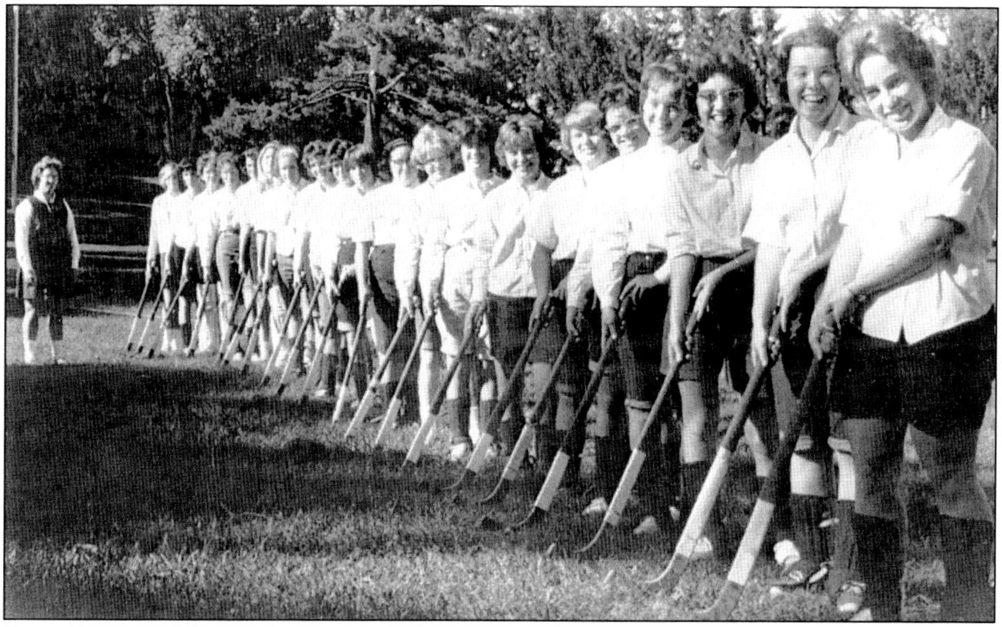

**Field Hockey.** This 1964 team includes seven seniors, five juniors, three sophomores, and five freshmen. They are, from left to right, Merlyn Courser, the coach; Janis Heine; J. Dutton, co-captain; R. Johnson; B. Stevens, co-captain; J. Howe; A. Carpenter; M. Pasell; B. Nutting; E. Hill; F. Nutting; A. Cushman; A. Campbell; D. Blair; P. Morin; K. Blair; S. Mallon; and N. Roy.

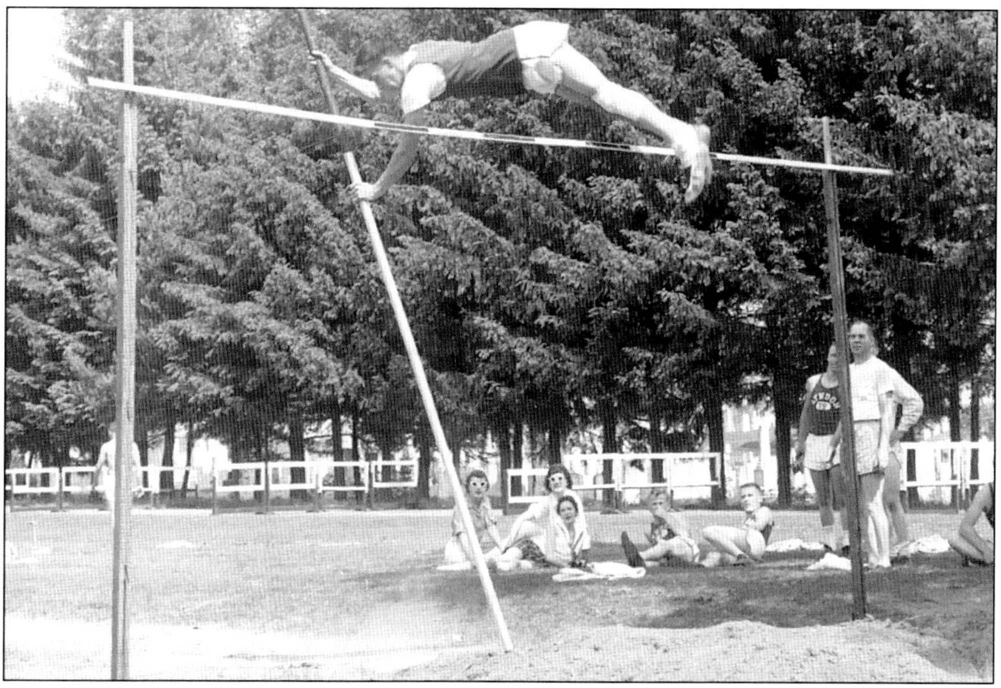

**Over He Goes.** An unidentified athlete participates in the pole vault event. For many years, an alumni track meet was held on Alumni Day, and this activity was scheduled to be repeated for Alumni Day 2000.

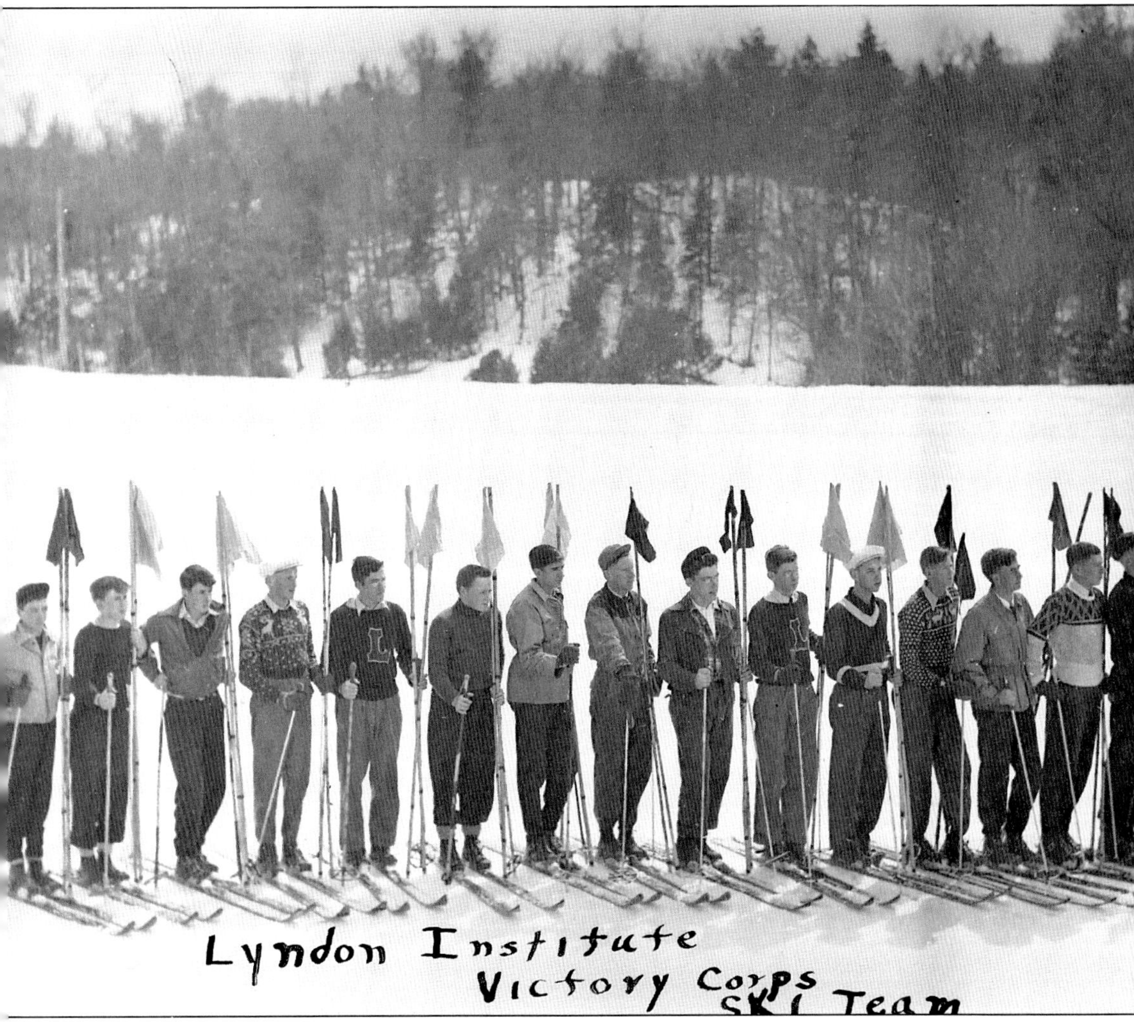


**SKIING FOR VICTORY.** In 1943, the faculty at Lyndon Institute initiated a Victory Corps program at the request of the United States Army. The objective in high schools throughout the country was to condition students for national service. The ski team went to the snow-covered hills and fields one afternoon a week to practice maneuvers somewhat like those practiced by the army mountain troops. The team includes, from left to right, George Guy, Howard Garfield, Norman Lavely, Doug Thompson, Elmer Brown, Dick Wheeler, Edgar Kellaway, Norman Leach, Raymond Mathers, Eddie Smith, Delmar Leach, Wayne Brown, Howard Wakefield, Duane Pierce, and Franz Smith.

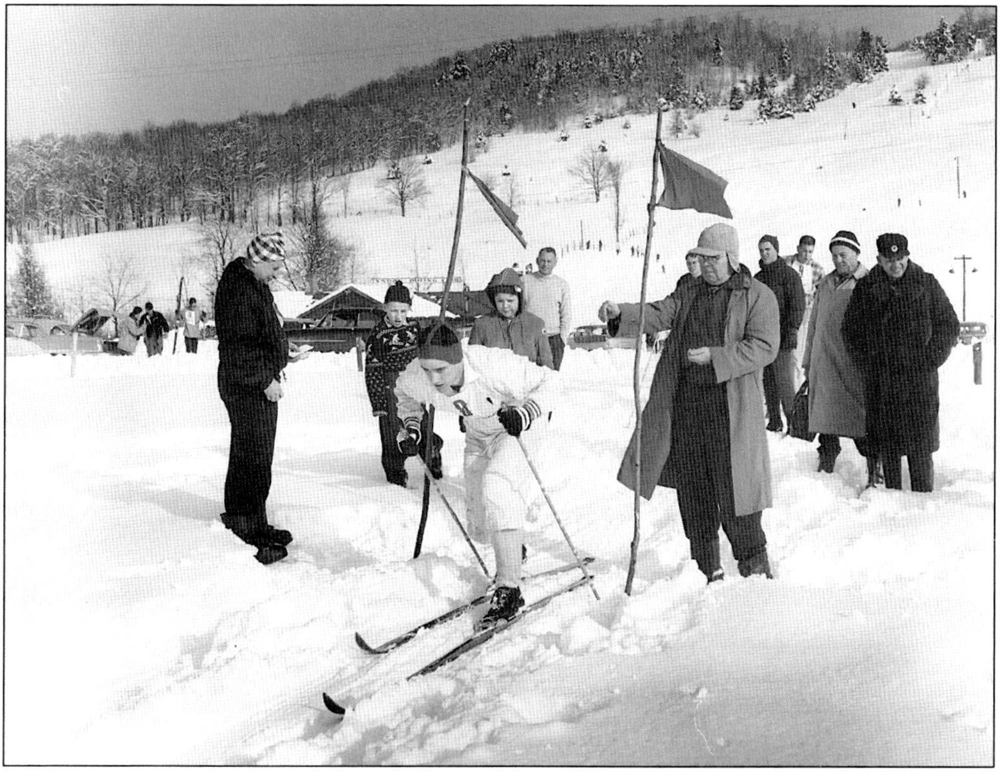

**ANOTHER HAT FOR HEADMASTER LEWIS.** Robert Lewis, headmaster from 1957 to 1963, and Lyndon Institute faculty member since 1924 as a history teacher, an athletic coach, an assistant headmaster, puts on his winter cap in 1961 to time races for an interscholastic ski meet at the Lyndon Outing Club. After retiring as headmaster, Lewis took charge of fund raising for the for the new Alumni Auditorium Gymnasium wing.

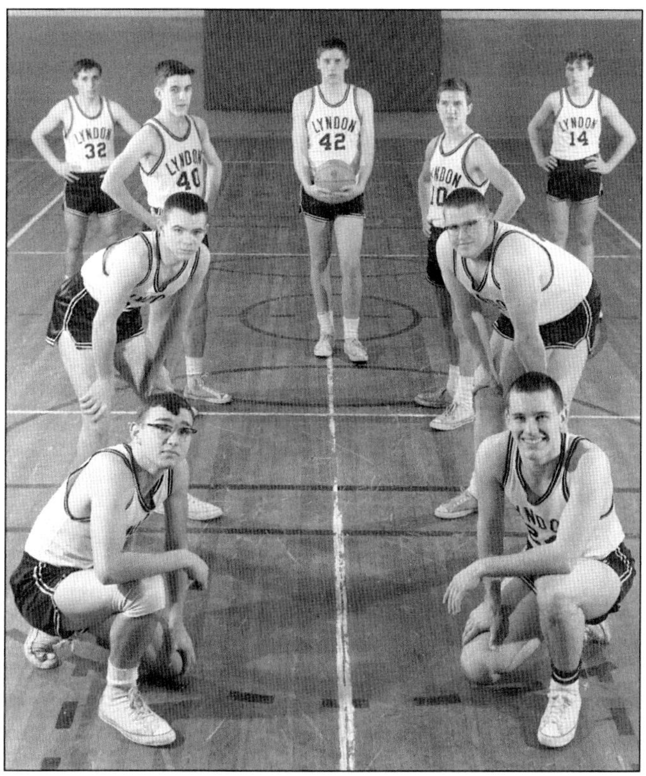


**BASKETBALL IN 1965.** Team members stop the game to pose for this photograph. They are Russell Lawrence, Gilbert Grant, Robert Mills, Rufus Winsor, Steven Douglas, Ray Ingalls, Gilbert Simpson, John Sharpley, and Stephen Gray.

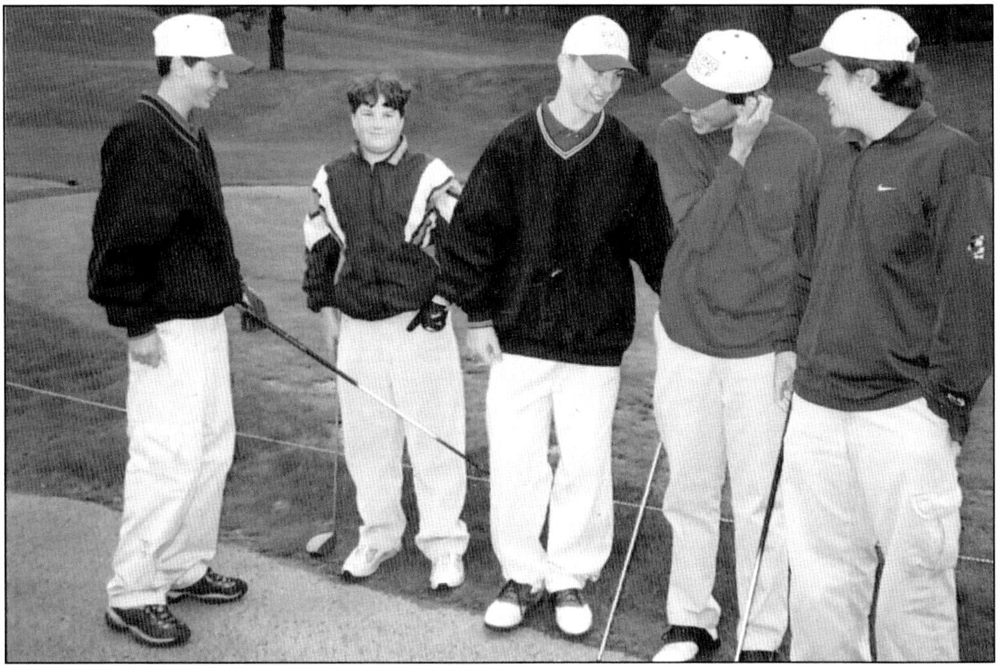

**FORE!** Golf was added to the sports curriculum in 1998. The following students are, from left to right, Justin Brittell, Aaron Cole, Eri Seguin, Aaron O'Brien, and Garrett Cota. During the season, they practice every day at the St. Johnsbury Country Club. There are about a dozen boys and a few girls on the golf team.

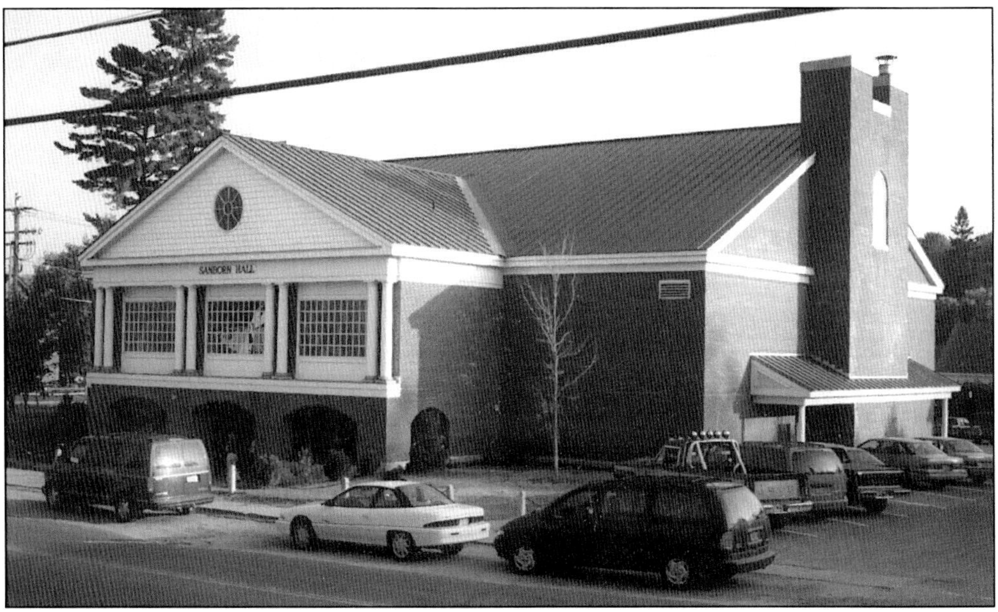

**THE ATHLETIC FACILITY.** The new Sanborn Hall, the field house, was built on the former Sanborn House site (see page 20), and dedicated on September 24, 1988, during halftime of the Montpelier-LI football game. It contains weight rooms, training facilities, locker rooms, a whirlpool, and a gymnasium primarily for basketball games and physical training. This added facility made it possible for more students to participate in sports activities.

# *Ten*

# CLUBS AND ACTIVITIES

There are many clubs at Lyndon Institute. Almost every course has a related club or organization that students may join, giving them the opportunity to practice some of the lessons they have learned in the classroom. Activities and clubs include Student Council, Vocational/Industrial, Future Business Leaders of America, Future Homemakers, athletics, and several scholastic and language clubs. A few are included here, as photographs were available.

One of the largest activities, which involved students, teachers, staff at Lyndon Institute, parents, and many other area people, was the centennial celebration of the chartering of the Lyndon Literary and Biblical Institution in 1867. The exciting day, June 10, 1967, Alumni Day, was ideal for a parade and the many events that occurred for this special time. Figures of the past were represented by people of the present. It was a privilege to have Theodore N. Vail's great-nephew Maj. Ira Vail, Mrs. Vail, and two children present for the occasion. Many people in the parade were descendants of former principals, trustees, or benefactors of the Lyndon Institute.

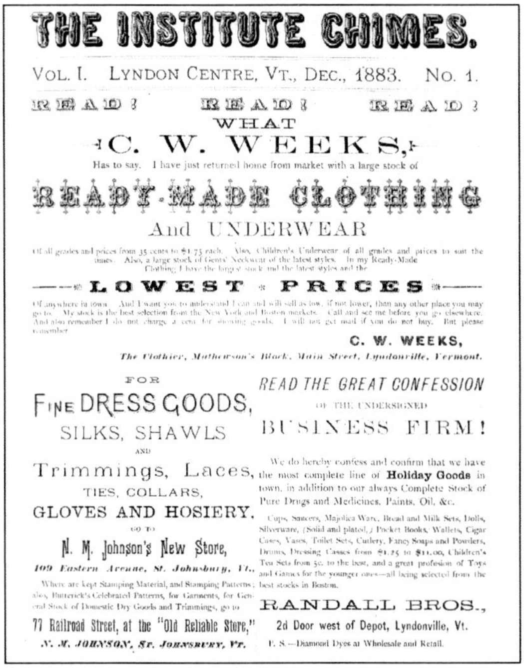

THE INSTITUTE CHIMES.

VOL. I. LYNDON CENTRE, VT., DEC., 1883. NO. 1.

READ! READ! READ!

WHAT

C. W. WEEKS,

Has to say. I have just returned home from market with a large stock of

READY-MADE CLOTHING

And UNDERWEAR

Of all grades and prices from 35 cents to $1.75 each. Also, Children's Underwear of all grades and prices to suit the times. Also, a large stock of Gents' Neckwear of the latest styles. In my Ready-Made Clothing I have the largest stock and the latest styles and the

LOWEST PRICES

Of anywhere in town. And I want you to understand I can and will sell as low, if not lower, than any other place you may go to. My stock is the best selection from the New York and Boston markets. Call and see me before you go elsewhere. And also remember I do not charge a cent for showing goods. I will not get mad if you do not buy. But please remember

C. W. WEEKS,

*The Clothier, Mathewson's Block, Main Street, Lyndonville, Vermont.*

FOR

FINE DRESS GOODS,

SILKS, SHAWLS

AND

Trimmings, Laces,

TIES, COLLARS,

GLOVES AND HOSIERY,

GO TO

N. M. Johnson's New Store,

*109 Eastern Avenue, St. Johnsbury, Vt.,*

Where are kept Stamping Material, and Stamping Patterns; also, Butterick's Celebrated Patterns, for Garments, for General Stock of Domestic Dry Goods and Trimmings, go to

77 Railroad Street, at the "Old Reliable Store,"

*N. M. JOHNSON, ST. JOHNSBURY, VT.*

READ THE GREAT CONFESSION

OF THE UNDERSIGNED

BUSINESS FIRM!

We do hereby confess and confirm that we have the most complete line of **Holiday Goods** in town, in addition to our always Complete Stock of Pure Drugs and Medicines, Paints, Oil, &c.

Cups, Saucers, Majolica Ware, Bread and Milk Sets, Dolls, Silverware, (Solid and plated,) Pocket Books, Wallets, Cigar Cases, Vases, Toilet Sets, Cutlery, Fancy Soaps and Powders, Drums, Dressing Cases from $1.25 to $11.00, Children's Tea Sets from 5c. to the best, and a great profusion of Toys and Games for the younger ones—all being selected from the best stocks in Boston.

RANDALL BROS.,

2d Door west of Depot, Lyndonville, Vt.

P. S.—Diamond Dyes at Wholesale and Retail.

**A STUDENT PUBLICATION.** In December 1883, students published Volume 1, No. 1 of *The Institute Chimes*, a quarterly in a small-magazine format. It contained editorials, school news, humorous tidbits, an occasional photograph, literary writings, and ads from supporting area businesses. This publication continued on and off for several years.

**GETTING DOWN TO BUSINESS.** In 1970, senior Kim Peck, left, and yearbook adviser and business practices teacher Marion Wakefield use the easiest way to organize the *Cynosure* photographs. The Class of 1924 was the first to publish the *Cynosure*, a word meaning the "center of attraction or attention." The word was on a vocabulary list in an English class. English and Latin teacher Theta Baker, was the first *Cynosure* adviser.

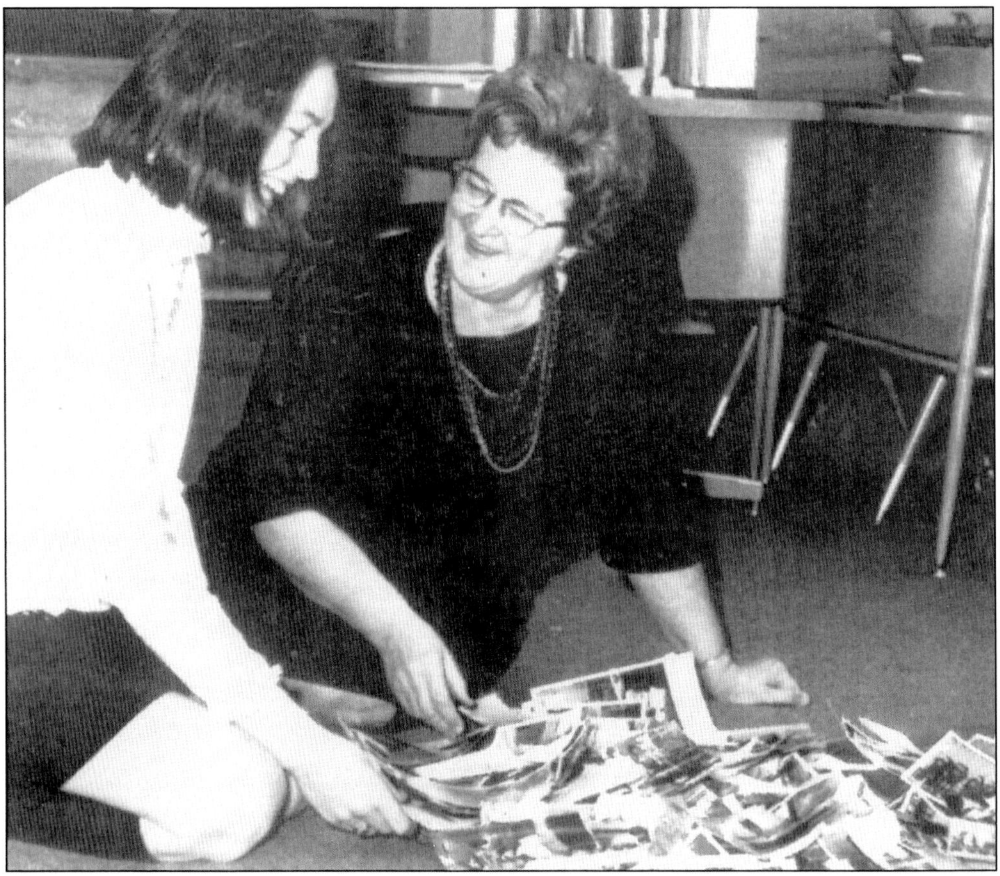

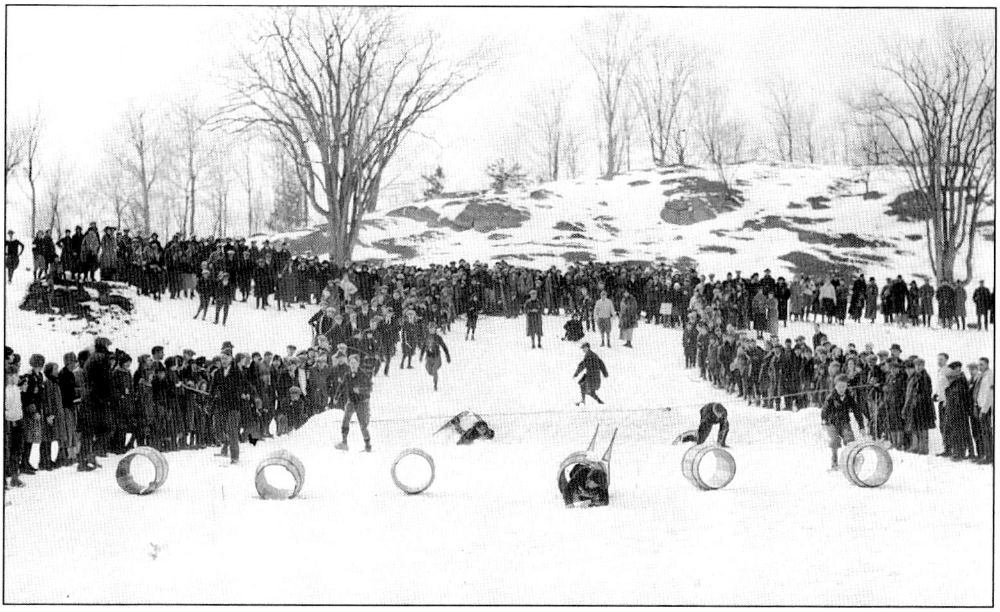

**ROLLING OUT THE BARRELS.** An interscholastic winter carnival at St. Johnsbury on February 21, 1925, drew a big crowd. Crawling through barrels on snowshoes doesn't look very easy, and it was probably hilarious to watch.

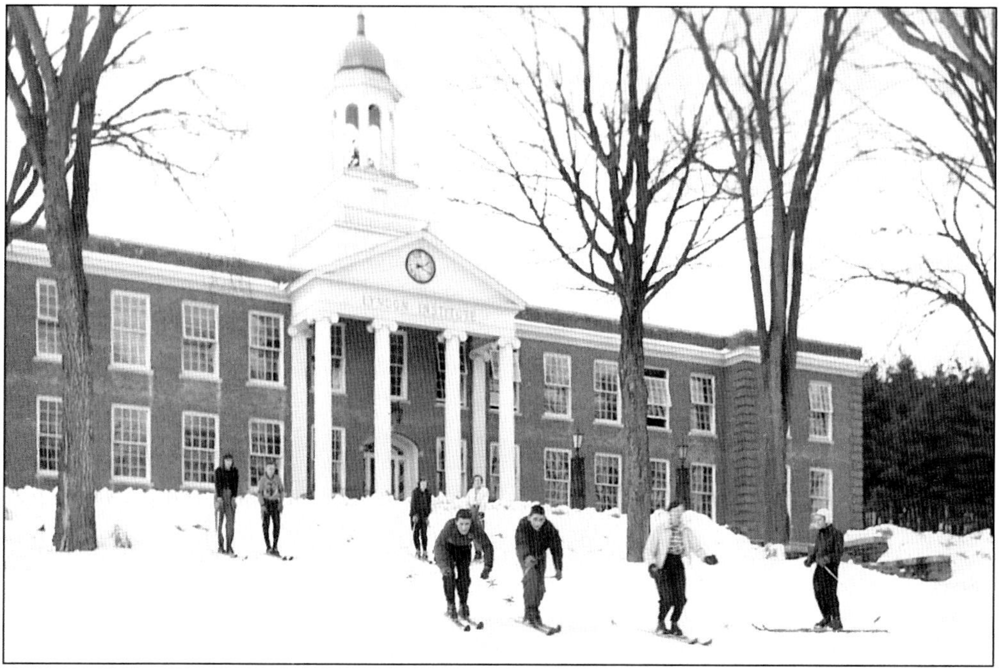

**SKIING AT LYNDON INSTITUTE.** This may be practice skiing, or it may be part of a winter carnival, *c.* 1938. Carnivals were held at Lyndon Institute with skating on the campus rink, snowshoeing on the meadow, tugs-of-war, and many other activities. In more recent years, the Lyndon Institute carnivals have been held at the Lyndon Outing Club. Evelyn Fuller, the French teacher, was an outdoor fan and one of the carnival coordinators. She is second from the right, wearing a white jacket and a beret.

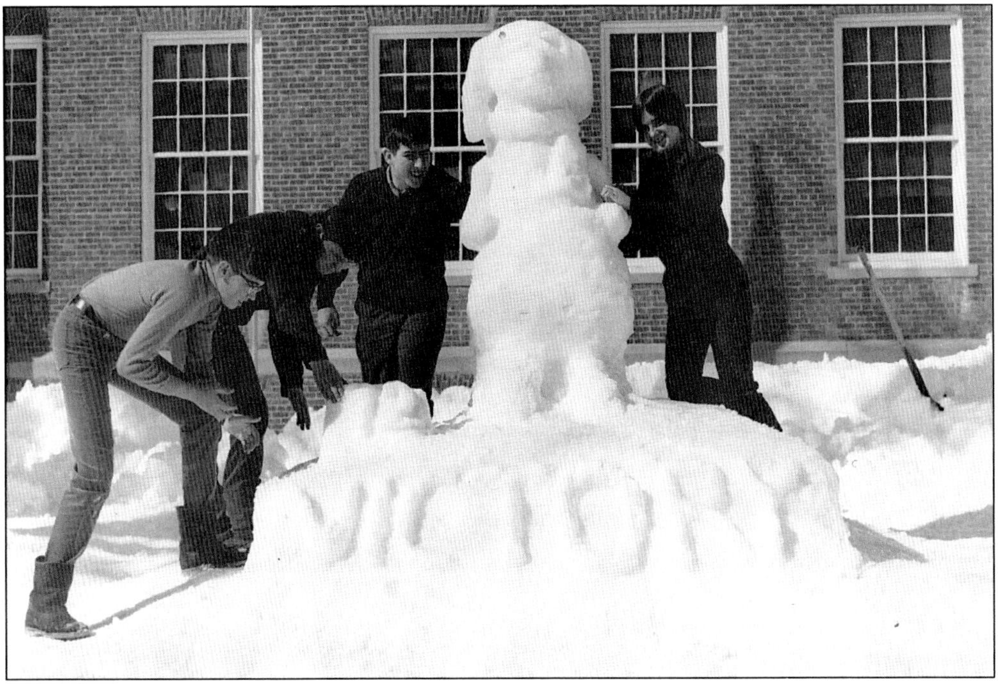

**SNOOPY STANDS FOR VICTORY.** Each class enters a snow sculpture somewhere on the campus for the Lyndon Institute winter carnival contests and activities. John Towle, Ronald Sylvester, and Kathy Devereaux, all from the Class of 1972, put the finishing touches on their creative efforts.

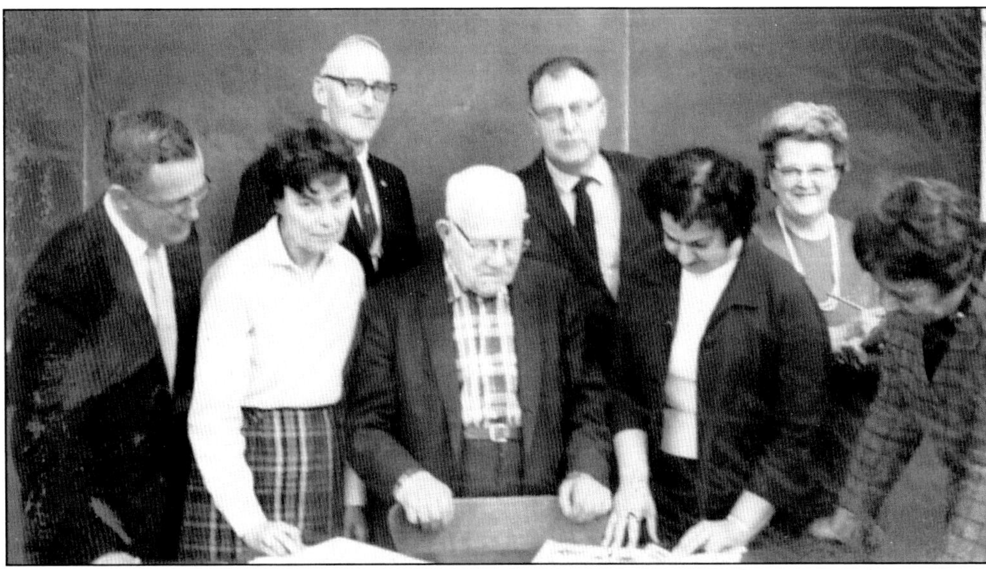

**THE CENTENNIAL PLANS.** Chairmen of the celebration committee, deep in conference, are, from left to right, as follows: (front row) Gerald Aubin '33, Harriet (Fletcher) Fisher '37, Arthur Simpson, art teacher Bertha Koury, and typing teacher Winifred King; (back row) Clair Holbrook, Herbert Gallagher '29, and business teacher Marion Wakefield. Bertha Koury drew the plans for 13 floats, each one representing an important phase in the 100-year life of the school. Parents, students, faculty, staff, and townspeople helped build and decorate the floats.

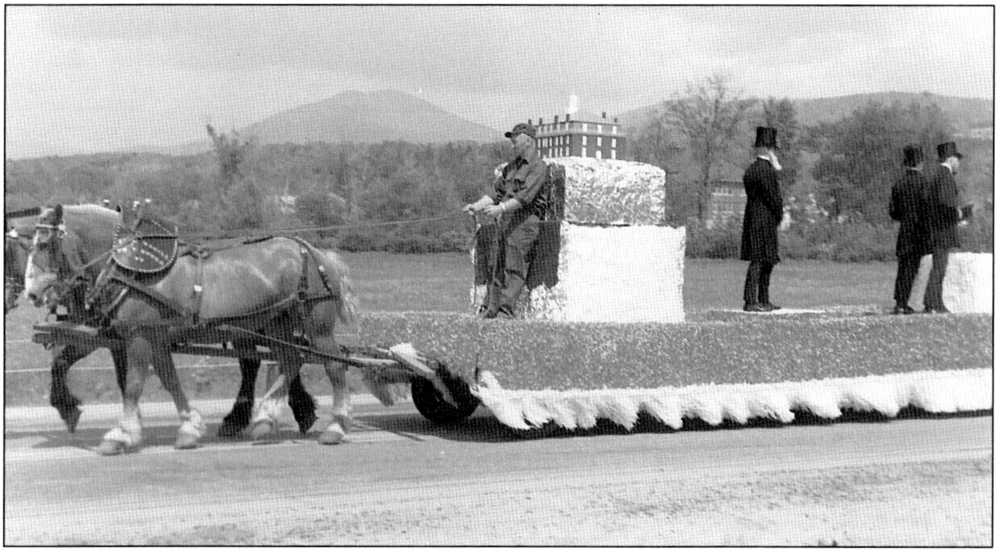

**The Charter Float.** The Lyndon Institute celebrated its centennial with a big parade and many other activities. The big parade was on June 10, 1967, Alumni Day. These men represent the 9 Baptist clergymen and the 13 businessmen who were the first corporators. The replica of the building on the float was made by Gerald Aubin '33, an instructor of mechanical drawing in the related math and pre-vocational shop. This float was sponsored by the Town of Lyndon. The driver is Freeman "Bill" Magill.

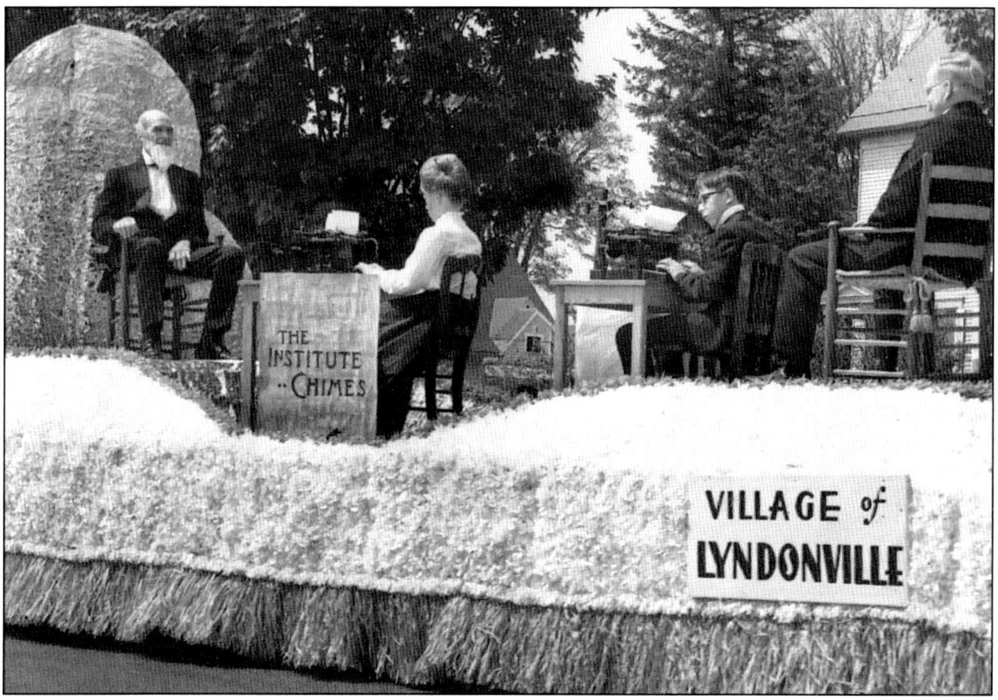


**The Business Department Float.** This float represents the 1880s and shows students of the commercial course at their Remington No. 2 typewriters. On the float is Paul Fisher '41, made up in white whiskers, representing benefactor Dudley P. Hall, president of the 1880 Lyndon Institute Board of Trustees. The Village of Lyndonville sponsored this float.

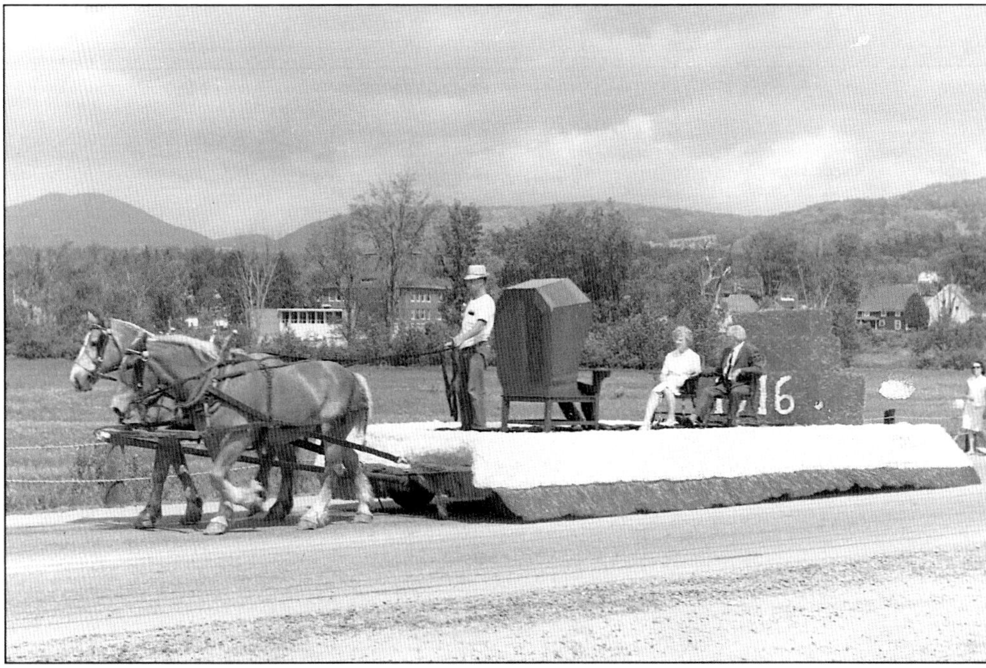


**A Chair for President Taft.** At graduation ceremonies in 1916, the school was honored by having as guest speaker the former president of the United States, William Howard Taft, a close friend of Theodore N. Vail. Taft was visiting Vail at Speedwell Farms. Vail had two fireside chairs built that were large enough to hold comfortably men of their build. The float was sponsored by the Vermont Tap and Die Company. The driver is David Mitchell.

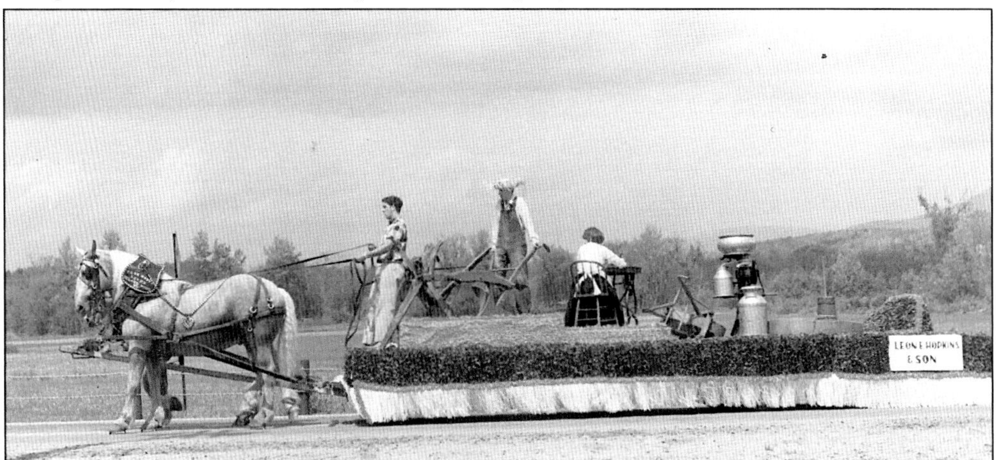


**Country Life.** Theodore Vail believed that young people could be taught scientific skills for improving farm and home life. This float represents the Agricultural School and the household economics department. The float was sponsored by Leon E. Hopkins & and Son, a business in coal, oil, and insurance. Hopkins was a 1917 graduate of the Agricultural School. The driver is Alan Ovitt of Island Pond.

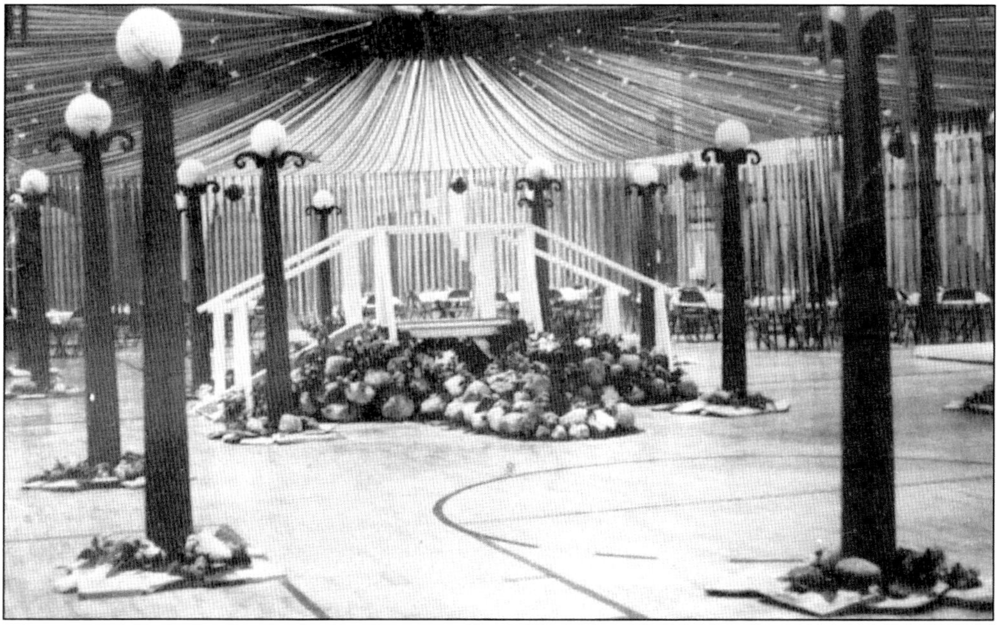

**The Senior Prom.** In 1970, art teacher Bertha Koury and the dance committee turned the gym into a special ballroom for the prom, which included lampposts, a bridge, and an arbor, all of which were enhanced by an abundance of flowers. The next night, the alumni enjoyed the same setting. Now, replacing the senior ball each year is a substance-free, all-night occasion of various activities. An event on the evening of Alumni Day includes a concert in the auditorium by John Padden's Alumni Band.

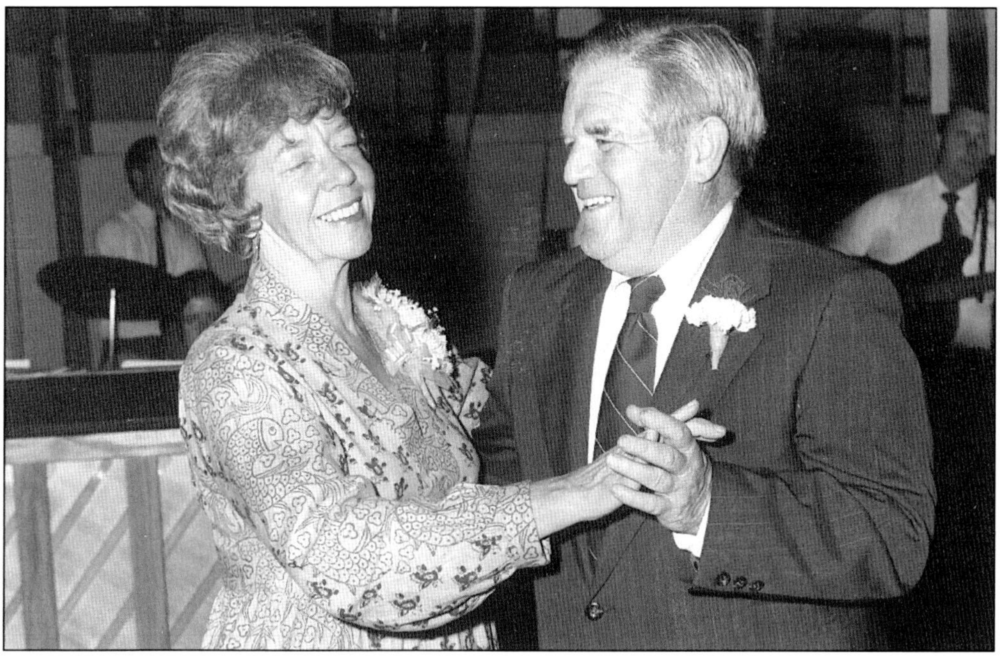

**May I Have This Dance?** Catherine Mallon dances with her husband Archie Mallon, headmaster, at the senior prom—they always attended during his tenure. She helped with the research and the gathering of information for the centennial celebration.

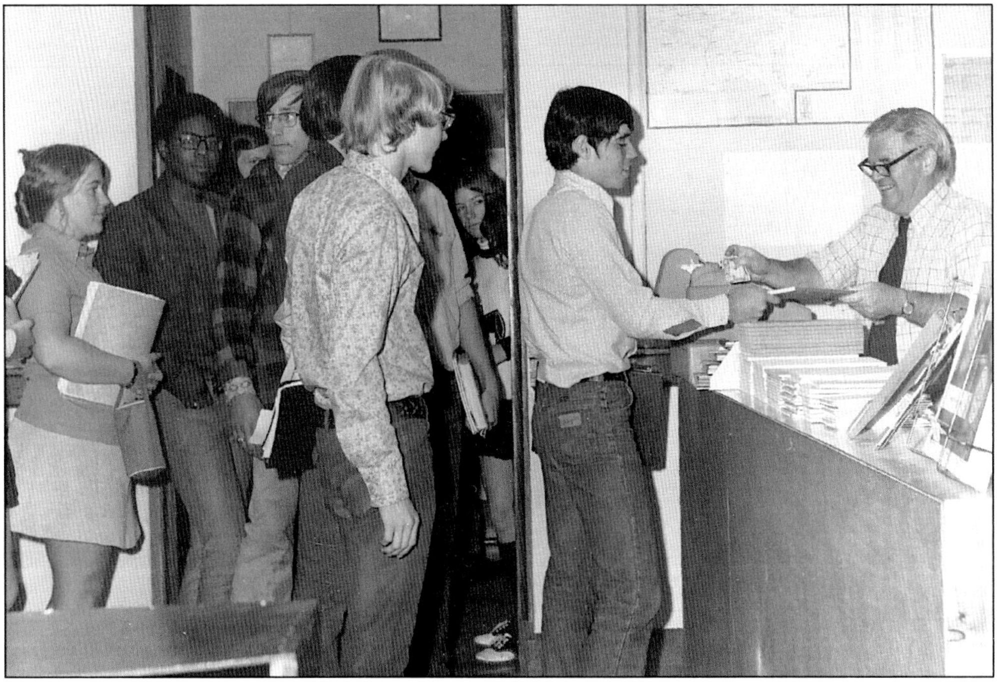

**ARCHIE MALLON MINDS THE STORE.** Pencils, notebooks, binders? What do you need? The headmaster takes the lunchtime shift at the cafeteria branch of the campus store to tend to students' needs.

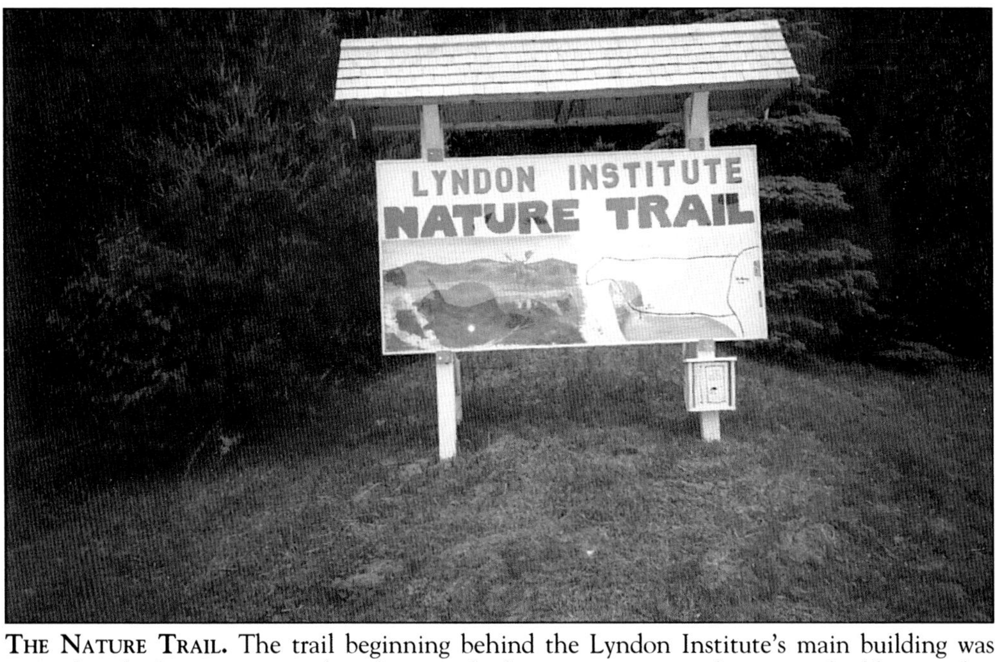


**THE NATURE TRAIL.** The trail beginning behind the Lyndon Institute's main building was created with the assistance of students in biology, environmental science, building trades, welding, computer science, art, design publishing classes; faculty; staff; and the Town of Lyndon zoning administrator. The trail was funded in part by the Earth and Us program. Site maps are available in a box at this sign and people take the well-marked trail on their own.

# *Eleven*

# GRADUATIONS AND ALUMNI ACTIVITIES

The bell in the Lyndon Institute tower tolls ten, and the strains of "Pomp and Circumstance" sound from the institute band on the campus. Members of the graduating class, the girls in white caps and gowns and the boys in maroon, march out the front door, following the marshals down the steps and the sloping walk to the campus for this important day in their lives. After the speeches the graduates, one by one, walk across the stage to receive a diploma. When the ceremonies are over, the air is suddenly filled with maroon and white caps, as the enthusiastic graduates hurl them high into the air.

When it rains, graduation is held at the Lyndon State College gymnasium or the Fenton Chester Arena, large enough to hold the many friends and relatives of the more than 100 graduates. In earlier years, graduations were held in the Music Hall in Lyndonville. Distinguished speakers have always given inspirational talks. Some have been governors, senators, and other well-known figures. In 1916, Theodore Vail invited his distinguished friend, the former president, William Howard Taft, to speak at the combined graduation of the Lyndon Institute and the Vail Agricultural School.

Graduates automatically become members of the Alumni Association. Many go off to college or jobs. As they grow older, they are more likely to come back for reunions. Reuniting classes often give glowing reports of the fun they have at the alumni activities and meeting again with old friends.

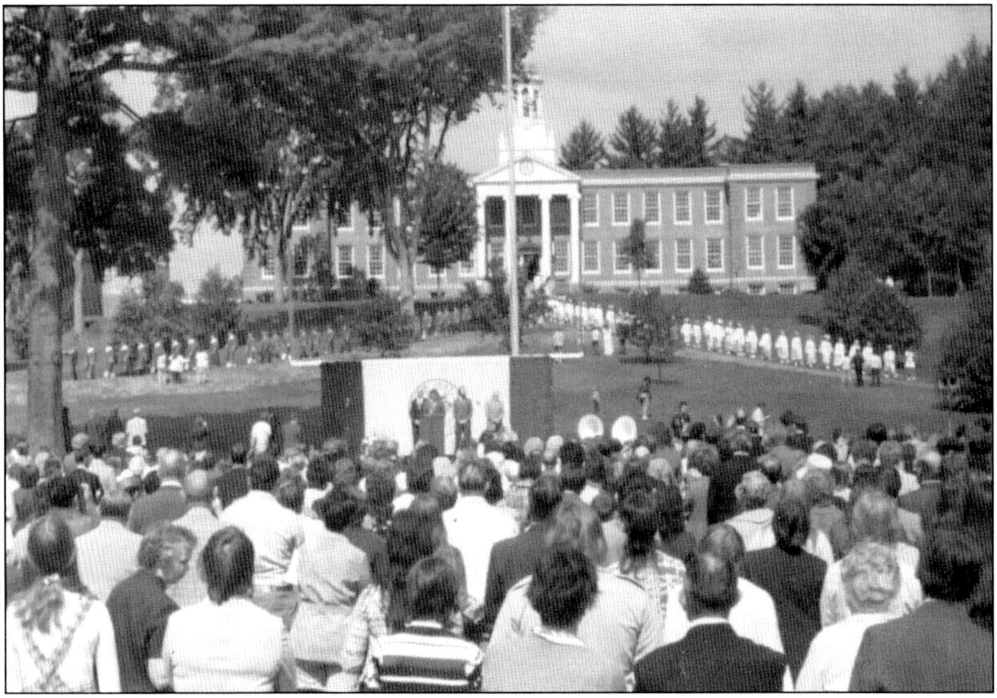

**The Graduation Walk.** Seniors proudly march down "the path to the future," the girls in white and the boys in maroon, the school colors, while parents, relatives, and friends watch, awaiting the graduation ceremonies on the campus. The disappointment is great if it rains and the ceremony has to be held inside.

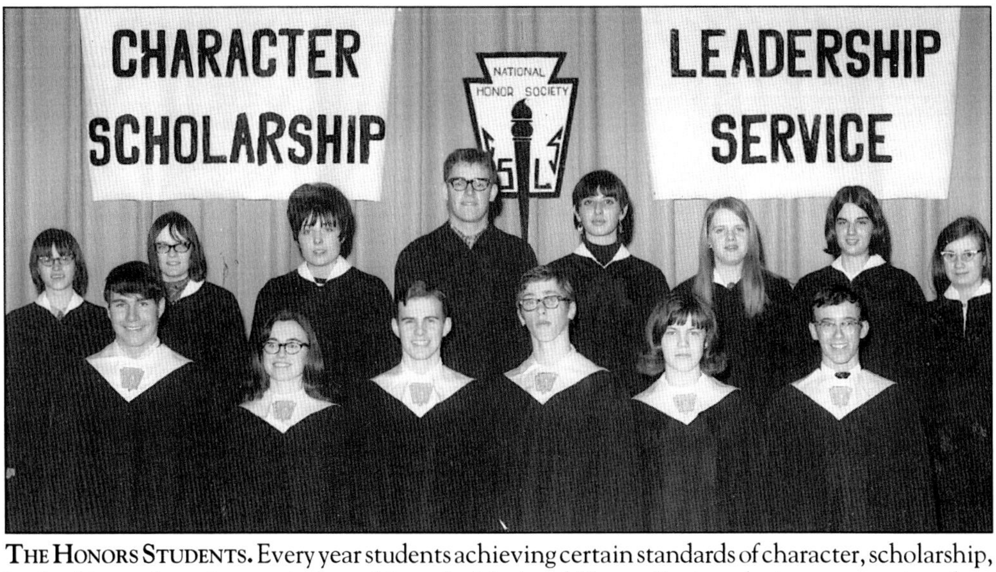


**The Honors Students.** Every year students achieving certain standards of character, scholarship, leadership, and service, are inducted into the National Honor Society during ceremonies when other awards and prizes are given out at an honors assembly. In 1967, they were, from left to right, as follows: (back row) Kathy LaBay, Donna Rossier, Nancy Brown, Stephen Bean, Mary Amster, Alice Campbell, Ellen Hill, and Mary Ann Bingham; (front row) Robert Pendleton, Judith Day, Earl Daniels, Stephen Elliott, Marilyn Worden, and Daniel Gibson.

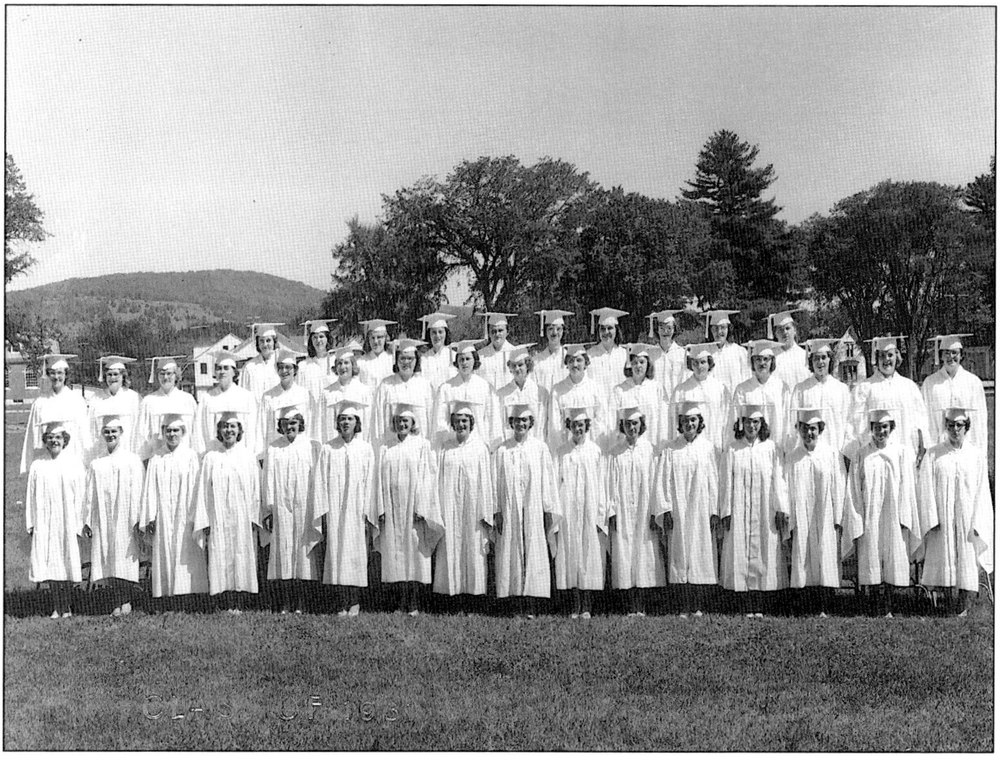


**Maroon and White.** The graduates of the Class of 1961 pose on the Lyndon Institute campus, the girls in white and the boys, below, in maroon.

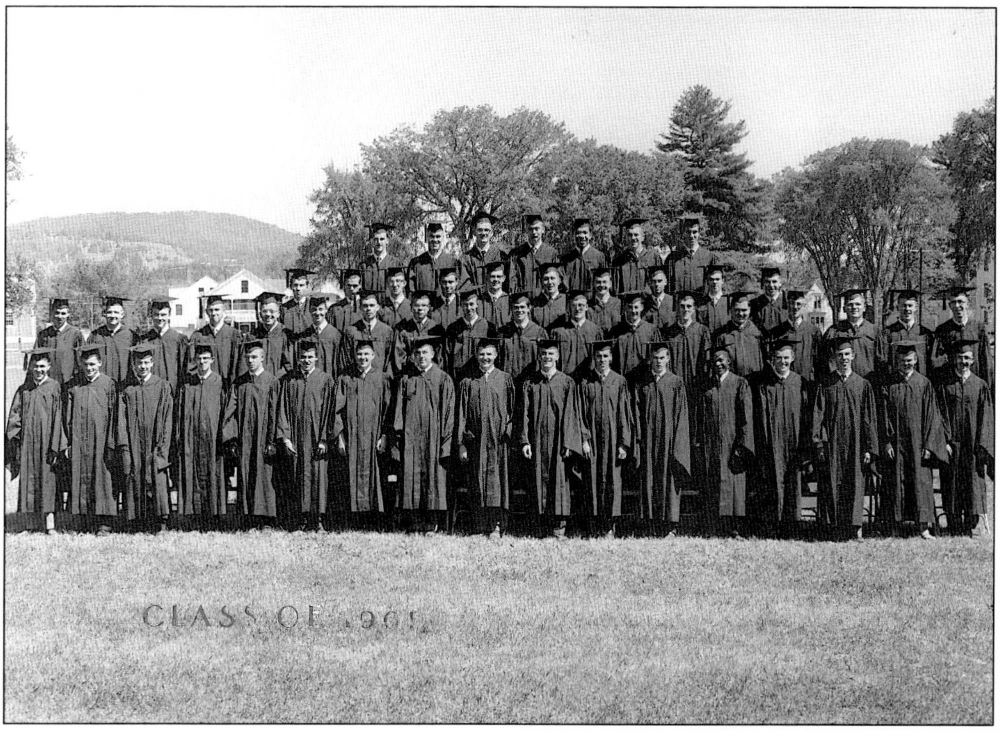

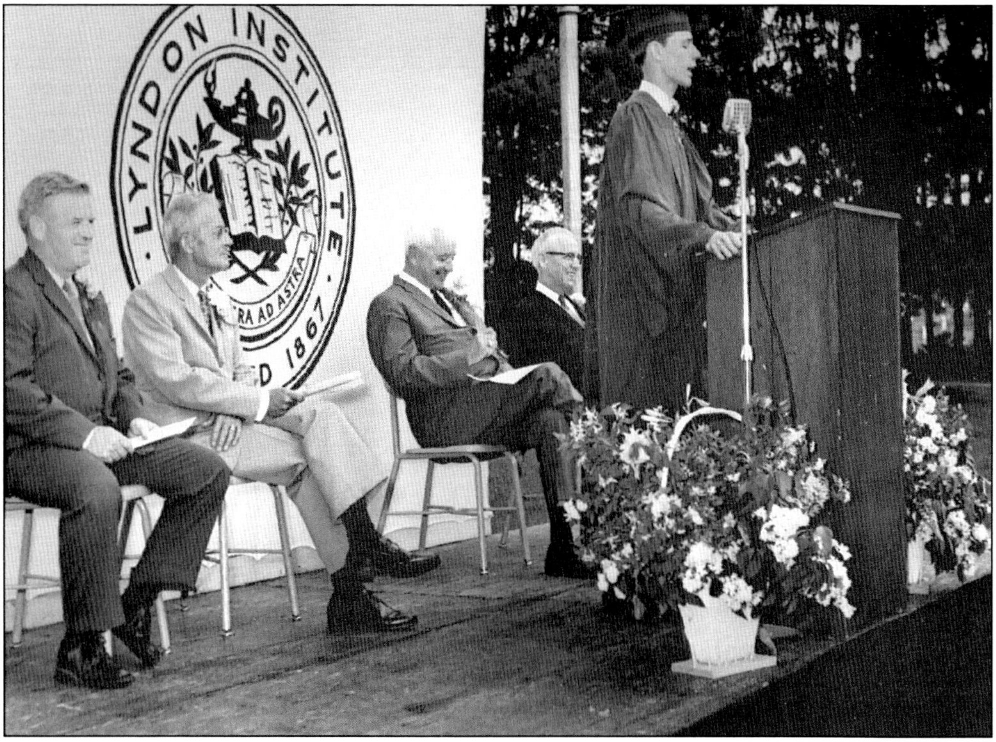


**GRADUATION DAY, 1968.** Danny Heath brought greetings from his class. Listening here are, from left to right, Archie Mallon,headmaster; John L. Norris Jr., trustee president; the Honorable Ernest W. Gibson, chief judge of the Unites States District Court; and the Reverend Axel Heath. Paraphrasing Sen. Robert Kennedy, Gibson urged the graduates to "dream things that are not, and then ask why not."

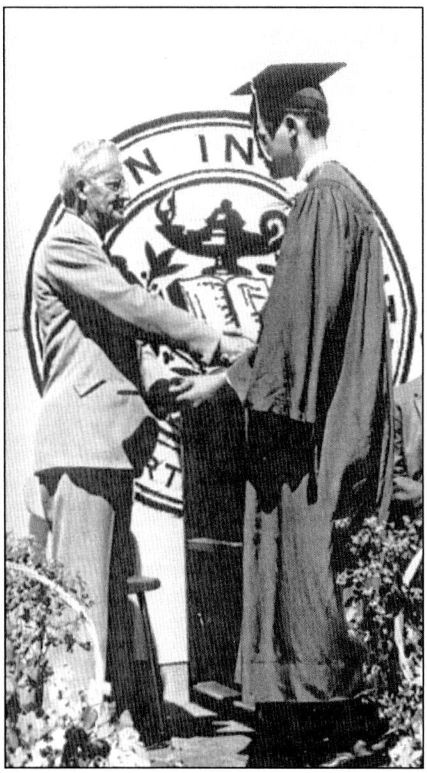

**THE MAGIC CIRCLE.** When a graduate, in this case Louis Burrington '68, steps in front this "magic circle"—the Institute seal—to receive a diploma, he or she knows the four years at Lyndon Institute have been accomplished successfully.

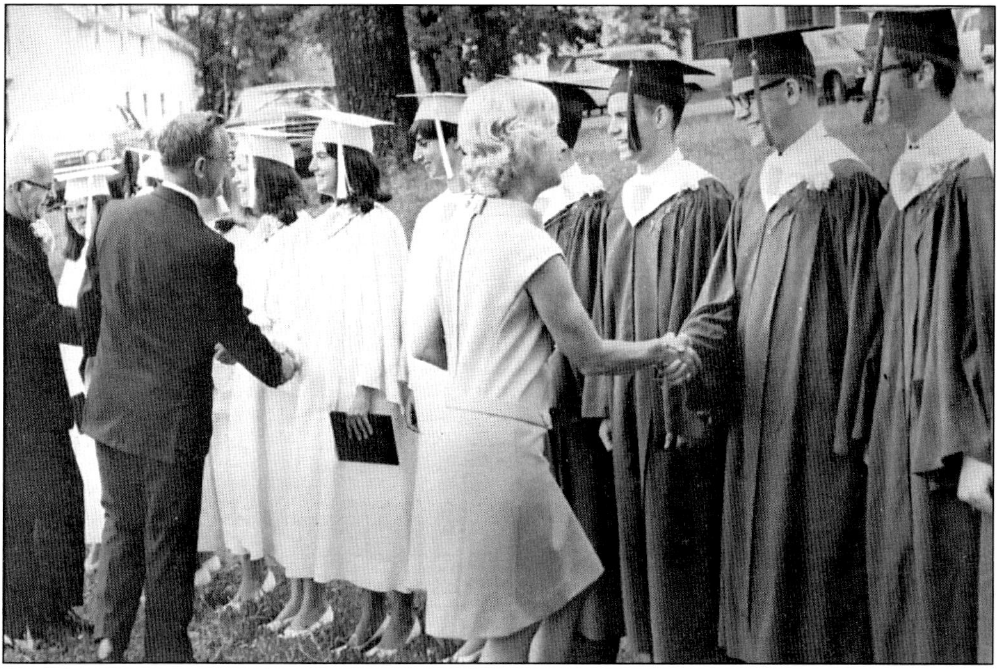

**The Receiving Line.** The 1967 graduates had the honor of being the Centennial Class of Lyndon Institute, which was chartered in 1867. With their tassels properly turned toward the left, they receive congratulations from the Reverend Clyde Campbell, left, and teachers Gerald Aubin '33 and Erma (Richardson) Akley '35. The 1967 graduates numbered 120.

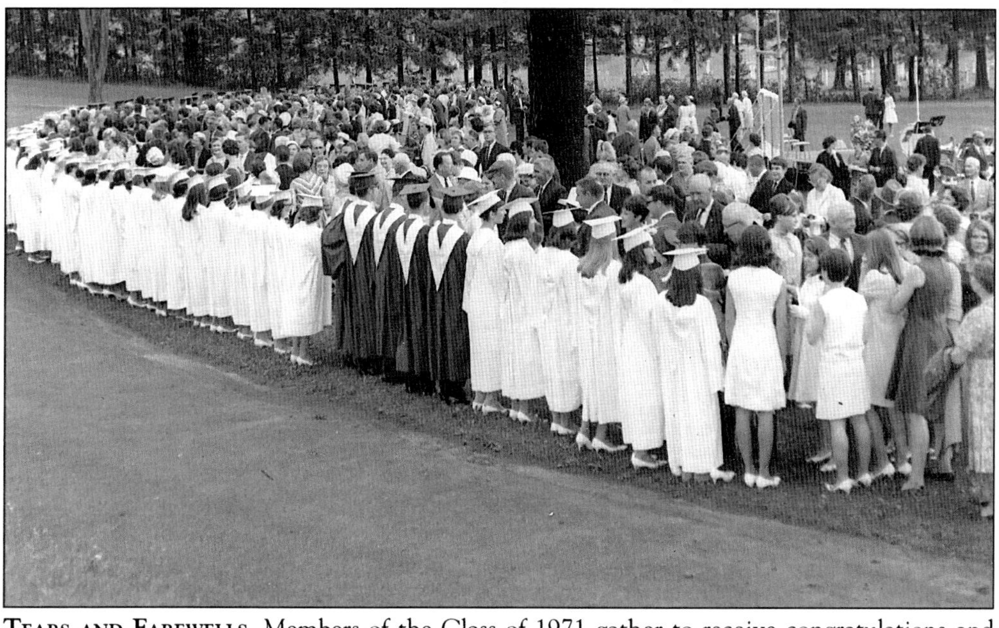

**Tears and Farewells.** Members of the Class of 1971 gather to receive congratulations and best wishes and to say goodbye to each other after the graduation ceremony. The young men with the shawls are members of the Honor Society, as are some young women whose shawls do not show up in this photograph. The line continues around toward the back, where the young men in maroon are barely visible behind the crowd. That year there were 121 graduates.

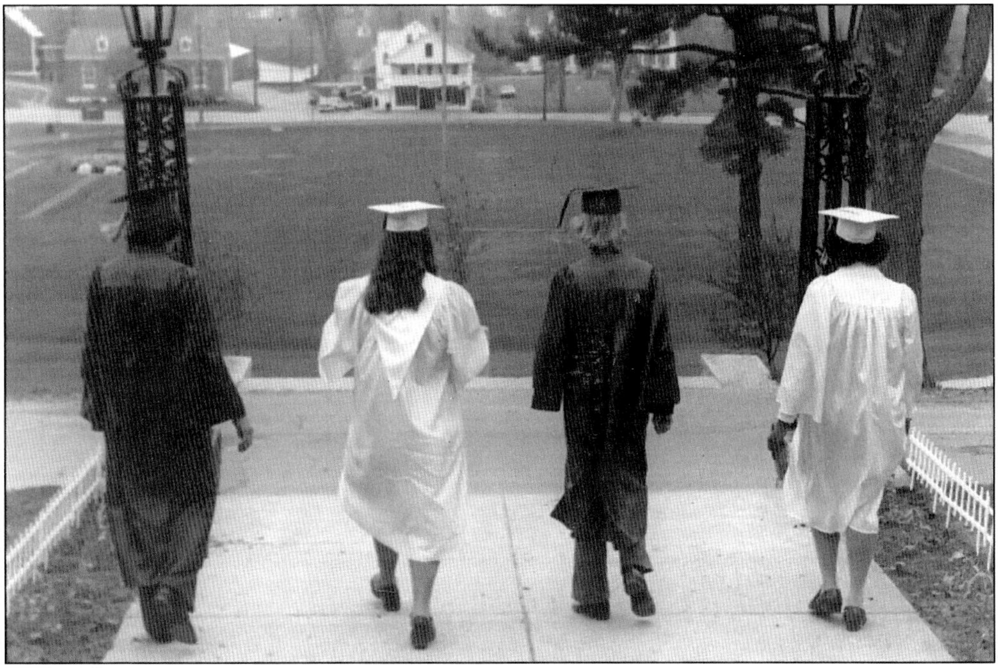

**Leaving Lyndon Institute.** These four members of the Class of 1975 step into the future from the front door of their alma mater. They are, from left to right, Sam Carleton, Sharolyn Weed, Brian Bean, and Nancy Williams. The graduates in 1975 numbered well over 100.

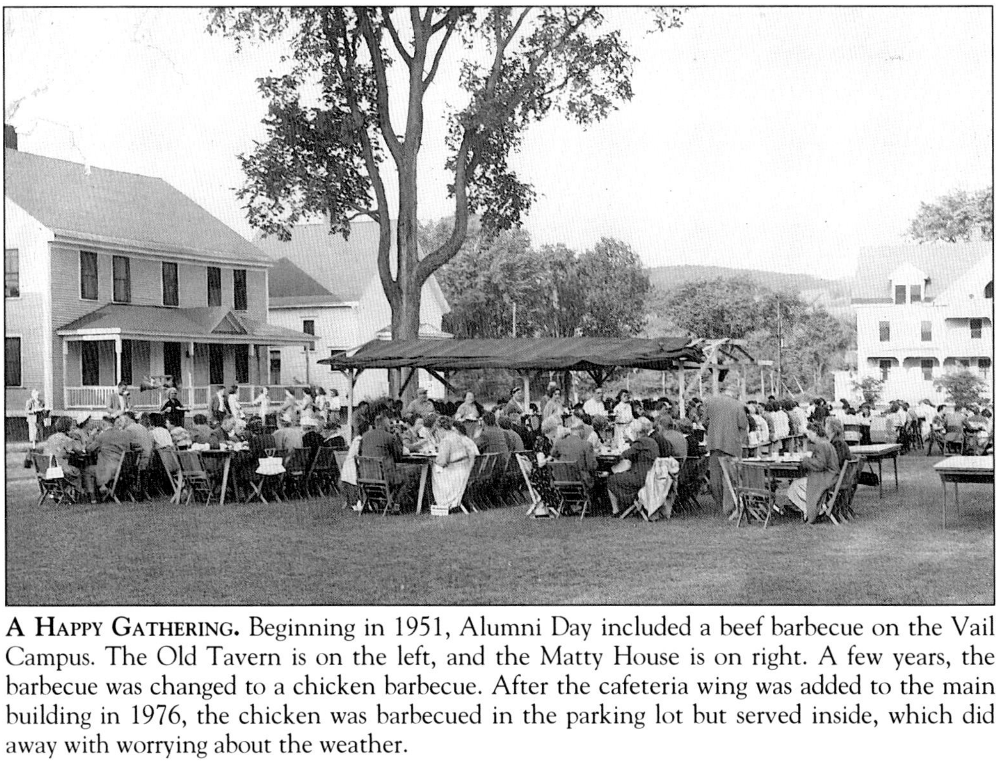

**A Happy Gathering.** Beginning in 1951, Alumni Day included a beef barbecue on the Vail Campus. The Old Tavern is on the left, and the Matty House is on right. A few years, the barbecue was changed to a chicken barbecue. After the cafeteria wing was added to the main building in 1976, the chicken was barbecued in the parking lot but served inside, which did away with worrying about the weather.

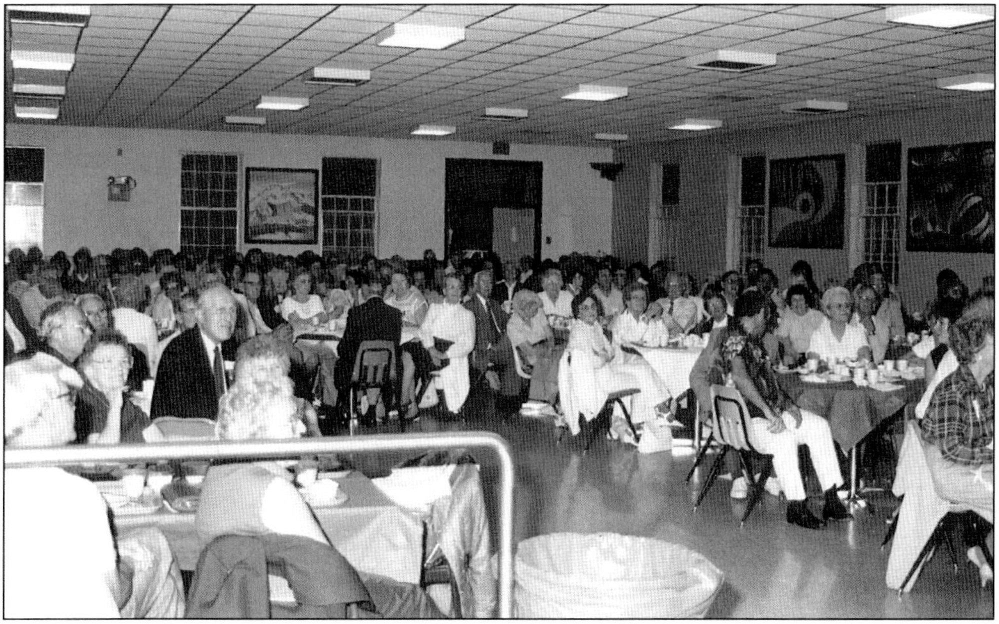

**The Reunion Luncheon.** This image shows the cafeteria in full use for some of the reunion class members who chose this location for their luncheon. Paul Aubin '31, facing right front, is easily identified. The walls are decorated with work from students in the art department.

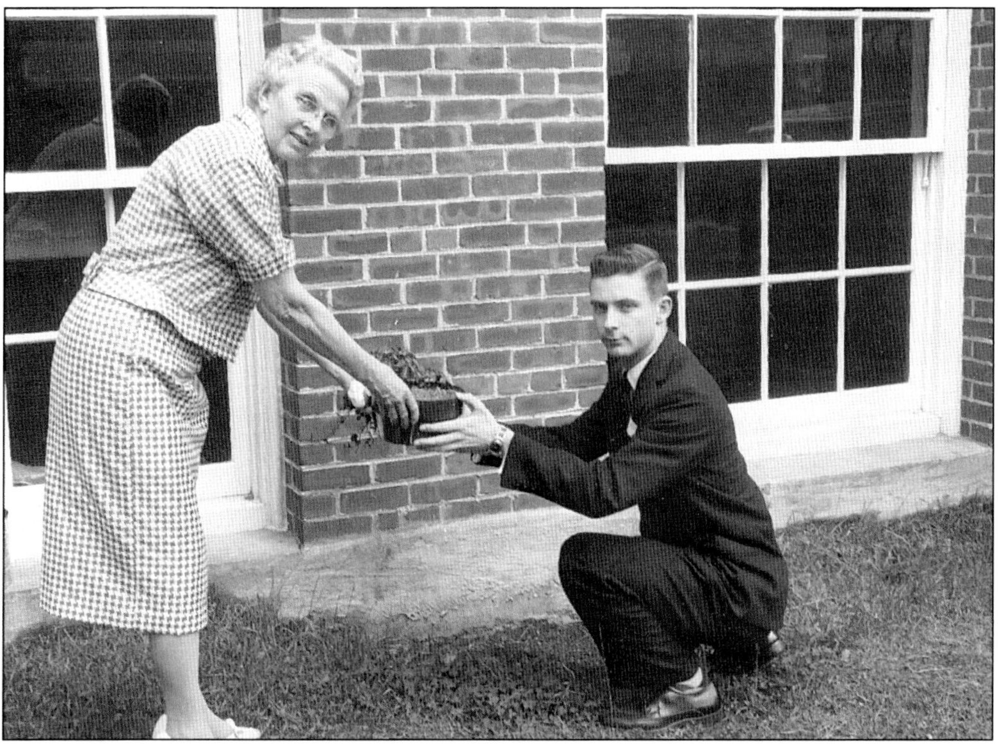

**Those Ivied Walls.** They will be ivied walls when this little plant takes root and grows. Kenneth Miller '59 and Helen McDowell Holthan '19 planted the ivy so that it would grow to cover a back wall of the main building

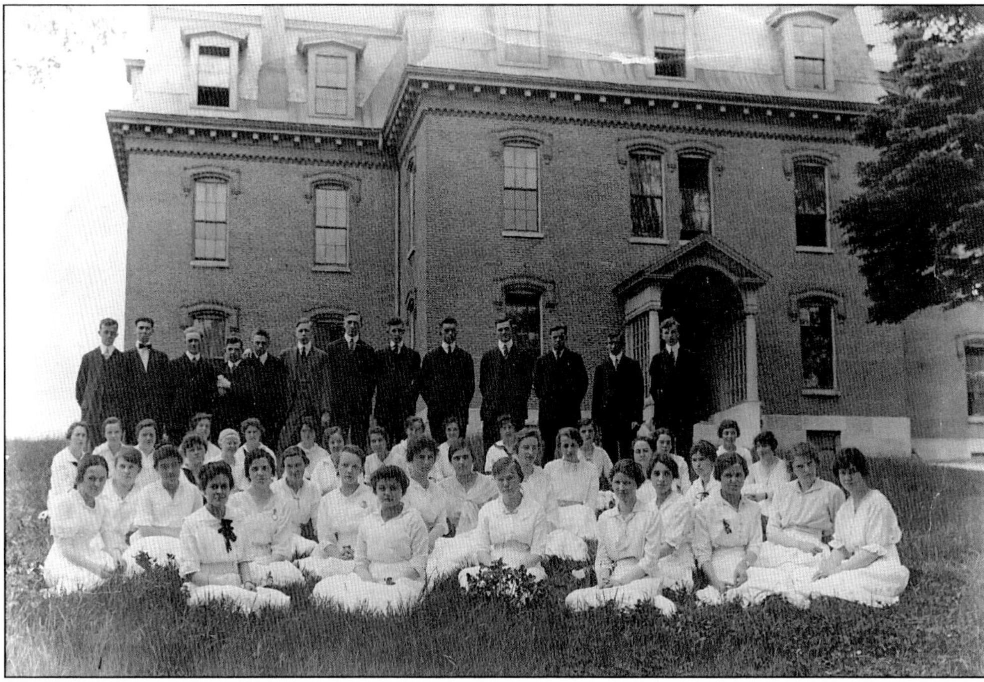

**The Class of 1916.** Fifty young men and women pose on the lawn of Thompson Hall. Before Lyndon Institute adopted the custom of wearing caps and gowns, white graduation dresses for the girls and suits for the boys was the tradition. Below, members of the same class attend their 45-year reunion at the Boulders, a restaurant and dance pavilion at Willoughby Lake in Westmore. A total of 36 people are pictured, but some of them are probably spouses.

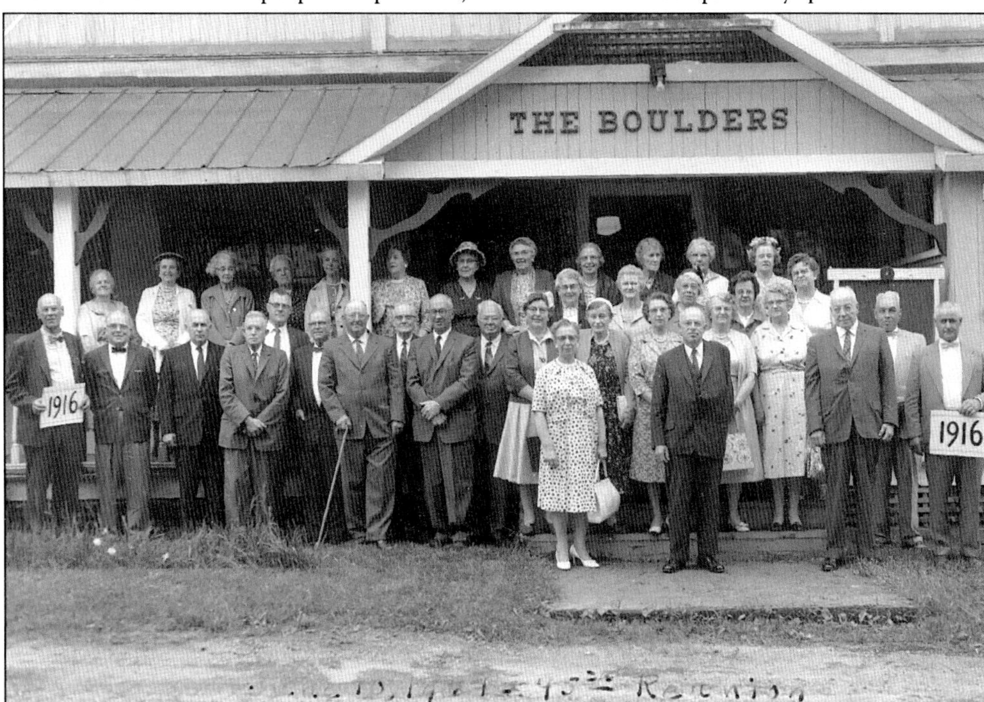

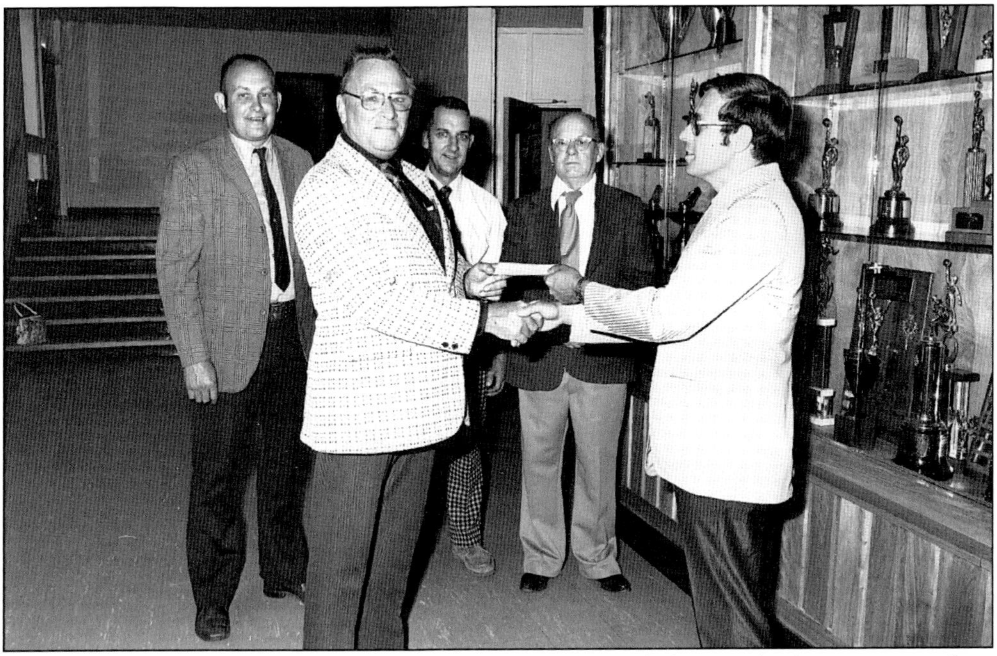

**The Presentation.** Members of the Class of 1936 donated their 40th class reunion gift to pay for an additional trophy case. Here, in front of an array of trophies, Philip Rich '36, front left, makes the presentation to Gerald Dennis, headmaster. Looking on are, from left to right, Robert Heath '58, assistant headmaster and coach; Carroll Gorham Jr. '55, alumni president; and Robert F. Pierce, Lyndon Institute treasurer.

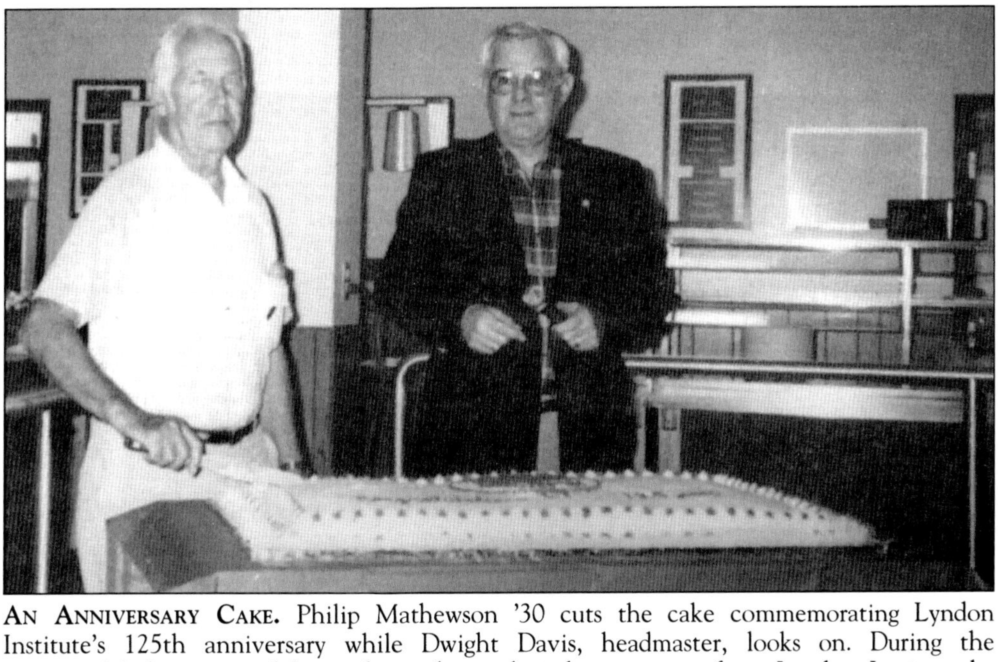

**An Anniversary Cake.** Philip Mathewson '30 cuts the cake commemorating Lyndon Institute's 125th anniversary while Dwight Davis, headmaster, looks on. During the summer, Mathewson and his wife reside in their home across from Lyndon Institute by Mathewson Pond, where his father, Ozias D. Mathewson, a former headmaster, and family lived for many years.

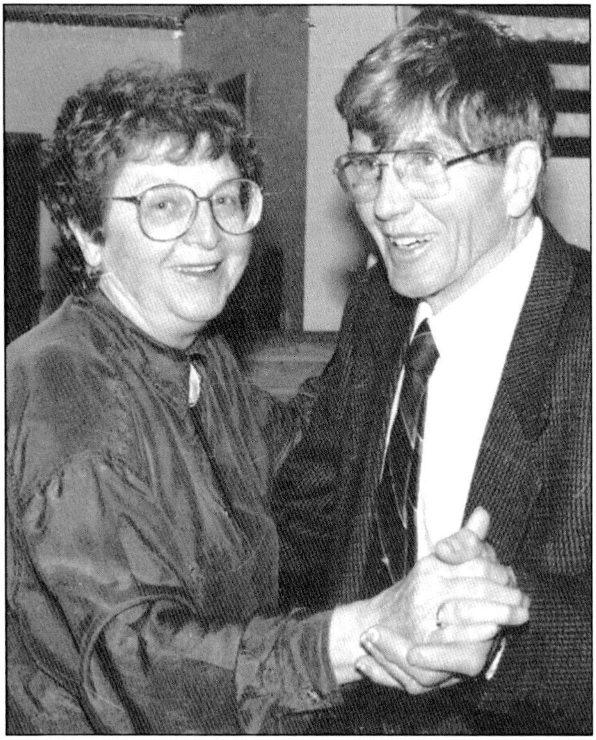

**A 50TH REUNION.** Howard and Helen (Gilman) O'Neil '43 wrap up their big day at the 1993 alumni dance, which was held at the Lyndonville Veterans Hall. They certainly are enjoying themselves.

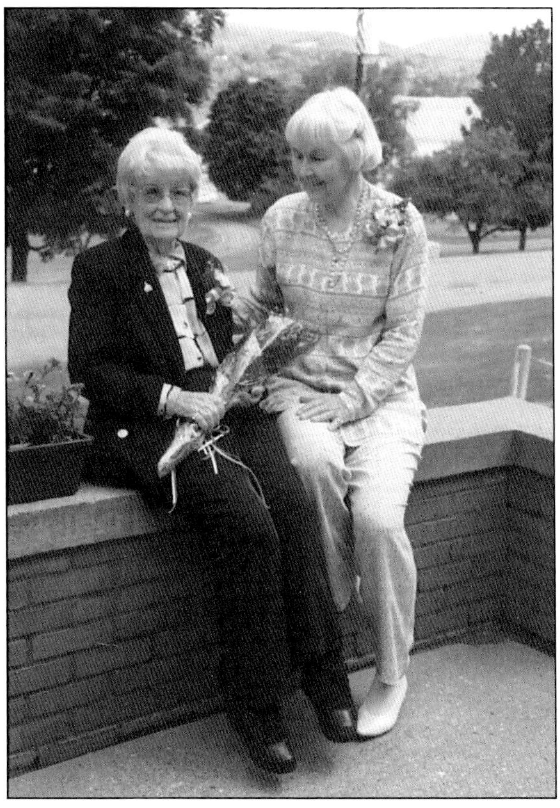

**HER 80TH REUNION.** Carolyn Darling Ahern '18, accompanied by her daughter Ann Qualmane, traveled from Waukesha, Wisconsin, in 1998 to celebrate her 80th reunion. She was at the annual Alumni Day luncheon and was presented with a corsage, the 1995 Alumni Directory, and other gifts. The daughter wrote later, saying that her mother was treated like "royalty" while revisiting her alma mater.

**AN ALUMNI GOLFER.** Since 1989, a golf tournament between St. Johnsbury Academy and Lyndon Institute has been an Alumni Day activity at the St. Johnsbury Club. Dan Daley '77, right, head of the Lyndon Institute math department, swings for his alma mater.A scoring system is worked out to see which school gets to keep the coveted Headmaster's Golf Challenging Cup, shown below, for a year.

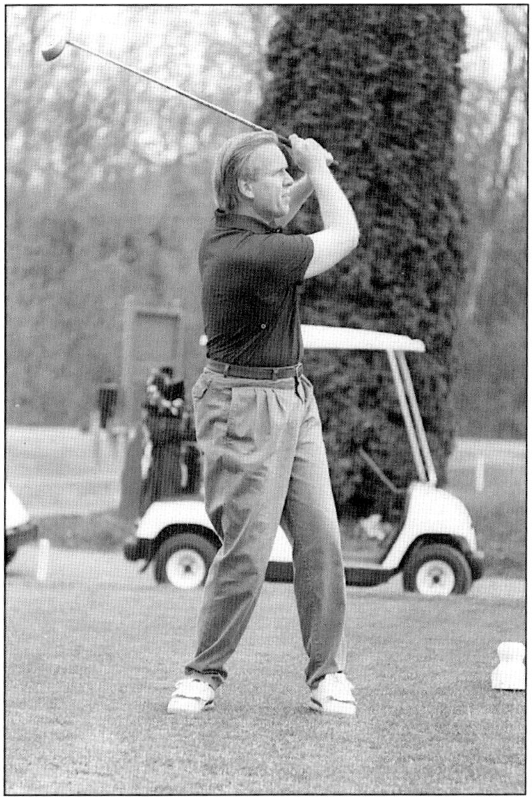

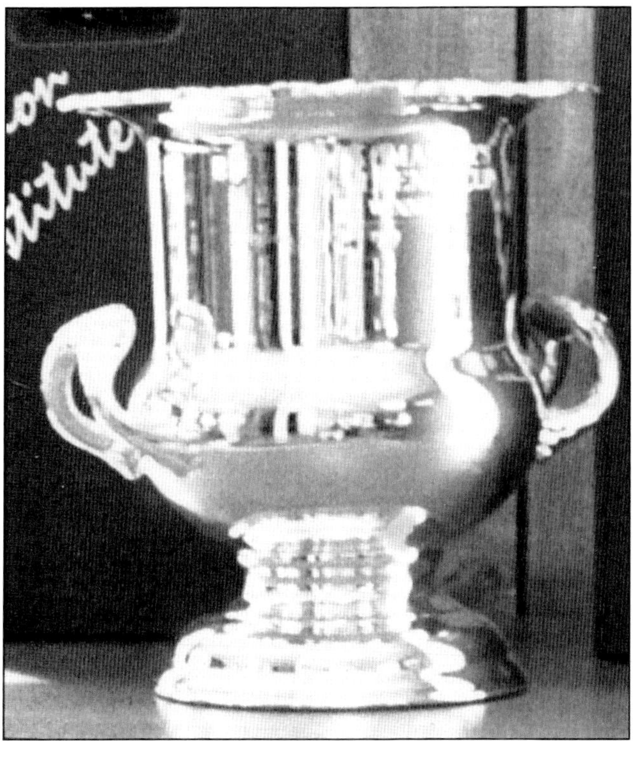

**THE COVETED CUP.** Sometimes it stays at St. J Academy for a year, sometimes at Lyndon Institute.

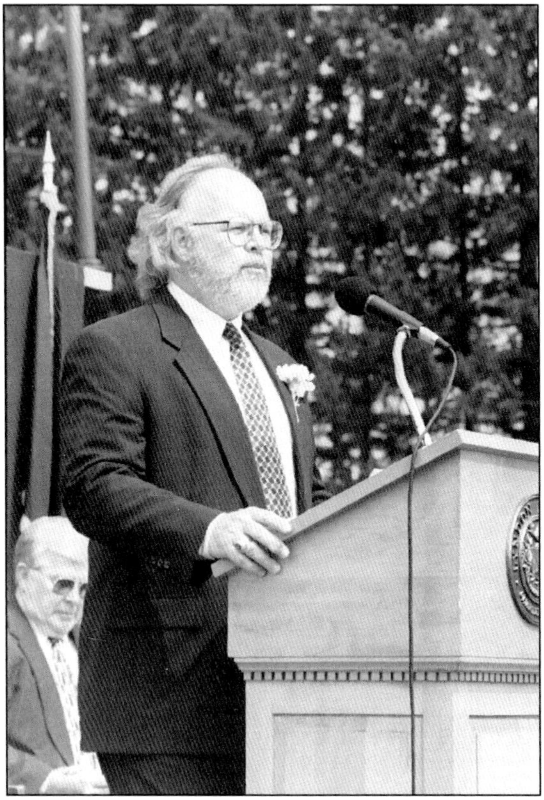

**A Recent Benefactor.** Lawyer Earl "Sam" Daniels III, Class of 1967, of Tucson, Arizona, was the speaker at the 1997 graduation. His generosity helped make it possible to construct a new building for all mathematics classes (below). Daniels Hall helped to relieve the pressure for needed classrooms.

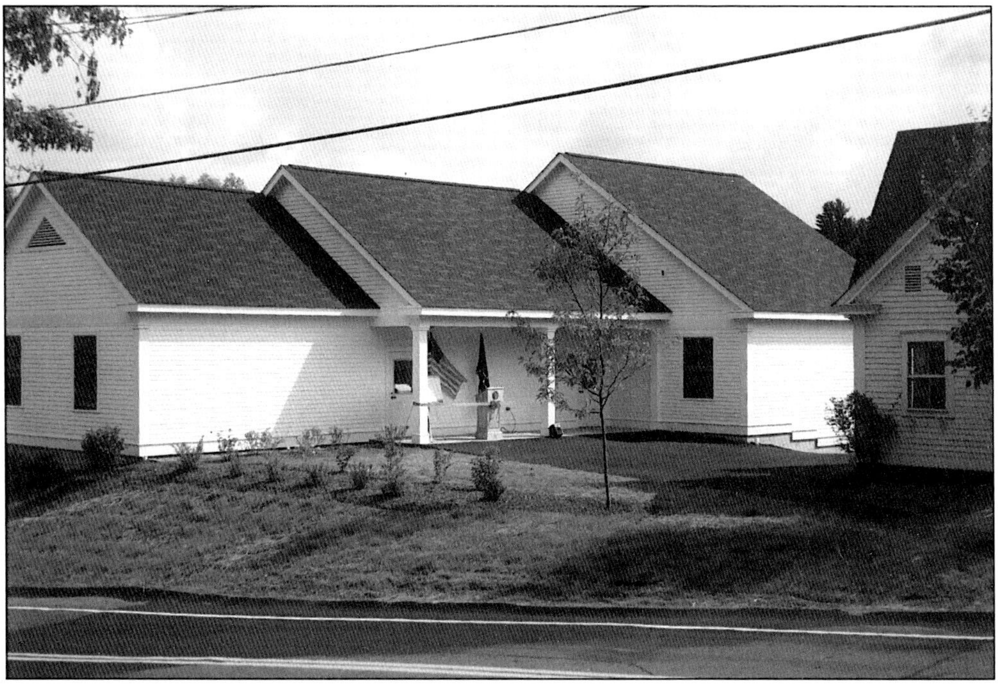

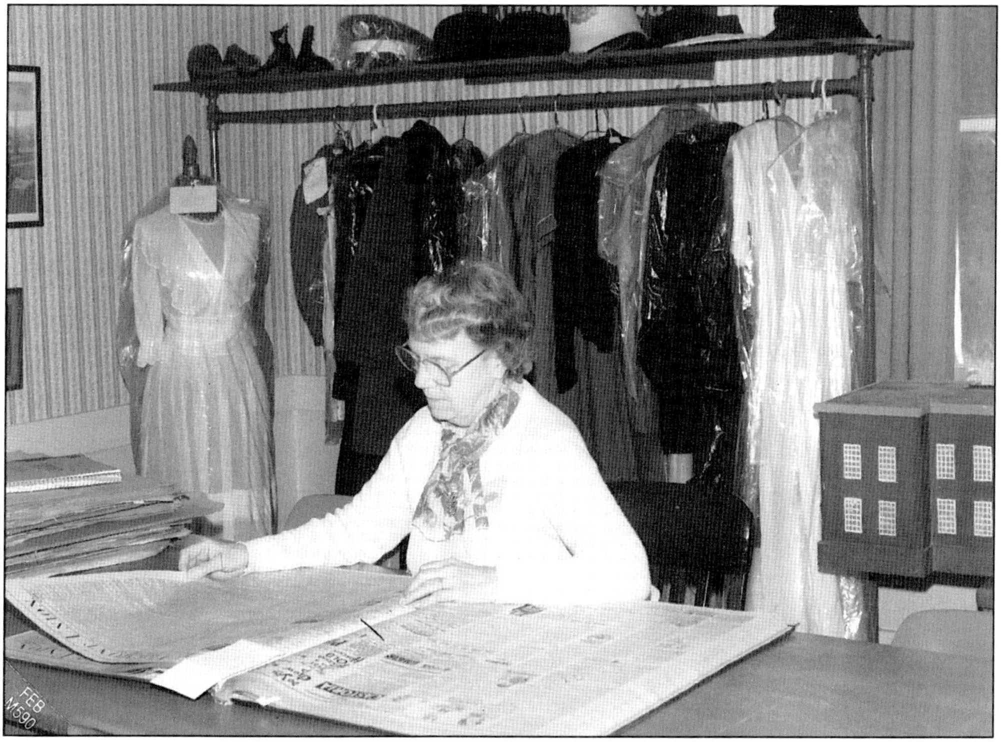

**THE ALUMNI MUSEUM CURATOR.** Norma (Gordon) Austin '40 enjoyed and devoted much of her time to organizing, cataloging, and displaying the Lyndon Institute's cherished artifacts. A retired nurse, she also volunteered in the cafeteria and in the LI bookstore. In 1983, the museum was maintained in the Mathewson House.

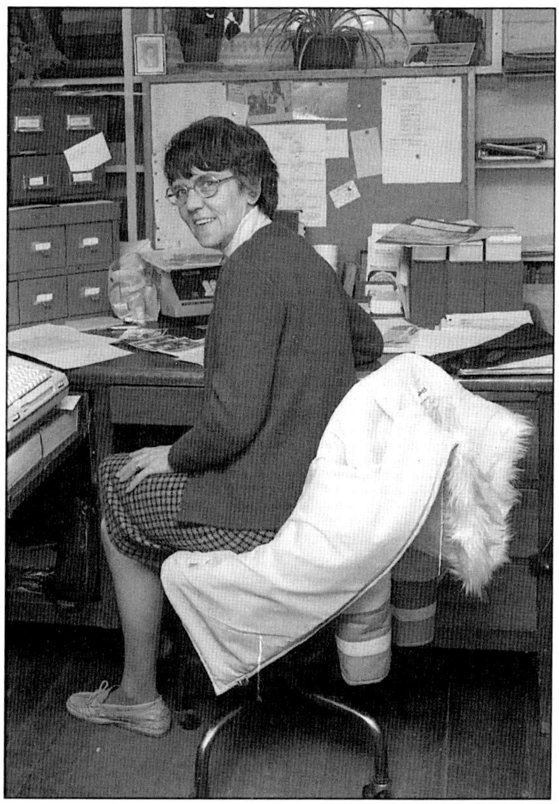

**THE CURATOR SUCCESSOR.** Gertrude (Angell) Grant, Class of 1949, carries on the work of maintaining the Lyndon Institute museum, now housed in the Theta Helen Baker Building. Part of her work is sorting the many photographs that come in from *Cynosures* and alumni (or alumni relatives) who pass on LI photographs and other memorabilia to the school museum. It is a never-ending task, but one that she is happy to do, just as Norma Austin was before her.

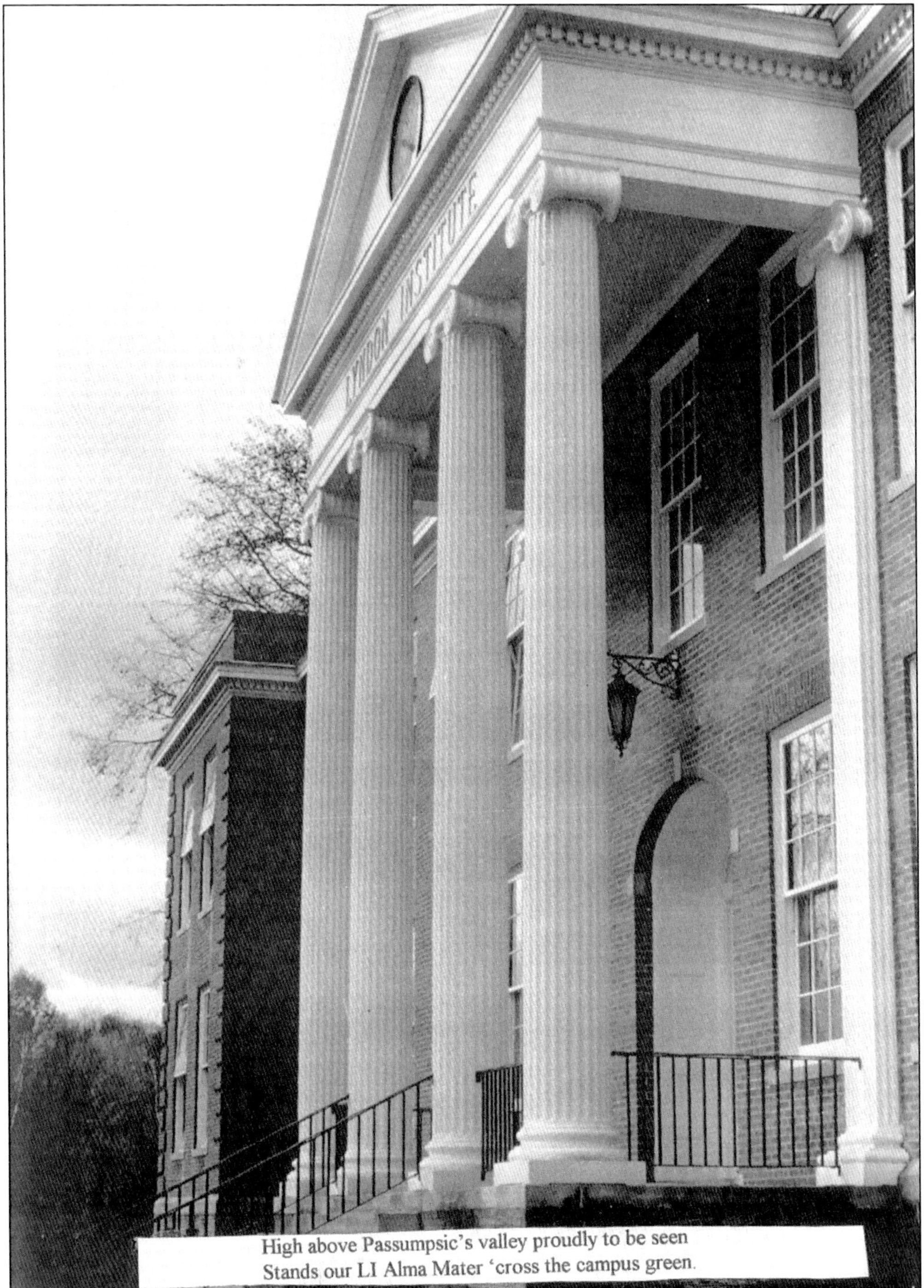


**STANDING PROUD.** These words come from Lyndon Institute's "Alma Mater."